J. Laurence Laughlin

The History of Bimetallism in the United States

J. Laurence Laughlin

The History of Bimetallism in the United States

ISBN/EAN: 9783743418776

Manufactured in Europe, USA, Canada, Australia, Japa

Cover: Foto ©ninafisch / pixelio.de

Manufactured and distributed by brebook publishing software (www.brebook.com)

J. Laurence Laughlin

The History of Bimetallism in the United States

THE HISTORY

OF

BIMETALLISM

IN THE

UNITED STATES.

BY
J. LAURENCE LAUGHLIN, Ph. D.,
ASSISTANT PROFESSOR OF POLITICAL ECONOMY IN HARVARD UNIVERSITY.

NEW YORK:
D. APPLETON AND COMPANY,
72 FIFTH AVENUE.
1895.

GRESHAM'S LAW.

"Oftentimes have we reflected on a similar abuse
  In the choice of men for office, and of coins for common use;
  For your old and standard pieces, valued and approved and tried,
  Here among the Grecian nations, and in all the world beside,
  Recognized in every realm for trusty stamp and pure assay,
  Are rejected and abandoned for the trash of yesterday;
  For a vile, adulterate issue, drossy, counterfeit and base,
  Which the traffic of the city passes current in their place!"
ARISTOPHANES, "FROGS," 891-898; FRERE'S TRANSLATION.

"Whilst each of the two metals was equally a legal tender for debts of any amount, we were subject to a constant change in the principal standard measure of value. It would sometimes be gold, sometimes silver, depending entirely on the variations in the relative value of the two metals; and, at such times, the metal which was not the standard would be melted and withdrawn from circulation, as its value would be greater in bullion than in coin."
RICARDO.

PREFACE TO THE SECOND EDITION.

THE various tables in this edition have been continued, so far as possible, to the latest dates. In Appendix VI, the exports of silver from the United States to the East for 1870–1885, and in Appendix VII, the total coinage of gold and silver by countries and by periods since 1850, have been inserted. Appendix VIII contains Dr. Soetbeer's estimate of the present consumption of gold and silver in the arts.

Of recent publications, Dr. Soetbeer's "Materialien zur Erläuterung und Beurtheilung der wirthschaftlichen Edelmetallverhältnisse und der Währungsfrage" (1885) is the most complete collection of statistics concerning gold and silver ever made. The second edition of his book (1886), which is even more valuable than the first, has been translated into English by Professor F. W. Taussig for the report of Mr. Edward Atkinson to the Department of State (December, 1887). Additional contributions to the subject may be found in the "Third Report of the Royal Commission on the Depression of Trade and Industry" (1886).

Congress has passed the act of February 19, 1887, for the retirement and recoinage of the trade-dollar, and also, in the sundry civil appropriation bill of August 4, 1886, a provision for the issue of silver certificates in denominations of one, two, and five dollars.

PREFACE TO THE SECOND EDITION.

The investigation of the relation of prices to the supposed scarcity of gold since 1873—to which public attention has been directed under the name of "appreciation of gold" —has been carried out by me since the first edition of this volume was issued, and gives the facts to substantiate the views very briefly expressed on that subject in these pages. This study was published in the "Quarterly Journal of Economics" (George H. Ellis, 141 Franklin Street, Boston), in April, 1887.

To the large number of persons who have kindly sent me their studies on the silver question I wish here to offer my acknowledgments.

J. L. L.

January, 1888.

PREFACE TO THE FIRST EDITION.

ALTHOUGH the plan of this book was conceived with the view of presenting simply a history of bimetallism in the United States, it has been necessary, in the nature of the subject, to make it something more than that. And yet it was my hope that the effect of an historical inquiry in suppressing some of the theoretical vagaries of the day might be realized by showing what our actual experience with bimetallism has been, in contrast with the assertions of some writers as to what it may be. The practical lessons from facts in such a subject are more instructive than the suppositions of theory. That the facts of our experience may be found in these pages in such a way as to enable just conclusions to be drawn by any judicially minded reader has been my aim throughout.

But it has also been necessary, in taking up the history of an economic subject like bimetallism, to deal with some matters of economic principle as well as with the facts to which they are applicable. An economic history could not be otherwise treated. In all such cases, however, I have tried to treat the question without the use of technical language, and in a manner intelligible to the ordinary reader.

And yet I have not made this volume a treatise on the theory of bimetallism. The theory has been discussed only so far as the hard facts of our own experience have directly borne upon some part of the theory.

In the pursuit of this object it will be found that there are some portions of the book which, at first glance, may not seem to be relevant to a history of bimetallism in our own country; but I trust that, if they are taken in connection with the thread of the history, they will be found to be absolutely essential to clear conceptions of the causes affecting the relative values of gold and silver. There are two illustrations of this method which will convey my meaning, and which have been put forward as important, even if they are somewhat new. The first is the extraordinary production of silver beginning near the close of the last century, and which I must consider as momentous as the well-known production of silver soon after the discovery of America. In order to discuss the effect of this surplus silver on the values of the precious metals, it was necessary to furnish the materials for comparison in other and earlier periods. This is the occasion for Charts IV, V, and VI. In truth, I think sufficient attention has not been paid to this part of the history of the precious metals by our writers. The second illustration, to which I wish to call attention, is the explanation in the chapters of Part II of the cause of the late fall in the value of silver. I can not but believe that the discussion as to the cause hitherto has been partial, disjointed, and unhistorical. I have made an attempt to supply what seemed to me a more rational explanation; and, if this explanation is accepted, it must materially alter the policy of the United States in regard to the coinage of silver. Our present attitude is utterly unjustifiable.

The explanation of the late fall in the value of silver, however, is intimately connected, to my mind, with an argument commonly heard, and urged with great ability and learning, in favor of bimetallism—the argument that gold has appreciated, and that there is not enough to satisfy the needs of trade. This position has been maintained, among others, by Mr. Goschen and Mr. Giffen in England, and by several writers and speakers in this country. I feel that this argument should not be passed by without pointing out an economic fallacy in it. The "appreciation of gold" is spoken of as if a change in the purchasing power of gold were a direct proof of the abundance or scarcity of gold. Nothing is more common than the presentation of tables of falling prices, and a conclusion drawn from the figures that gold has "appreciated." It is perfectly true that, as prices fall, a gold dollar buys more of commodities, and in this sense, that the gold coin has appreciated in value. But in all such arguments the implication is conveyed that this increased purchasing power of gold, when prices fall, is due to a diminishing supply of gold (or to an increased demand for it). This, I contend, is a complete *non sequitur*. When prices fell after the panic of 1857 the gold dollar bought perhaps seventeen per cent more than before the disturbance; but every one knows that the gold supply was increasing in an untold quantity. And yet the gold dollar had as certainly "appreciated" as it has since 1873. This makes it necessary to say that no direct inference whatever can be drawn from tables of prices as to the quantity of gold in existence at a given time. All economists know that prices are affected by purchasing power of any kind; that purchasing power, or demand for goods, comes not merely from the actual amount of money in the hands of the public, but also from the amount of credit used; and that the rapid use of money, banking devices, paper money, credit-substitutes for gold and silver, checks, drafts, and book-credits, all go to increase the demand for goods, if offered, and so act to increase prices. So that, even if the supply of metallic money were to remain exactly the same, prices might vary, owing to changes in the other factor affecting prices, namely, credit. Since 1873 a great collapse of credit and confidence has occurred; and it can not be argued logically that, therefore, because prices have fallen, gold is becoming scarce. It may, or may not, be true that gold is scarce, but it is not proved solely because prices have fallen.

Moreover, even if credit and the supply of money had remained exactly the same, the purchasing power of gold might have increased. The value of gold increases if its power to purchase other commodities increases; and if diminishing rates for transportation, new and improved processes of manufacture, the introduction of labor-saving machinery, the opening up of fertile agricultural lands, take place, as they have taken place on an extraordinary scale in late years, the prices of all articles exchanged against gold must fall—and fall, too, without implying any change whatever in the existing quantity of gold. That is, the purchasing power of gold may increase solely because of changes affecting the articles against which the gold is exchanged. In this way, if "appreciation of gold" means an increase of its purchasing power, then gold has "appreciated"; but that is nothing new. In fact, changes in the value of gold are constantly taking place. After any disturbance of trade, gold, or any money (not merely gold alone), "appreciates." And it is fallacious to connect with the words "appreciation" of gold any inference whatever as to its scarcity.

In order to prove that gold has increased in value from causes affecting the quantity alone, the *onus probandi* lies on any one to show that no changes have taken place in any of the uses of credit in any of its forms, that no changes have taken place in the cost of production of the commodities in the list whose prices may be given, and, after all this allowance has been made, it must be shown that gold prices have fallen. I do not believe any human being is capable of carrying on such an investigation. No one, in the nature of things, can know what changes are going on in all the articles exchangeable for gold.

I have also wondered why bimetallism should have drawn so much attention when its whole economic purpose may be accomplished in a more certain and effective way by the multiple standard. Money has three chief functions to perform: as a medium of exchange (to transfer value), as a common denominator of value (to compare values), and as a standard of deferred payments. Now, bimetallism is concerned only with this last function. Its chief end is to secure, as its advocates claim, a less changeable standard for paying long contracts; and to accomplish this an international league is indispensable to even a shadow of success (even if this could cause success). But, as we have found out by the monetary conferences of 1878 and 1881, this is a very difficult end to accomplish. Now, the same object can be attained by the separate action of individual states, irrespective of the action of others, by creating a legal unit of payment derived from the prices of a sufficient number of staple articles. By this means a long contract would be paid at its maturity with exactly the same purchasing power which was borrowed at the beginning. In brief, the multiple standard would take away all reason for bimetallism. The avocation of the bimetallist would be gone.

J. LAURENCE LAUGHLIN.

HARVARD UNIVERSITY, CAMBRIDGE, MASS., *October*, 1885.

CONTENTS.

PART I.

THE UNITED STATES, 1792–1873.

CHAPTER I.—*Arguments of the Bimetallists and Monometallists.*

	PAGE
§ 1. The inductive process applicable in this investigation	3
§ 2. The main arguments of the bimetallists	3
§ 3. The main arguments of the monometallists	5
§ 4. The United States experiment a favorable one for study	8
§ 5. Subdivisions of our subject	8

CHAPTER II.—*The Silver Period, 1792–1834.*

§ 1. Situation before the adoption of the Constitution	10
§ 2. Why Hamilton recommended bimetallism	13
§ 3. Choice of a ratio between gold and silver	15
§ 4. The system as adopted in 1792	20
§ 5. Gresham's law and the disappearance of gold	24

CHAPTER III.—*Cause of the Change in the Relative Values of Gold and Silver, 1780–1820.*

§ 1. The theory that the English demand for gold caused not a fall in silver, but a rise in the value of gold	32
§ 2. The value of money a ratio	37
§ 3. Did prices show a rise in the value of gold?	38
§ 4. A disproportionate increase in the supply of silver as compared with that of gold the true cause of a fall in its value	41
§ 5. Paradoxically, when the annual supply was declining, the value of silver was also falling	50

CHAPTER IV.—*Change of the Legal Ratio by the Act of 1834.*

§ 1. Condition of the circulation before 1834	52
§ 2. Various proposals to amend the coinage	57

§ 3. Choice of the ratio of 1 : 16 60
§ 4. Tendency to the disappearance of silver 64
§ 5. Debasement of the gold standard by the act of 1834 69
§ 6. Act of 1837, changing the alloy to one tenth 73

Chapter V.—*The Gold Discoveries and the Act of 1853.*

§ 1. A serious fall in the value of gold 75
§ 2. The disappearance of silver coins 76
§ 3. The single gold standard accepted 79
§ 4. Principles governing a subsidiary coinage as contained in the act of 1853 82

Chapter VI.—*The Gold Standard, 1853-1873.*

§ 1. The single gold standard to 1862 86
§ 2. The displacement of gold and subsidiary coins in 1862 by depreciated paper 87
§ 3. The resumption of specie payment in silver small coins . . . 89

Chapter VII.—*The Demonetization of Silver.*

§ 1. Influence of the act of 1873 92
§ 2. Silver dollar demonetized by act of 1874 93
§ 3. The charge that silver was demonetized surreptitiously . . . 95
§ 4. The trade dollar 101

PART II.

The Late Fall in the Value of Silver.

Chapter VIII.—*The Production of Gold since 1850.*

§ 1. The reason for the digression of Part II. 109
§ 2. The effects of the new gold to be discussed only as they influence the values of the precious metals 110
§ 3. Statement of the facts of the gold production 111
§ 4. The preference for gold to silver in commercial nations . . . 113
§ 5. Production of gold and silver in 1493-1850 compared with the yield in 1850-1875 115
§ 6. Effect on the value of silver 116
§ 7. France receives gold and gives up silver 118

Chapter IX.—*India and the East.*

§ 1. The passion of Eastern nations for ornaments 122
§ 2. Their demand for silver as a medium of exchange 124

CONTENTS. xv

	PAGE
§ 3. Amount of silver sent to the East	125
§ 4. Considerations affecting the future demand for silver in India	128
§ 5. The effect of the Indian demand on the relative values of gold and silver	130

CHAPTER X.—*Germany Displaces Silver with Gold.*

§ 1. The opportunity presented to Germany for changing a silver to a gold currency	135
§ 2. The measures adopted for this purpose	137
§ 3. Amount of silver thrown on the market	140
§ 4. German demand for gold	144

CHAPTER XI.—*France and the Latin Union.*

§ 1. Origin of the Latin Union, 1865	146
§ 2. Monetary experience of France	150
§ 3. Suspension of silver coinage, 1874	153
§ 4. Subsequent attitude of the Latin Union	156

CHAPTER XII.—*Cause of the Late Fall in the Value of Silver.*

§ 1. The extent of the fall	161
§ 2. Causes of the fall assigned by the Committee of the House of Commons	164
§ 3. The increased gold production since 1850 the cause of the fall in silver	167
§ 4. This cause traced in the monetary events since 1850	170

PART III.

THE UNITED STATES, 1873–1885.

CHAPTER XIII.—*Silver Legislation in 1878.*

§ 1. Acceptance of the act of 1873	179
§ 2. Disregard of the European situation	180
§ 3. The provisions and legislative history of the Bland bill	181
§ 4. Conditions in the United States preceding the act of 1878	186
§ 5. Reasons for the passage of the measure	188
§ 6. The Matthews resolution and the Silver Commission	201

CHAPTER XIV.—*The Present Situation.*

§ 1. Forces which keep the silver dollar at par	205
§ 2. The trade dollar discontinued	208
§ 3. The Treasury and the banks	210
§ 4. Attempts to preserve the gold basis	214

APPENDICES.

Appendix I.—*Production of Gold and Silver in the World.*

		PAGE
A.	1493-1850	217
B.	1850-1875	218
C.	1876-1883	219

Appendix II.—*Relative Values of Gold and Silver.*

A. Ratios of gold to silver, by periods, 1501-1875 220
B. Ratios of gold to silver, by years, 1687-1832 221
C. Ratios of gold to silver, by years, 1833-1884. Pixley and Abell . . 223
D. Average yearly price of standard silver per ounce in London, 1833-1884 224
E. Monthly London prices of silver in pence, 1871-1884 224
F. Ratios of gold to silver, by months, 1845-1880 225
G. Method of computing ratios from London prices of silver . . . 225
Method of computing the value of a dollar of 412½ grains from New York prices of silver 226

Appendix III.—*Coinage Laws.*

A. Laws of the United States relating to coinage 227
B. The French monetary law of 1803 236
C. German monetary laws of 1871 and 1873 237
D. Treaty of 1865 forming the Latin Union 245

Appendix IV.

Coinage of Gold and Silver at the United States Mint, 1793-1884 . 249

Appendix V.

Equivalent in Gold of the Silver Dollar of 412½ Grains, 1834-1884 . . 251

Appendix VI.

Flow of Silver to the East, 1835-1880 252

Appendix VII.

Coinage of Gold and Silver at the French Mint, 1850-1875 . . . 254

Appendix VIII.

Consumption of Gold and Silver in the Arts 255

Index 257

INDEX OF CHARTS.

		PAGE
I.	Ratio of Gold to Silver, 1780–1833	19
II.	Coinage of Gold and Silver at the United States Mint, 1793–1833	31
III.	Movement of Prices of Forty Articles, 1782–1865, with additional line from 1857 to 1885 . . .	38
IV.	Relative Production of Gold and Silver, 1493–1880	42
V.	Relative Quantities of Gold and Silver produced, 1560–1660	47
VI.	Relative Quantities of Gold and Silver produced, 1761–1820	47
VII.	Ratio of Gold to Silver, 1820–1860	61
VIII.	Coinage of Gold and Silver at the United States Mint, 1834–1860	69
IX.	Production of Gold and Silver since 1493 . . .	76
X.	Relative Production of Gold and Silver, 1493–1850, and 1851–1875	116
XI.	Excess of Exports and Imports of Gold and Silver from and into France, 1849–1882	119
XII.	Net Imports of Gold and Silver into British India, 1855–1882	126
XIII.	Ratio of Gold to Silver, by years, 1687–1884 . .	161
XIV.	Monthly Fluctuations in the Price of Silver, 1876–1879	173
XV.	Fall in the Value of Silver, 1870–1884 . . .	180
XVI.	Coinage, and Distribution of Silver Dollars within and without the United States Treasury, 1878–1885 .	210

PART I.

THE UNITED STATES, 1792–1873.

PART I.
THE UNITED STATES, 1792-1873.

CHAPTER I.

THE ARGUMENTS OF BIMETALLISTS AND MONOMETALLISTS.

§ 1. THE conflicting opinions of the day in regard to the adoption of bimetallism by the United States, and the disregard of the facts within our own experience, make it desirable that these facts should be investigated historically, and the results presented in a simple form for general use. Monetary science, moreover, will gain by any honest attempt to collect accurate data which may serve in the process of verification of economic principles, enabling us either to confirm the truth of previous conclusions, or to demonstrate their divergence from actual facts. In a monetary investigation of this kind induction is our main dependence; here, in truth, as we seek the means for verification, is the proper field for the historical method.

In order, however, to place the present history in its proper light—in order that it may bear to some purpose on the bimetallic discussion—it has seemed fit to give a very brief *résumé* of the main arguments[1] of both parties to the controversy.

§ 2. I. BIMETALLISM has been proposed under two such widely differing conditions that the following general division of arguments may properly be adopted:

---

[1] See also S. Dana Horton's "Gold and Silver," chap. iii.

A. National Bimetallism.
B. International Bimetallism.

(A.) (1) The selection of both gold and silver by an individual state as legal payment of debts to any amount at a ratio fixed without regard to the legal ratios of other states may be defined as national bimetallism. An example of this system is to be found at present in the United States, where, although no other country of importance has the same ratio (and although the legal ratio does not correspond with the market value of the two metals), we have a proportion of $1:16$. Such a system is not upheld by any economic writer of repute. Whenever it is advocated in the United States (2) it has been urged from a strong belief that, if we do not use silver, there will not be enough of the precious metals in existence to perform the exchanges; or (3) with the expectation of inducing other countries to adopt bimetallism; (4) or to sustain the price of silver; (5) or to force the cheaper metal into use as an easy means of scaling debts and of relieving debtors of a part of their burdens. The theories of national bimetallism, as thus advocated, are widely different from the tenets of another school of writers, who are also known as bimetallists.

(B.) An agreement between the chief commercial nations of the world on one given ratio (e. g., $15\frac{1}{2}:1$) would, in the opinion of this other school, keep the value of silver relatively to gold invariable, and so cause the concurrent use of both metals in all the countries of such a league. This may be termed international bimetallism, to distinguish it from the other body of theories. (6) The essential part of this theory is that the legal provision for the use of silver in the coinage of each state creates a demand for silver; and that, inasmuch as other states of the league have the same ratio, no reason could exist why either silver or gold should leave one country for another. (7) In close connection with this argument it is urged that the "compensatory action" of a double standard will prevent that extreme fluctuation of the standard of prices which is made possible by a single standard; since, as prices follow the metal which is for the time the cheaper, the latter will feel a demand just in proportion as the other metal loses it. (8) The desire to use gold, it is held, should be discountenanced, as tending not only to lower the value of silver, but to concentrate the monetary demand of the whole civilized world upon gold; and that, as its quantity would be alone insufficient for the needs of commerce, the value of gold must increase, and the prices of all things diminish, to the great discouragement of business enterprise. There would be a "gold famine" the effects of which would be intolerable.[1] (9) This same school also present very strongly the opinion that the general demonetization of silver would so increase the value of gold, and the value of the unit in which the enormous public debts of the world must be paid, that it would entail a heavy loss to the taxpayers.

(10) Other writers, still, urge that the two precious metals were designed by a Higher Power as media of exchange, and that it is a mistake arbitrarily to set up one of them as a standard by which other commodities are to be measured, and to discard the other.[2]

§ 3. II. MONOMETALLISM is not a belief in the sole use of gold. Its advocates regard gold as the least variable of the two metals, as best suited for large payments; and believe that silver, as a heavier and cheaper metal, should also be used for smaller payments, but not as an unlimited legal tender. (1) Monometallists hold that "national bimetallism" is an impossibility for any length of time, since, as soon as one metal in the market falls slightly below the legal ratio, the other

---

[1] These arguments may be most conveniently found in F. A. Walker's "Political Economy," and "Money, Trade, and Industry"; and in S. Dana Horton's "Silver and Gold," and the "Report of the International Monetary Conference of 1878." See also the French Report of the Mon. Confer. of 1881, in index "Bimétallisme."

[2] "Providence seems to have originally adjusted the relative values of the precious metals."—Sir Roderick Murchison, quoted by Ernest Seyd in "Decline of Prosperity," title-page. The following words of Turgot are often quoted: "Gold and silver were constituted, by the nature of things, money and universal money, independently of all convention and all law."

metal will be driven out of circulation, and the country will really have only a succession of single standards, alternating between gold and silver. (2) They believe that one country alone can not hold up the value of silver against the tendencies of many countries to disuse it; and if it should try, the holders of silver bullion would gain at the expense of the single country, which is sacrificing itself by buying silver which will depreciate on its hands; (3) that, if it is an object of the United States to induce other countries to join us in a league, we can best force that policy on them by withdrawing from our isolated and unsupported position until the others manifest a disposition to join us; (4) and that the movement to force silver upon the United States at the present ratio of 1:16 is a disguised form of the policy which a few years ago led to the "greenback" heresy, and is intended to favor owners of silver mines, and dishonest debtors who wish a cheaper unit of payment, at the expense of national honor and credit.

It would be hard to say what the monometallists hold in regard to international bimetallism, since it is largely a matter of theory and of future potentiality. Monometallists do not—as is so often said—believe that gold remains absolutely stable in value. They hold that there is no such thing as "a standard of value" for future payments in either gold or silver, which remains absolutely invariable; but that, so long as we must use one of the two, gold is preferable, inasmuch as it has proved in the past more steady in value than silver. (5) They admit that a general agreement of states to coin silver at a ratio higher than the present market value would have an effect to raise its value; but, while it is extremely doubtful whether this league could overcome natural forces, it is denied that such a league is politically possible, and the experience of the conferences of 1878 and 1881 is cited to show it. (6) As regards the "compensatory action" of a double standard, it is denied that this can act without alternately changing the standard from a single standard of gold to a single standard of silver—and this is not regarded as a "double standard." There can be no "compensation" except as one metal drives out the other. While it may prevent extreme fluctuations of the standard of prices, it brings more frequent fluctuations, each of which is sufficient to drive one metal out of circulation. (7) The tendency to disuse silver is, they claim, due to natural causes affecting the demand, and the legislation hostile to silver but registers the wishes of commerce. (8) The fall of prices since 1873 is used to prove an appreciation of gold; but it is denied that prices depend directly on the quantity of money, and that it can not be said that because prices fall money has appreciated. The fall of prices, used to indicate an increase in the value of gold, is found to depend quite as much on a collapse of credit, and lessened cost of production of the commodities against which gold is exchanged, as on any relative scarcity of gold. (9) As regards national debts, it is distinctly averred that neither gold nor silver forms a just measure of deferred payments, and that if justice in long contracts is sought for, we should not seek it by the doubtful and untried expedient of international bimetallism, but by the clear and certain method of a multiple standard, a unit based upon the selling prices of a number of articles of general consumption. A long contract would thereby be paid at its maturity by the same purchasing power as was given in the beginning.

(10) Far from being true that the value [1] of any metal is providentially fixed, it depends, on the contrary, on the power of that metal to satisfy the demands of commerce as an artificial medium of exchange to save us from barter; as countries grow in wealth, it is found that, as an historical fact, commercial centers, where transactions are large, prefer

---

[1] "Between gold and silver, therefore, there is not any fixed proportion as to value, established by Nature, any more than there is a fixed proportion established by Nature between lead and iron, or between wheat and tobacco. Nature does not say that one ounce of gold shall always be worth so many ounces of silver any more than she says that a certain number of pounds of iron shall always be worth so many pounds of lead, or that a bushel of wheat shall always be worth a fixed quantity of tobacco."—Raguet, "Currency and Banking," p. 219.

gold to silver; consequently, the value of a metal, merely as affected by its demand, can not remain the same. Moreover, the supply of a metal can very seriously disturb its permanent value. No commodity, not even gold, has any sacerdotal qualities which keep its value invariable.

§ 4. In regard to some of the above differences of opinion, the history of bimetallism in the United States will, in my opinion, give such teaching as ought to settle all cavil or dispute. The experience of this country has been unique. No experiment of bimetallism has ever been inaugurated under circumstances more favorable for its success; and no hostility or suspicion attended its progress. No fairer field for its trial could have been found; and its progress under such conditions makes its history peculiarly instructive. We have had in this country a legal and nominal double standard from the establishment of the Mint in 1792 to the present day, with the exception of the years between 1873 and 1878; and in this period of about ninety years we have had almost every possible experience with our system. Has it proved a success in the past? What lessons does it offer for the future?

It will be remembered that the question of bimetallism has been actively discussed only since the great fall of silver in 1876, and that great animation and warmth have been shown both by its friends and foes. An experience of bimetallism, therefore, under no attacks and under friendly auspices, during the years preceding 1876, for more than three quarters of a century, ought to furnish us lessons which we can readily accept, because they are drawn from results caused by normal conditions, and not vitiated by any suspicion of prejudice against silver. A ship which had proved unseaworthy in fair weather would not be a secure refuge in stormy seasons. Has our system proved successful under these fair and normal conditions?

§ 5. In detailing the events of our history in the following pages it will be found convenient to divide the time into

certain periods, distinguished by important legislation and by the consequent effects :
  I. Silver period, 1792–1834.
  II. Gold period, 1834–1853.
  III. Gold period, 1853–1873.
  IV. Single gold standard, 1873–1878.
  V. Transition period, 1878–1885.

Part I will include the first three periods, from 1792 to 1873 ; Part II will offer a statement of the antecedent facts, and an explanation, of the late extraordinary fall in the value of silver, which was most marked in 1876 ; and Part III will include the history of the periods in the United States from 1873 to the present day, with a statement of the present situation.

CHAPTER II.

THE SILVER PERIOD.

§ 1. In the time before the adoption of the Constitution the circulating medium of the colonies was made up virtually of foreign coins. During the war of the Revolution the "Spanish milled dollar" was the unit of common account.[1] The paper money, it was at first expected, was to be redeemed in this medium. But as regards coins of a denomination other than the Spanish dollar, there were a variety of them in circulation. In keeping accounts, next in order of common usage to the dollar came the pound and shilling, which was the natural consequence of our English origin; but the shilling stamped by some of the colonies, although forming a considerable part of the money in circulation, varied widely in value.[2] Besides these kinds of money there were also English, French, Spanish, and Portuguese coins, which in 1776 were assigned[3] the following relative values:

---

[1] Cf. J. K. Upton's "Money in Politics," chap. iii.

[2] The Spanish dollar equaled 5 shillings in Georgia; 8 shillings in North Carolina and New York (12½ cents); 6 shillings in Virginia, Connecticut, New Hampshire, Massachusetts, and Rhode Island (16⅔ cents); 7 shillings 6 pence in Maryland, Delaware, Pennsylvania, and New Jersey; 32 shillings 6 pence in South Carolina. This accounts for the present reckoning of 12½ cents to a "shilling" in New York, Ohio, etc., and of 16¾ cents in New England and Virginia ("nine pence" still being used as the equivalent of 12½ cents). The persistence, to the present day, of the units of account of a century ago, although the coins representing them have long passed out of existence, is one of the striking facts in monetary history.

[3] "Report of 1878," p. 422. It is to be kept in mind, however, that the Spanish dollar with which this comparison was made varied in weight.

	Weight.		Value.
	Dwt.	grains.	Dollars.
English guinea	5	6	4 2/3
French "	5	5	4 5/9
Johannes	18	0	16
Half Johannes	9	0	8
Spanish pistole	4	8	3 2/3
French "	4	4	3 1/2
Moidore	6	18	6
English crown	......		1 1/9
French "	......		1 1/9
English shilling	......		2/9

From 1782 to 1786 the colonies began seriously to consider the difficulties arising from the variety of different coins in circulation, and their deleterious effects on business and methods of accounts, to the extent that they proposed a special American coinage with the dollar as the basis. In 1782 Robert Morris, Superintendent of Finance, made proposals[1] for the establishment of an American Mint, which were approved by the Congress of the Confederation. He faced the question at once, Of what metal should the dollar be made? He urged the use of silver alone,[2] for, he said, both gold and silver could not be used, because the ratio between the two metals was not constant.

Jefferson advocated the decimal denominations in the system of coins, and urged the dollar[3] as a unit. He adds in regard to the ratio:

"The proportion between the values of gold and silver is a mercantile problem altogether"; and further remarks: "Just principles will lead us to disregard legal proportions altogether, to inquire into the market price of gold in the several countries with which we shall principally be connected in commerce, and to take an average from them. Perhaps we might with safety *lean to a proportion somewhat above par for gold*, con-

[1] "Report of the International Monetary Conference of 1878," pp. 425–435. In referring to this authority I shall hereafter call it the "Report of 1878."

[2] "Report of 1878," pp. 430, 431.

[3] Ibid., pp. 437–443. "The unit or dollar is a known coin, and the most familiar of all to the mind of the people. It is already adopted from South to North, has identified our currency, and therefore happily offers itself as a unit already introduced."

sidering our neighborhood and commerce with the sources of the coins and the tendency which the high price of gold in Spain [16 : 1] has to draw thither all that of their mines, leaving silver principally for our and other markets. It is not impossible that 15 for 1 may be found an eligible proportion."

Morris had stated the ratio in America to be about 1 : 14½ at this time. The proposals of Morris and Jefferson were, however, not carried into effect.

In 1785 the strong desire for a metallic currency, coupled with the belief that silver could be most easily obtained, was evident in a "Report[1] of a Grand Committee of the Continental Congress":

"In France, 1 grain of pure gold is counted worth 15 grains of silver. In Spain, 16 grains of silver are exchanged for 1 of gold, and in England 15¼. In both of the kingdoms last mentioned gold is the prevailing money, because silver is undervalued. In France, silver prevails. Sundry advantages would arise to us from *a system by which silver might become the prevailing money.* This would operate as a bounty to draw it from our neighbors, by whom it is not sufficiently esteemed. Silver is not exported so easily as gold, and it is a more useful metal."

Congress again accepted the dollar as a unit, and other coins of decimal proportions to the dollar, but nothing was done.

April 8, 1786, the Board of Treasury,[2] although they mention that the ratio then prevailing in America was 1 : 15·60, made three reports, showing the following adjustment of the coins:

	Weight of silver dollar.	Weight of gold dollar.	Ratio between silver and gold coins.
	Grains fine.	Grains fine.	
Report No. 1	375·64	24·6268	1 : 15·253
Report No. 2	350·09	23·79	1 : 14·749
Report No. 3	521·73	34·782	1 : 15

The first report was followed, and the board ordered to draft an ordinance for the establishment of a Mint, which was ac-

---

[1] "Report of 1878," pp. 415–449.
[2] Samuel Osgood and Walter Livingston. See "Report of 1878," pp. 449–453.

cepted October 16, 1786. Nothing, however, was carried into effect before the adoption of the Constitution. The colonies remained, consequently, until 1792, with a circulating medium of foreign coins, composed almost entirely of silver, and subject to the regulations of the foreign governments which issued them.

§ 2. The establishment of a double standard[1] in the United States is due to Alexander Hamilton. His "Report[2] on the Establishment of a Mint" remains the best source of information as to the reasons for adopting the system which has continued, with a slight break, from that day to this. As was to be expected, the arguments urged at the present time in favor of bimetallism had not occurred to Hamilton. He did not enter into a general discussion of the effects of a double standard, such as we might expect from a modern bimetallist. In speaking of gold and silver, he was emphatic in stating his belief that if we must adopt one metal alone, that metal should be gold, and not silver (at variance, as we have seen, with the views of Robert Morris in 1782); because, said Hamilton,[3] gold was the metal least liable to variation. In fact, we find in his report thus early in our history an expression of that preference for gold over silver, whenever the former can be had, which has since then played no little part among the influences acting on the relative values of the two metals.

---

[1] For the first instance of a double standard in this country see the experiment of the colony of Massachusetts in 1762. Cf. Upton, "Money in Politics," p. 21.

[2] Dated May 5, 1791. It is given in full in "Report of 1878," pp. 454-484.

[3] "Gold may, perhaps, in certain senses, be said to have a greater stability than silver; as, being of superior value, less liberties have been taken with it in the regulations of different countries. Its standard has remained more uniform, and it has, in other respects, undergone fewer changes; as, being not so much an article of merchandise, owing to the use made of silver in the trade with the East Indies and China, it is less liable to be influenced by circumstances of commercial demand. And if, reasoning by analogy, it could be affirmed that there is a physical probability of greater proportional increase in the quantity of silver than in that of gold, it would afford an additional reason for calculating on greater steadiness in the value of the latter."

"As long as gold, either from its intrinsic superiority as a metal, from its rarity, or *from the prejudices of mankind*, retains so considerable a pre-eminence in value over silver as it has hitherto had, a natural consequence of this seems to be that its condition will be more stationary. The revolutions, therefore, which may take place in the comparative value of gold and silver *will be changes in the state of the latter* rather than in that of the former."

This prophecy of Hamilton's was fulfilled to the letter within a few years after the words were uttered.

But in these words also we find the excuse for the adoption of a system of bimetallism which, after the expression of a preference for gold, might have seemed undesirable. If a farmer is seeking for one of two pieces of land, he will be obliged to select that which is within his means. The United States was in the same position as the farmer. There was a general scarcity of specie in the new country, and it was a difficult matter to perform the exchanges with ease. Not only was there no prejudice against silver, but it was the metal most in common use. The whole object of the Secretary was to secure a metallic medium in abundance; silver, being in use, must, of course, be retained, and gold brought in also, if possible. The double standard was preferred, therefore, because it afforded a moral certainty of the retention of silver and a possibility also of adding gold to the money of the land. It would not do, says Hamilton, to adopt a single silver standard, for that would act "to abridge the quantity of the circulating medium." It was hoped to utilize the existing quantity of silver, and yet keep the gold also. Although he preferred a single standard of gold, he must be content to take what he could get; and silver was most easily secured for the new currency. There is, he adds, an extraordinary supply of silver in the West Indies,[1] and

---

[1] "But our situation in regard to the West India Islands, *into some of which there is a large influx of silver directly from the mines of South America*, occasions an extraordinary supply of that metal, and consequently [since our trade with the West Indies was important] a greater proportion of it in our circulation than might have been expected from its relative value."

this will render it easier for the United States to obtain a supply of that metal. He had little conception of the coming effect on his system of this "extraordinary supply" of silver from the South American mines. The scarcity of metallic money was the fact which influenced him in his recommendation of a double standard—a natural scarcity, too, for the country yet felt the effects of the havoc caused by the worthless continental paper which had driven specie out of use. Like the farmer of limited means, who preferred the better although more expensive land, but took the cheaper piece because it was within his reach, Hamilton naturally adopted the poor-country plan,[1] and, in order to secure a metallic currency, took measures to retain silver, the best he could get (with the hope of keeping gold also).

§ 3. Having, for these reasons, fully decided to adopt a double standard, the Secretary was obliged to face the chief difficulty in the problem—the selection of a legal ratio between gold and silver. Here was the rock on which, as we shall see hereafter, his system was inevitably bound to go to pieces.

In selecting a ratio between gold and silver in our coinage there is not a reasonable doubt but that, in spite of later charges, Hamilton fully intended to keep as closely as possible to the market ratio in the United States.

"There can hardly be a better rule in any country for the legal than the market proportion, if this can be supposed to have been produced by the free and steady course of commercial principles. The presumption in such case is, that each metal finds its true level, according to its intrinsic utility, in the general system of money operations."

---

[1] In the Report of the Committee to Congress in 1785 (see p. 12) the same idea was uppermost. They saw that the French ratio of $1:15$ attracted silver to France from England and Spain, where silver had a less value (viz., $1:15\cdot2$ in England and $1:16$ in Spain); consequently it was urged that a ratio like the French, or even $1:14\cdot75$, would be likely to draw silver to the United States from England and Spain, and thereby increase the chances of gaining enough of this metal to satisfy our needs. Jefferson also, in 1782, seeing that France lost gold, but England and Spain lost silver, thought it well to adopt a ratio of $1:15$, because, as our commerce was chiefly with Spain, we should receive silver readily from Spain, where the ratio was unfavorable to silver [$1:16$].

Having decided to adopt the market ratio, he found an alternative between (1) the market ratio of "the commercial world" and (2) the market ratio solely of the United States. He frankly admitted his inability to discover the former. "To ascertain the first with precision would require better materials than are possessed, or than could be obtained, without an inconvenient delay."[1] Here he committed a grave financial error. No system of bimetallism has been able to exist for any length of time in a country trading with foreign states, if the Mint ratio was not in agreement with the market ratio of the chief commercial nations. Hamilton certainly did not then foresee this difficulty. On a matter of monetary principles he was wholly wrong. He should have made the inquiry in regard to the relative values current in "the commercial world" with great care; for, if he had no time to conduct such an investigation, it was certain that his bimetallic system would soon be disturbed. But, as we shall soon learn, he was led to that which was right in fact, although, on a matter of principles, he was wholly in error.

The object he set before him, then, was the ascertainment of the current ratio between gold and silver in the United States, irrespective of the relative values of the two metals in foreign lands. This, however, was no easy matter. Morris had stated the ratio to be 1 : 14$\frac{3}{4}$, and Jefferson 1 : 14$\frac{1}{2}$; but Hamilton found that there was a customary ratio[2] between gold and silver coins in the United States of 1 : 15·6, although

---

[1] Mr. Upton, it seems to me, is in error when he says ("Money in Politics," p. 39): "He admitted that if the ratio between the metals should not prove to be the commercial one, there was hope of retaining only the overvalued metal in circulation. He asserted his belief, however, that 1 : 15 *would prove to be the commercial ratio.*"

[2] Hamilton explains the prevalence of this ratio by the fact that it arose from a custom existing in years before of comparing gold coins with earlier issues of Spanish Seville pieces (386$\frac{4}{5}$ grains of pure silver), which contained more pure silver than the Spanish dollars current in 1791. The Board of Treasury also ("Report of 1878," p. 449) gave 1 : 15·6 as the ratio in common use in 1786.

THE SILVER PERIOD.

this ratio was not based on the weight of Spanish dollars coined at this time.[1] The weight of the Spanish dollars varied, in truth, within very wide limits, and yet had the same nominal value. As early as 1717 the assays of Sir Isaac Newton, at the English Mint, gave the following results:

Seville piece of eight.................... 387 gr. pure silver.
Mexican piece of eight.................. 385½ "   "
Pillar dollar.............................. 385¾ "   "
New Seville piece of eight............. 308 $\frac{7}{16}$ "   "

The Spanish government issued its later coins of less weight than its older ones.[2] Then, also, worn coins contained less silver than fresh ones, so that for many reasons the dollar did not represent any definite weight of silver. In speaking of these coins, Hamilton remarks:

"That species of coin has never had any settled or standard value, according to weight or fineness, but has been permitted to circulate by tale, without regard to either, very much as a mere money of convenience, while gold has had a fixed price by weight, and with an eye to its fineness. This greater stability of value of the gold coins is an argument of force for regarding the money unit as having been hitherto virtually attached to gold rather than to silver.

"Twenty-four grains and six eighths of a grain of fine gold have corresponded with the nominal value of the [silver] dollar in the several States, without regard to the successive diminutions of its intrinsic worth.

"But if the [silver] dollar should, notwithstanding, be supposed to have the best title to being considered as the present

---

[1] In 1782, Robert Morris reported that the best assays to his knowledge made the dollar in general circulation to contain about 373 grains of pure silver. In 1785, a committee reported, and Congress adopted, a plan for a dollar of 362 grains, but it was not carried out. The Board of Treasury, in 1786, proposed a dollar of 375·64 grains. See "Report of 1878," pp. 431, 447, 449.

[2] Gallatin, in a letter to Mr. Ingham, Secretary of the Treasury (December 31, 1829), says: "The present rate (1 : 15) was the result of information clearly incorrect respecting the then relative value of gold and silver in Europe, which was represented as being at the rate of less than 15 to 1, when it was in fact from 15·5 to 15·6 to 1" ("Report of 1878," p. 591). But Hamilton did not attempt to adjust his ratio according to the ratio prevalent in Europe.

unit in the coins, it would remain to determine what kind of dollar ought to be understood."[1]

It seemed, therefore, to be definitely understood that $24\frac{3}{4}$ grains of fine gold stood as the recognized equivalent of a silver dollar; and with this starting-point Hamilton, having already selected the ratio of 1 : 15 between the coins, would be led *a priori* to determine that the silver dollar ought to contain 15 × $24\frac{3}{4}$ grains of fine silver, or $371\frac{1}{4}$ grains. And, in all probability, this was the process by which he arrived at his conclusion. He announced that the later issues of dollars from the Spanish mint had contained 374 grains of fine silver, and the latest issues only 368 grains, which implied a current market ratio in the United States (if these dollars exchanged for $24\frac{3}{4}$ grains of fine gold) of from 1 : 15·11 to 1 : 14·87, or a mean ratio of about 1 : 15. Of this ratio Hamilton says it is "somewhat more than the actual or market proportion, *which is not quite* 1 : 15." But, throughout his inquiry, no one can doubt but that he was honestly seeking for a ratio as near as possible to that existing in the markets of the United States. He certainly can not be charged with an intention of underrating gold.

In later years, however, Hamilton was vehemently attacked by Benton[2] (during the controversy on the second United States Bank) because of an alleged intention to favor silver in preference to gold by his ratio, in order to drive out gold and encourage the use of paper substitutes for the less portable and heavier metal, silver. There seem to be no just grounds for this reflection on Hamilton's purposes. Benton, in his day, saw gold disappearing; but the cause of it was as unknown to him as it was to Hamilton, although it was in operation in 1791, when bimetallism was adopted. To learn what this cause was, it will be suitable first to give a statement from sources now accessible to us of the actual

---

[1] "Report of 1878," p. 456.
[2] Ibid., p. 484. Cf. also Horton's note, p. 460.

CHART I.

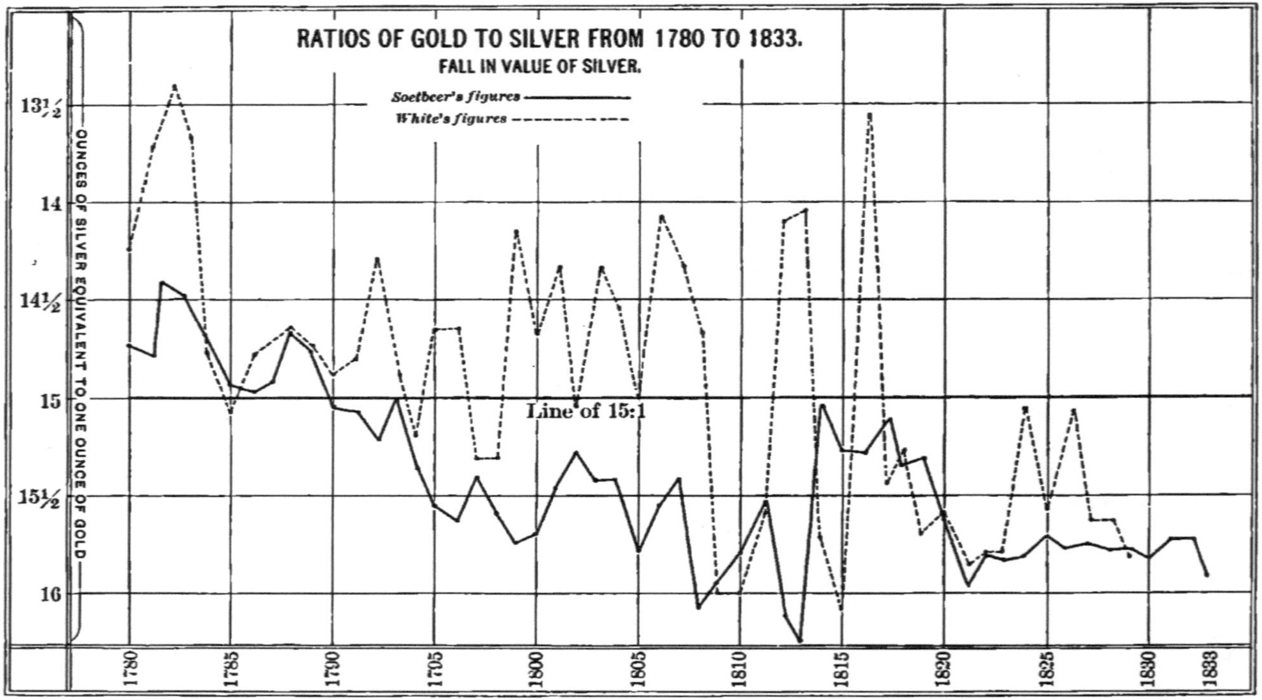

RATIOS OF GOLD TO SILVER FROM 1780 TO 1833.
FALL IN VALUE OF SILVER.
Soetbeer's figures
White's figures
OUNCES OF SILVER EQUIVALENT TO ONE OUNCE OF GOLD
13½
14
14½
15
15½
16
Line of 15:1
1780
1785
1790
1795
1800
1805
1810
1815
1820
1825
1830
1833

ratios of gold to silver during this time, when a coinage system was being established.

The relative values between gold and silver, computed by Dr. Soetbeer from absolutely credible sources in the official quotations twice a week of the prices of silver at Hamburg, are the most reliable. About 1780, Hamburg was a much more important silver market than was London, although in later years the English city has easily taken the lead of all other markets. Another table of ratios was compiled in 1829 by John White, cashier of the United States Bank, covering the years from 1760 to 1829. It is unquestionably full of errors, and quite untrustworthy, but has been quoted by various American writers and officials as if it were trustworthy. For this reason, in the discussion of the years from 1780 to 1800, both tables[1] will be quoted, and the reader can make his own comparisons:

The movement of silver relatively to gold, as shown by these tables, may be best seen in Chart I. A downward tendency in the value of silver relatively to gold, beginning soon after 1780, is the marked characteristic of this period. The horizontal line drawn across the chart indicates the place of the ratio of 15 : 1 proposed by Hamilton, and it can be seen by comparison with this line whether the market ratios corresponded with 1 : 15. The line based on the Hamburg

Year.	Soetbeer.	White.
1780	14·72 : 1	14·30 : 1
1781	14·78 : 1	13·70 : 1
1782	14·42 : 1	13·42 : 1
1783	14·48 : 1	13·66 : 1
1784	14·70 : 1	14·77 : 1
1785	14·92 : 1	15·07 : 1
1786	14·96 : 1	14·76 : 1
1787	14·92 : 1	14·70 : 1
1788	14·65 : 1	14·58 : 1
1789	14·75 : 1	14·76 : 1
1790	15·04 : 1	14·88 : 1
1791	15·05 : 1	14·82 : 1
1792	15·17 : 1	14·30 : 1
1793	15·00 : 1	14·88 : 1
1794	15·37 : 1	15·18 : 1
1795	15·55 : 1	14·64 : 1
1796	15·65 : 1	14·64 : 1
1797	15·41 : 1	15·31 : 1
1798	15·59 : 1	15·31 : 1
1799	15·74 : 1	14·14 : 1
1800	15·68 : 1	14·68 : 1

---

[1] These tables are collected and given in full in Appendix II, together with Cashier White's figures, and critical notes on some of the ratios. All the evidence we have goes to confirm the Hamburg quotations as generally reliable, and to show White's figures to be almost utterly worthless.

[2] See, for critical note on these years, Appendix II.

quotations shows that the market ratios remained at about the line of 1:15 in the years from 1790 to 1793, the very time during which our system was established; but it will be noticed at once that, after 1793, silver began a steady fall relatively to gold, and never thereafter in this period did it return to the ratio of 1:15. It was a very short time, indeed, that the ratio of "the commercial world" remained near Hamilton's choice. Of this gradual tendency of silver to change its value relatively to gold Hamilton, of course, did not know. Had he known of it, he must have foreseen the subsequent action of Gresham's law (by which the cheaper metal drives out the dearer), and the establishment of a single silver standard, instead of the single gold standard which he preferred. Without knowing it, he was dealing with a metal even then shifting in value; and, without intending it, he established a ratio which could accord with the market rate for only a very inconsiderable time. Hamilton's attempt was like that of a man who should try to build a house on the banks of the great glaciers in the Alps, which slowly but constantly move onward within their mountain channels, and who should yet expect to maintain fixed and unchanged relations in his house with the surface of the moving ice.

§ 4. Having supplied ourselves with a knowledge of the actual condition of things on which Hamilton was erecting his bimetallic system, we can now look closer into the plan which was adopted by Congress and put into operation in 1792. His report[1] draws the following conclusions, on which the act was based:

"That the unit in the coins of the United States ought to correspond with 24 grains and ¾ of a grain of pure gold, and with 371 grains and ¼ of a grain of pure silver, each answering to a dollar in the money of account. The former is exactly agreeable to the present value of gold, and the latter is within a small fraction of the mean of the two last emissions of dollars—the only ones which are now found in common cir-

---

[1] See "Report of 1878," p. 478.

culation, and of which the newest is in the greatest abundance. The alloy in each case to be one twelfth of the total weight, which will make the unit 27 grains of standard[1] gold and 405 grains of standard silver."[2]

In carrying out this plan in the act of April 2, 1792, Congress[3] deviated slightly from the recommendations. The alloy in the silver dollar was not made one twelfth, but about one ninth, by fixing the standard weight at 416 grains. The original silver dollar, therefore, weighed 416 grains (not 412½), and contained 371¼ grains of pure silver. No gold dollar pieces were authorized; but the eagle, or ten-dollar piece, was made the basis of our gold coins. The eagle was to contain 270 grains of standard coin and 247·5 grains of pure gold; so that one gold dollar would have weighed 27 grains, and contained 24·75 grains of pure gold. Fifteen times 24·75 grains gives 371¼ grains, the weight of pure metal in the silver dollar, making the ratio between the pure metals in our coins 1 : 15, as intended by Hamilton. The ratio, of course, is never estimated on the standard weights in the coins.

The subsidiary silver coins, or those of denominations below one dollar, were established of a weight and fineness corresponding to that of the dollar piece. That is, two halves,

---

[1] "Standard" is the term applied to the pure metal mixed with the alloy. The actual weight of a finished coin, of course, contains a certain weight of fine or pure metal, plus the alloy. England, Spain, Portugal, and France then put an alloy of one twelfth of the total, or standard, weight into their gold coins. (See "Report of 1878," p. 466.) The origin of this fraction is in the use of carats. Twenty-four carats fine is a standard of pure gold, and these countries adopted as the standard of fineness in their gold coins twenty-two carats, or $\frac{22}{24}$, or $\frac{11}{12}$. Reduced to the decimal system, $\frac{11}{12}$ is 916·66 thousandths fine.

[2] Although Hamilton recommended the same alloy for silver as for gold coins, for some reason Congress did not carry out the suggestion. Instead of adding alloy to 371¼ grains of pure silver, so as to make the standard weight 405 grains (which would have been one twelfth alloy), Congress fixed the standard weight of the silver dollar at 416 grains, thus establishing a fraction a little more than one ninth of alloy (or, in the decimal system, 892·43 thousandths fine). The same was true of the subsidiary silver coins, or denominations below one dollar.

[3] For the provisions of the act at length, see Appendix III.

four quarters, ten dimes, or twenty half-dimes, contained as many grains (371¼) of pure silver as did the one-dollar piece. Therefore, as we shall see later, whenever anything happened to affect the circulation of the dollar piece, it equally affected the subsidiary coinage. This, as is now well known, was an error, and subsequently resulted in the disappearance of all coins used for "small change."

It was also enacted (Sec. 14) that "it shall be lawful for any person or persons to bring to the said Mint gold and silver bullion, in order to their being coined." These words contain the important privilege known as "Free Coinage," by which is meant the right of any private person to have bullion coined at the legal rates. If the Government reserves to itself this right, there would not be free coinage. This is a matter of importance, because through it alone can Gresham's law have an immediate effect. If there is a profit in sending one of two legal metals to the Mint, and in withdrawing the other, with the result of displacing one of the metals in circulation with another, it is necessary, of course, that access to the Mint should be free to any one who sees this chance of profit.

Free coinage, however, is to be distinguished from the absence in the act of any charge for "seigniorage," as expressed in the words: "And that the bullion so brought shall be there assayed and coined as speedily as may be after the receipt thereof, and that free of expense to the person or persons by whom the same shall have been brought." Seigniorage is a charge exacted from persons for coining their bullion into coins at the Mint; but no such charge was exacted in this act of 1792.

The legal-tender power was granted to both gold and silver coins, and subsidiary coinage as well, to an unlimited extent, in these words (Sec. 16): "All the gold and silver coins which shall have been struck at, and issued from, the said Mint shall be a lawful tender in all payments whatsoever, according to the respective values hereinbefore declared, and those of less than full weight at values proportional to their respective weights." As regards the subsidiary coins this was an error, from the point of view of all later experience. That subsidiary coins should be an unlimited tender to any amount, however, when of equal value with the dollar piece, could not create much annoyance.

Such was the bimetallic system established, soon after the foundation of our Government, in 1792. There probably never was a better example of the double standard, one more simple, or one for whose successful trial the conditions could have been more favorable. There was no prejudice among the people against the use of either gold or silver. The relative values of the two metals had been fairly steady for a long time in the past. At the start everything seemed fair. The real difficulty which the future disclosed was one inherent in a system based upon the concurrent use of two metals, each of which is affected by causes independent of the other. The difficulty was certainly not, as some would have us believe, in the selection of a wrong ratio. Knowing, as we now do, that the ratio between gold and silver began to change, as if for a long-continued alteration of their relations, at the very time when Hamilton was setting up a double standard, and learning, as we have, that he declined, from lack of time, to ascertain the market ratio for "the commercial world," we are prepared to find that, as he was wrong in theory, he was also wrong in the ratio he selected with so narrow a view. This, however, is not true. It happened that the ratio he adopted, on the sole ground that it was near to the current relation [1] in the United States, was also, by a piece of good fortune, as near as could be expected to the ratio of "the commercial world." By reference to the Hamburg tables it will be seen that European prices during the four years from 1790 to 1793 (inclusive) gave a market ratio of almost exactly 1 : 15. Indeed, if Hamilton had taken the European market into account, it is difficult to understand

---

[1] Jefferson approved of Hamilton's choice of 1 : 15. Cf. "Report of 1878," p. 486.

what other ratio he could properly have adopted.[1] As a matter of fact, his legal ratio corresponded with the market ratio when his plan went into operation. As a matter of Hamilton's own monetary skill, it was surely but a hand-to-mouth policy; for a ratio different from that of the commercial world would have been wholly unjustified by correct monetary rules.

§ 5. We must now accompany the new coinage system in the course of its experience during the first period of its history. The young and promising offspring of Hamilton started well, but soon began to limp, and then to walk on only one leg. We must therefore investigate the cause of this trouble. In calling attention to Chart I it was noticed that the relative values of gold and silver began to change soon after 1780; that relatively to gold the value of silver fell (or, not to prejudge the case, the value of gold rose relatively to silver) until in the last five years of the century the ratio remained in the vicinity of 1 : 15·5. By continuing the table of figures from 1800 to 1833, the period represented by the chart, it will be possible to see the extent and direction of further changes in this season of trial for the new system. As already observed, the market value, according to Hamburg prices of silver, never rose after 1793 to the

Year.	Soetbeer.	White.
1801	15·46 : 1	14·33 : 1
1802	15·26	15·09
1803	15·41	14·33
1804	15·41	14·54
1805	15·79	15·00
1806	15·52	14·12
1807	15·43	14·33
1808	16·08	14·66
1809	15·96	16·00
1810	15·77	16·00
1811	15·53	15·58
1812	16·11	14·09
1813	16·25	14·04
1814	15·04	15·71
1815	15·26	16·15
1816	15·28	13·52
1817	15·11	15·44
1818	15·35	15·28
1819	15·33	15·68
1820	15·62	15·57
1821	15·95	15·84
1822	15·80	15·77
1823	15·84	15·77
1824	15·82	15·05
1825	15·70	15·55
1826	15·76	15·05
1827	15·74	15·63
1828	15·78	15·63
1829	15·78	15·81
1830	15·82	....
1831	15·72	....
1832	15·73	....
1833	15·93	....

---

[1] Even if we take the untrustworthy figures of White, we find that the ratio was below 1 : 15, and had been since 1786. Therefore it can not be charged by Benton that Hamilton favored silver by the ratio of 1 : 15, since this ratio gave gold an exchange value in the coins greater than that in the market (so far as White's table goes).

ratio of 1 : 15 (indicated by the horizontal line), within this period which extends to 1833 (although it came nearest to it in 1814 and 1817). After 1820 there was a lower level in the relative value of silver to gold, indicating a more or less permanent change in the relations of the two metals, at a rate between 1 : 15½ and 1 : 16. The decline after 1793 was steady, broken by a rally in 1803–1805, and followed by a fall below 1 : 16 in 1813. These are the simple facts, taken from the most trustworthy sources, concerning the relative values of gold and silver in the first period after Hamilton established his system in 1782. Thus was fulfilled his prophecy: "The revolution, therefore, which may take place in the comparative value of gold and silver *will be changes in the state of the latter* rather than in that of the former."

Without stopping now to consider the cause of this change in the relations of gold and silver, it will be best to explain the effects of this change—no matter what its cause—upon the coinage of the United States. The situation now resembles that of a man who, having balanced a lever on a fulcrum, and then, after having lengthened one arm and shortened the other, should expect the lever to balance on the fulcrum in the same manner as before. We now have an illustration of Gresham's law—that when two metals are both legal tender, the cheaper one will drive the dearer out of circulation. This can not operate, however, unless there is "free coinage," and unless there is such a divergence between the mint and the market ratios of gold and silver as will secure to the money-brokers a profit by exchanging one kind of coins for the other. But, as we have already seen, "free coinage" existed, and a profitable difference [1] between the mint and the market ratios in the United States appeared about as early as 1810.

---

[1] Mr. Baring, the banker, testified: "A very slight difference of one tenth or one fourth per cent would determine the use of one metal or another."—Quoted by C. P. White, p. 43 of "H. R. Report No. 278," vol. ii, 1833–1834, 1st session, 23d Congress. In speaking again of this report I shall describe it as "Report No. 278, 1833–1834."

The operation of Gresham's law is in reality a very simple matter. If farmers found that in the same village eggs were purchased at a higher price in one of two shops than in the other, it would not be long before they all carried their baskets to the first shop. Likewise, in regard to gold or silver, the possessor of either metal has two places where he can dispose of it—the United States Mint, and the bullion market; he can either have it coined and receive in new coins the legal equivalent for it, or sell it as a commodity at a given price per ounce. If he finds that silver in the form of United States coins buys more gold than he could purchase with the same amount of silver in the bullion market, he sends his silver to the Mint rather than to the bullion market. By reference to Chart I, it will be seen that the market value of silver relatively to gold had fallen to 1:16, while at the Mint the ratio was 1:15. That is, in the market it required sixteen ounces of silver to buy one ounce of gold bullion; but at the Mint the Government received fifteen ounces of silver, and coined it into silver coins which were legally equivalent to one ounce of gold. The possessor of silver thus found an inducement of one ounce of silver to sell his silver to the Mint for coins, rather than in the market for bullion. But as yet the possessor of silver had only got silver coins from the Mint. How was he to realize his gain? Will people give the more valuable gold for his less valuable silver coins? To some minds there is a difficulty in understanding how a cheaper dollar is actually exchanged for a dearer dollar. This also is simple. The mass of people do not follow the market values of gold and silver bullion, nor calculate arithmetically when a profit can be made by buying up this or that coin. The general public know little about such things, and if they did, a little arithmetic would deter them. These matters are relegated by common consent to the money-brokers, a class of men who, above all others, know the value of a small fraction and the gain to be derived from it. Ordinary persons hand out gold or silver, when they are in concurrent circulation, under the supposition that the intrinsic value of gold is just equal to the intrinsic value of silver in the coins, according to the legal ratio expressed in the coins. If, under such conditions, silver falls as above described, the money-broker will continue to present silver bullion at the Mint, and the silver coins he receives he can exchange for gold coins as long as gold coins remain in common circulation— that is, as long as gold coins are not withdrawn by every one from circulation. Having now received an ounce of gold in coin for his fifteen ounces of silver coin, he can at once sell the gold as bullion (most probably melting it, or selling it to exporters) for sixteen ounces of silver bullion. He retains one ounce of silver as profit, and with the remaining fifteen ounces of silver goes to the Mint for more silver coins, exchanges these for more gold coins, sells the gold as bullion again for silver, and continues this round until gold coins have disappeared from circulation. When every one begins to find out that a gold eagle will buy more of silver bullion than it will of silver dollars in current exchanges, then the gold eagle will be converted into bullion and cease to pass from hand to hand as coin. The existence of a profit in selling gold coins as bullion, and presenting silver to be coined at the Mint, is due to the divergence of the market from the legal ratio, and no power[1] of the Government can prevent one metal from going out of circulation. Like the farmers with their eggs, under the operation of Gresham's law silver will be taken where it is of the most value (the United States

---

[1] A vivid illustration of this fact is given in Macaulay's "History of England," chap. xxi. About 1691, new coins were issued of full weight to take the place of the worn and clipped coins which caused so much wrangling in every bargain; but the old coins and the new were equally received by the state for government dues. There was, therefore, a premium on clipping the new coins, if the old and clipped coins were an equally good tender for taxes. The new coins disappeared as fast as they came from the Mint. Men and women were hanged in numbers for this kind of money-making, but the trouble went on as before, until the proper remedy was applied in 1695 by ceasing to receive the worn and clipped coins for more than their value by weight.

Mint), and gold will be sold[1] where it brings a greater value than as coin (the bullion market).

In the preceding explanation of Gresham's law I have described the process which began to make itself felt as early as about 1810. The date itself is of importance, because some writers have explained the operation of Gresham's law and the disappearance of gold by causes[2] which can be admitted as the true ones only if the date were as late as 1819, the year when the English Resumption Act was passed. There are, however, indisputable proofs that the change in the relations of the two metals was apparent long before 1819, and, consequently, long before the English demand could have been felt. Mr. Lowndes introduced the question of the disappearance of gold from the currency by a resolution[3] in the lower house of Congress as early as November 27, 1818. Benton[4] distinctly sets an earlier date by stating that "it was not until the lapse of near *twenty years after the adoption of the erroneous standard of 1792* that the circulation of that metal [gold], both foreign and domestic, became completely and totally extinguished in the United States." This would

---

[1] "The most extreme instance which has ever occurred was the case of the Japanese currency. At the time of the treaty of 1858, between Great Britain, the United States, and Japan, which partially opened up the last country to European trades, a very curious system of currency existed in Japan. The most valuable Japanese coin was the kobang, consisting of a thin oval disk of gold about two inches long and one inch and a quarter wide, weighing two hundred grains, and ornamented in a very primitive manner. It was passing current in the towns of Japan for four silver itzebus, but was worth in English money about 18s. 5d., whereas the silver itzebu was equal only to about 1s. 4d. Thus the Japanese were estimating their gold money at only about one third of its value, as estimated according to the relative values of the metals in other parts of the world. The earliest European traders enjoyed a rare opportunity for making profit. By buying up the kobangs at the native rating they trebled their money, until the natives, perceiving what was being done, withdrew from circulation the remainder of the gold."—Jevons, "Money and Mechanism of Exchange," p. 84.

[2] See *infra*, chap. iii, § 5.

[3] On which a report was made January, 26, 1819. 3 Finance, p. 398.

[4] "Thirty Years' View," vol. i, chap. cv. Speech on the revival of the gold currency.

fix the time at about 1812. This is corroborated by Crawford,[1] Secretary of the Treasury, who asserts that a change in the relative values had taken place *many years* before 1820. When we recall that such a process as the substitution of one metal by another must be comparatively slow, especially in a new and sparsely settled country, the causes must have been at work some time before, if we read in a report to Congress in 1821: "On inquiry, they find that gold coins, both foreign and of the United States, have, in a great measure, disappeared."[2] It seems, therefore, to be clear that gold began to disappear as early as 1810, if not before, and that little of it was in circulation by 1818.[3] Indeed, since 1793 there existed in the relative values of gold and silver a strong reason why gold should not circulate in the United States, and why Mr. Lowndes should have said[4] in 1819:

---

[1] "It is believed that gold, when compared with silver, has been *for many years* appreciating in value."—In a "Report on the Currency," February 24, 1820. Cf. "Report of 1878," p. 519. "*In the autumn of the year 1820* [November 25] an article, written by me, was published in your gazette ['National Gazette'] explaining *the cause of the disappearance of gold from the United States.*"— Condy Raguet, "Currency and Banking," p. 207.

[2] And they add: "There is a continual and steady drain of that metal from this country." See "Report of 1878," p. 554.

[3] "It is a notorious fact that there is at this moment a traffic carried on between the United States and Canada more destructive to our national interest than an evasion of the embargo, or even partially supplying the enemy with provisions, as its effects are so much more extensive. *We mean the taking from this country an immense quantity of* GOLD to Canada, and receiving therefor British Government bills. It is well known that thousands of pounds sterling are daily offered on the exchange; and such is the demand at this moment for gold that it will bring upward of 4 per cent advance for the purpose of the above-mentioned traffic."—From the "Boston Patriot," in "Niles' Register," vi, p. 46, 1814.

[4] 3 "Finance," p. 399. Mr. Ingham (Secretary of the Treasury, in a report to the Senate, May 4, 1830), in discussing this, says that, although Lowndes attributed the fact to an error in the selection of a ratio by Hamilton, "it does not appear from the market price in the United States, during the whole of that time [1792–1819], that gold was more valuable for exportation than silver. On the contrary, it will be observed, by reference to Table B [White's untrustworthy table], that in England, prior to 1810, the ratio of gold to silver had for fifty years averaged at less than 1 to 14·75, and at no period of ten years as

"It can scarcely be considered as having formed a material part of our money circulation for the last twenty-six years. In fact, the situation has been thus distinctly described:[1]

"Our national gold coins were seldom if ever used as currency. Silver, which, by the act of 1792, rated quite as high as its commercial value, was the only national coin much used by our citizens. On our Northwestern and Southern frontiers, and in some Atlantic cities, foreigners occasionally scattered foreign gold coins. But these did not form any considerable portion of the circulating medium, except perhaps at the Southwest. As they were valued by weight, their circulation was highly inconvenient and often the subject of imposition. Their value was constantly fluctuating, according to the rates of exchange on Europe, where they were a legal tender in payment of balances due from us."

In fact, the result of careful inquiry reveals to us that gold coins were seldom seen during the largest part of this period from 1792 to 1834. Even when bank-paper was used, the reserves of the banks were generally in silver, not in gold.[2] Whatever the cause of the change in the relative values, certain it is that gold disappeared, and that the United States had but a single silver currency as early as 1817, and probably earlier.

These conclusions are fortified by the returns of gold and silver coinage at the United States Mint. In the exposition of Gresham's law it was explained that the metal which had fallen in value would be presented at the Mint to be coined, while the dearer metal would go into the melting-pot, or be exported. Inasmuch as silver had fallen in value relatively to gold, it was to be expected that, to some extent, even in a new community where specie was scarce, silver would be brought to the Mint in preference to gold. And this is what we find to be the fact. After 1805 the coinage of silver dis-

---

high as 1 to 15." He then admits "the fact that it [gold] did not then [prior to 1819] circulate." Cf. "Report of 1878," p. 576, for the context.

[1] "H. R. Report," p. 5, No. 513, 24th Congress, 1st session, March 26, 1836.

[2] C. P. White says, in 1832: "For the last fifteen years our currency has been exclusively bank-notes (except for small change), subject to redemption, on demand, with *silver*."—" Report No. 278," p. 24, 1833-1834.

CHART II.

Coinage of Gold and Silver at the United States Mint, 1793-1833. Ratio, 1 : 15.

Silver, ⬜   Gold, ⬛

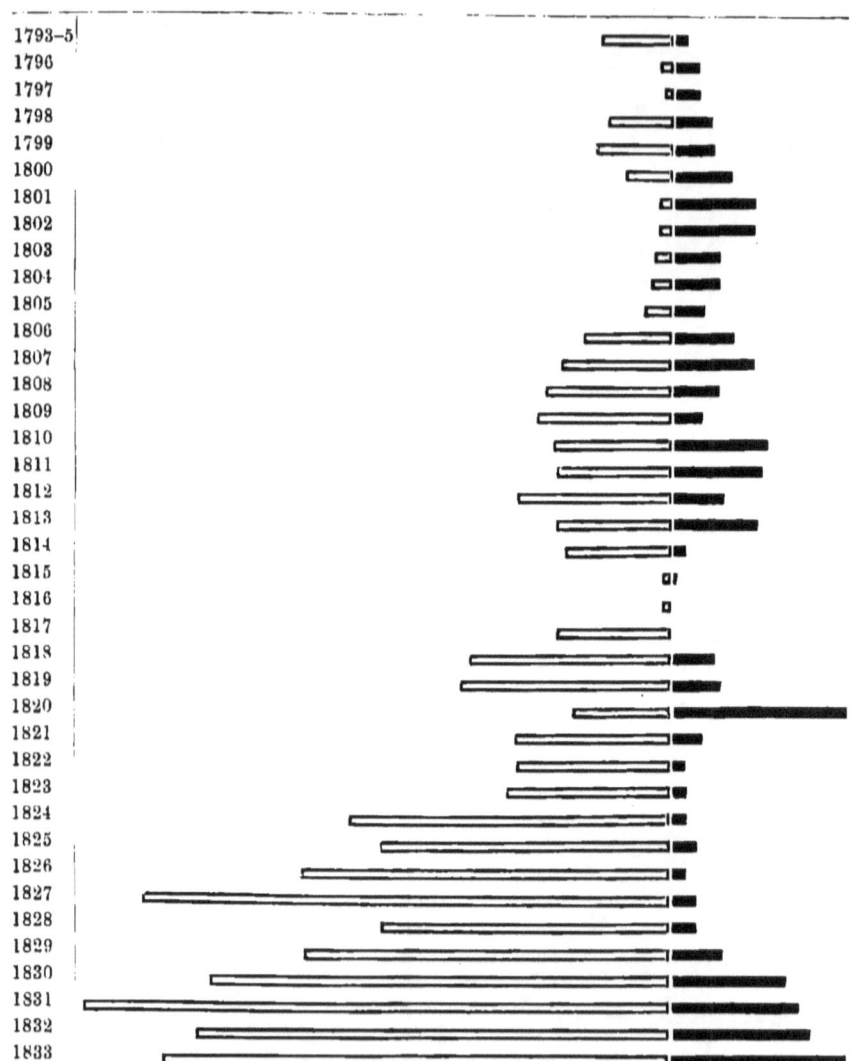

tinctly increased, without an increase of gold coinage, while soon after the war of 1812 the coinage of gold almost entirely ceased, but the issue of silver coins steadily multiplied during the remainder of this period. This can be most easily seen in Chart II. The length of the dark lines away from the perpendicular line shows the value of gold coined (estimated in dollars) each year,[1] while the open lines, extending in an opposite direction, show the same for silver.[2] So distinct a change in the relative amounts of gold and silver coinage since 1805 is in itself cumulative proof that there was such a variation of the market from the Mint ratio as to send silver to the Mint for coinage in preference to gold as early as 1806. And this, too, although American dollar pieces ceased to be sent out from the Mint after 1805, and were not coined from that time to 1836. The mass of silver coins issued were in the form of half-dollars, which contained proportionally the same weight of silver as the dollar piece.

In summing up, we find that, in fact, the ratio of 1 : 15 was in accordance with the market ratio at the time of the establishment of the Mint in 1792, but that Hamilton was attempting to set up the new system on the slope of a declining value of silver relatively to gold; and that this downward movement was unknown to the statesmen of that day. The divergence of the market from the Mint ratio brought Gresham's law into operation as early as the period from 1805 to 1810, and before 1820 it had virtually driven gold out of use as a medium of exchange.

---

[1] The exceptional gold coinage in 1820 was due to special importations of gold by the Bank of the United States, in order to bring about specie payments.

[2] See Table of Annual Coinage at the United States Mint, Appendix IV.

CHAPTER III.

CAUSE OF THE CHANGE IN THE RELATIVE VALUES OF GOLD
AND SILVER, 1780-1820.

§ 1. THE problem before us in this chapter is economic as well as historical. Having seen in the preceding chapter the effects of a change in the relative values of gold and silver upon our monetary system, it will now be necessary to find an explanation of the causes which produced this change.

The position has been taken by some writers that the divergence of the market from the Mint ratio, in the period we are speaking of, was, in fact, a rise in the value of gold relatively to silver, not a fall in the value of silver relatively to gold. The cause of this increased value of gold, they assert, was due to the demand of England for gold with which to resume specie payments in accordance with the act of 1819. In the well-known and elaborate reports[1] of Mr. Campbell P. White to Congress in 1832 we find the theory well developed:

"There were certainly no indications that gold was rated too low in our standard of 1 to 15 *earlier than 1821, when the English demand commenced.* The fact of concomitance in events is not relied upon as a proof of effective agency; but *a great demand for gold and an increased relative value for gold being coeval circumstances,* and in accordance with the universally admitted principle that a new or sudden increase of demand will enhance prices, it appears to be a natural and rational inference that the British demand for gold was the cause of increasing the value in respect to silver."

---

[1] "H. R. Report No. 278," 1833-1834, contains them all. For this extract see "Report," March 17, 1832.

CHANGE IN THE VALUE OF SILVER. 33

Condy Raguet[1] believed that the change of the market ratio had at least been brought to general notice by the English demand for gold. The theory of Mr. C. P. White has been revived of late by Mr. S. Dana Horton,[2] who says: "The concurrent circulation of the metals at 15 : 1 (with that *vis inertiæ* which is one of the unsettled problems of money) did not succumb to the influences of foreign demand until the drain began for the resumption of gold payment in England." He substantiates his position by quoting[3] the following table of average prices, computed by Professor Jevons, to show that the English demand for gold caused a shrinkage in gold prices of commodities. The effect of this English demand is traced in Mr. Horton's argument by giving estimates of the supply of gold and silver then existing, and then comparing with the existing supply the amount of gold collected by England, in order to show how large the demand was in proportion to the supply. It is estimated[4] by him that the amount of gold used as a medium of exchange in western Europe in 1810

Year.	Gold price.
1815	109
1816	91
1817	117
1818	132
1819	112
1820	103
1821	94
1822	88
1823	89
1824	88

---

[1] "It was in the early part of the year 1818—when the subject of the resumption of cash payments by the Bank of England (which had been suspended since 1797) occupied the attention of the British public and prepared the way for the act of Parliament to that effect, which was adopted in 1819—that a change in the relative value of gold and silver in the market of the trading world *first became generally apparent in the United States.*"—" Currency and Banking," p. 222. Bolles, following Raguet, says on one page: "Not until 1818, when the question arose of resuming cash payments by the Bank of England, did the fact clearly appear in this country that a change had occurred in the relative value of gold and silver "; but on the next page he asserts that " of the two metals it was apparent, even before the war of 1812, that gold was more desirable for exportation than silver."—" Financial History of the United States," pp. 502, 503.

[2] "Report of 1878," p. 460, note. Cf. also ibid., pp. 701-709. In these pages Horton gives a short statement of his position in convenient form. In his volume, " Gold and Silver" (1877), pp. 74-98, he developed this theory more fully.

[3] "Gold and Silver," p. 83.

[4] Ibid., pp. 81, 83, 84.

was $665,000,000, and that the accumulations of England for resumption purposes created a new demand for from $125,000,000 to $150,000,000 of gold, while the annual production at that time was only $7,500,000. "When, however, the process of obtaining gold [for England] from abroad had had time to exert its full effect on prices, and gold was actually substituted for paper, the fall took place, as depicted in the table of prices, giving for 1821–1824 an average of 90 in the place of 116—a difference of level of nearly 23 per cent."

While every one must admit the effect of a new demand upon an unaltered world's supply of gold to increase its value, it does not seem to me safe to believe that gold rose in value relatively to silver because of the English demand. To begin with, I must deny the worth of any guesses as to the existing supply of gold at any time; they are at most guesses, and, in the nature of things, can not be more than the most vague approximations. No statistics of this kind will do to build a theory upon. It is a different thing with the annual supply, since it is comparatively easy to ascertain the sums produced by the mines.

I am inclined to think, moreover, that in this case too much is made of a demand such as that of England at this time, which, in truth, only shifted a part of the existing stock of the metals from one part of the commercial world to another. England was only reclaiming that share of gold which the proportion of her transactions to the total transactions of the Western world warranted. She could have had no more before the restriction act in 1797, and she could retain no more permanently in her circulation in 1822. During the continuance of the Restriction Act England let her gold go, and other countries obtained a greater amount than before in proportion to their transactions. About 1820–1822 the old relation was resumed—except so far as transactions (or a general demand for money) throughout the commercial world had increased or changed. Was the accumulation of gold by England then, in its essence, a *new* demand on the existing stock of the world, taking into account the total demand of the world as well as the total supply? If it was not, then the perturbations of prices which may have been caused by the refluent tide of gold into England would soon settle themselves in accordance with the new and permanent distribution of gold. If Mr. Horton had shown that transactions, or general demand for gold as a medium of exchange, had increased by 1820 as compared with 1797, without a corresponding change in the supply of gold, or in economizing expedients or substitutes for gold, then he might have had ground for asserting that gold had risen in value. This he has not done.

Granting, however, all the influence which Mr. Horton ascribes to the English demand, it will be observed that he locates[1] the effect on prices of the increased value of gold in the years 1821-1824. But, from the evidence we have already collected, there is not a shadow of a doubt but that the change in the value of silver relatively to gold was felt in the United States before the war of 1812, and that, as Raguet says, gold had disappeared from circulation by 1818. Therefore, even without questioning all that Mr. Horton claims in regard to the effect on prices of the English demand for gold, it applies to a period (1820-1830) which lies outside of the time (1810-1820) when the disturbing causes we are now discussing were operating to drive gold out of circulation in the United States. Inasmuch as the change in the ratio between gold and silver was apparent in the period from 1810-1820, the cause of the change must therefore have been one which could have had nothing to do with the English demand for gold which took effect later, in 1820-1830. In short, some other cause[2]

---

[1] "Silver and Gold," p. 83.

[2] Gallatin also denies the validity of Horton's theory in the following words: "It is erroneously that the exportation of American gold coins, *which commenced in the year 1821*, has been ascribed to that extraordinary demand [in England for purposes of resumption]. That exportation has been continued uninterruptedly after that cause had ceased to operate, and, as will be seen hereafter, is due to the alteration from that epoch in the rate of the exchanges."
—Quoted by C. P. White in "Report No. 278," 1833-1834, p. 42.

than is assigned by Mr. Horton was at work to produce a divergence in the values of gold and silver, which certainly had a marked effect before 1816, the year when silver was made a subsidiary metal in the English coinage, and long before England began to collect any gold whatever for her resumption of specie payments in 1819–1822.[1] A glance at Chart I will show, even if we take the untrustworthy figures of White, that the change in the relative values of gold and silver had occurred so long before the English demand could have produced an effect that Mr. Horton's position seems to me entirely untenable.

Mr. Horton, however, goes still further, and asserts[2] that there was a rise in the value of gold, "because," he says, "as far as I can ascertain, the change of ratio was really a rise of gold, not a fall of silver. I am aware of no evidence that the general value of money as shown by averages of prices was less in 1820–1830 than it was in 1770–1780. Whatever scanty researches on this subject have come to my knowledge indicate a lower range of prices in the former than in the latter period." So far as the periods concern us, the comparison should be made between 1780–1790 and 1810–1820, since the ratio between gold and silver had distinctly changed in the latter period; and the former period gives a just means of comparison because it includes the fairly quiet years before the great continental wars with France. It will be our part, then, to discover, so far as possible, what change prices underwent in this period; but before doing so it will be best

---

[1] "The Resumption Act of 1819 continued the restriction of cash payment to February, 1820, and thereafter ordered the redemption by the bank of its notes, when demanded, in a quantity of not less than sixty ounces of gold (over $1,000) in gold bullion, at a discount for paper of about $3\frac{7}{8}$ per cent till October, 1820; from that date till May, 1821, at about 2 per cent discount; and thereafter, till May, 1823, at par, but still in bullion; while after the latter date all notes were to be paid in gold coin on presentation.

"The bank was, however, permitted to pay in bullion at higher rates in fixed periods, and in gold coin after May 1, 1822. A subsequent law permitted full redemption after May 1, 1822."—Horton, "Gold and Silver," p. 80.

[2] "Report of 1878," p. 701.

to explain briefly the economic principles on which relations of prices and money depend.

§ 2. Value, we know, is a ratio. The value of an ox, estimated in sheep, is the number of sheep for which the ox will exchange. If one ox exchanges for twenty sheep, an ox is twenty times as valuable as one sheep, or a sheep is one-twentieth as valuable as an ox. So with gold or silver. When the number of grains of silver in a dollar is exchanged for goods, value of the silver is expressed in the quantity of other things for which it will exchange, as, for example, two bushels of oats. On the other hand, the value of the oats is the quantity of silver they will purchase. Value, it is thus seen, is a relation. There must always be some other thing with which to compare the given commodity. For instance, in comparing silver with gold, the value of silver relatively to gold is the number of grains of gold for which a fixed amount of silver will freely exchange. If at any time more silver than before is needed to buy the same quantity of gold, this means that either silver has fallen in value relatively to gold, or that gold has risen in value relatively to silver. Now, however, if gold had remained nearly stable in its power of purchasing other commodities in general—that is, bought about the same amounts as before of various things other than silver; and if more grains of silver were needed than before to buy a given number of grains of gold—then, of course, it would be said that silver had fallen not merely with regard to gold, but to commodities in general. But, on the other hand, if silver fell in its value relatively to gold, and all other commodities likewise fell in relation to gold, then, of course, it will be said that gold has risen in value not merely with regard to silver, but to commodities in general. The amount of money, such as gold and silver given for an article, is its price. If gold rises in value, less of it is needed to buy other goods, therefore prices fall. In other words, if gold prices fall, the value of gold, provided we leave credit out of question, has increased relatively to commodities in general. With this brief exposition we may now go on to the study of our facts.

§ 3. It is incumbent on us, first, to discover whether, in the period from 1780 to 1820, gold gained or lost in its general purchasing power over ordinary goods. That is, whether gold prices rose or fell in 1810–1820, as compared with 1780–1790. But we must keep in view that prices are the result of two factors—(1) the amount of money taken in connection with its rapidity of circulation, and (2) the extent of credit and speculation. Every one knows that credit is purchasing power, and that prices rise and fall wholly through the use of credit in seasons of an expansion or depression of confidence. The fall of prices which takes place after a commercial crisis is due more to a collapse of credit than to any contraction in the actual quantity of the money-factor. If, in studying this question, we suppose that the play of credit should be considered as about equal in the two periods for comparison, 1780–1790 and 1810–1820, then we may fairly draw an inference as to the purchasing power of gold from tables of prices. On no other basis can the conclusion as to the value of gold be worth anything. In fact, for this reason, ordinary inferences from tables of prices are misleading in the extreme. For the present comparison the prices for this period have been arranged by Prof. Jevons[1] and reduced to a scale of 100, which represents the prices of forty commodities in 1782. The results are presented herewith in Chart III, to which has been added the line representing the index-numbers computed by the "London Economist." The latter are based on the figure 2,200, which is the sum of the scales of 22 articles, each by itself having 100 as a basis. The average prices of 1845–1850 are taken as the standard (2,200), and the movement of the line shows the subsequent departure of prices from that basis. This completes a chart of the movement of prices to the present day; although it is to be regretted that the prices are not calculated in the same way, both by Mr. Jevons and the

---

[1] First published in the "London Statistical Journal" in June, 1865, vol. xxviii, pp. 294–320, and reprinted in "Investigations in Currency and Finance" (1884), pp. 144–149.

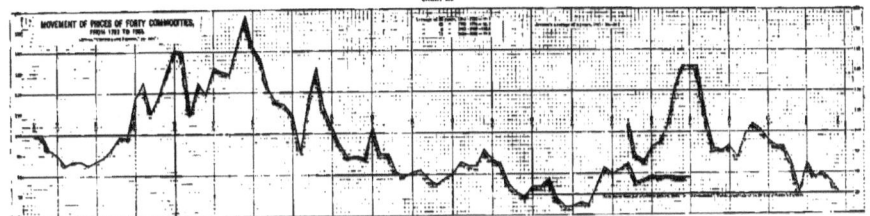

"Economist," thus presenting a continuous table without the break since 1850. In the figures given by Prof. Jevons we have the following results condensed in the accompanying table. So far as these figures prove anything, when we compare the period in which our ratio of 1 : 15 was established by Hamilton with the period from 1810-1820, during

Period.	Average prices.
1782–1792	90·5
1810–1820	118·9
1820–1830	92·5

which gold disappeared from the United States, it surely can not be said that gold prices fell (thus indicating an increased value of gold). Although our concern is not with the years from 1820-1830, yet even in this period we do not find that prices were lower when compared with those of 1782-1792. And in Mr. Horton's discussion it will be observed that he only wishes to show a fall of prices in 1821-1825. I can therefore believe that the English demand had only a temporary influence on the value of gold, and that the purchasing power of gold depended upon the demand of the commercial countries taken as a whole, and not upon that of England alone. I must also believe that a change in the relative values of gold and silver was sufficiently made out as early as 1810, and that it had its effect in driving gold out of circulation in the United States before 1820. Moreover, as we have not been able to find that the general purchasing power of gold (as expressed in the figures referred to by Mr. Horton) in 1810-1820 was less than in 1782-1792, we can not believe that gold had risen in value (in the former period). Therefore it seems to be inevitable that there was a fall in the value of silver, not merely with reference to gold, but with reference to commodities in general. On the contrary, we have seen, by the tables given herewith and by Chart III, that gold prices in the period just preceding 1820 were, if anything, higher than in 1782-1792. That is, so far as these prices go for anything, it was rather to be said that gold had fallen slightly, rather than risen, in its purchasing power, or, in other words, had fallen in its value relatively to other goods.

It does not appear from Mr. Jevons's figures, then, that

the value of gold had risen by 1820 as compared with 1782–1792. Some confirmatory testimony is offered by Dr. Edmund Schebek in the tables[1] of prices of a few articles in Continental markets:

PERIOD.	WHEAT.			CORN.			BARLEY.			GRAIN.		
	Average price.		Comparison with the foregoing period.	Average price.		Comparison.	Average price.		Comparison.	Average price.		Comparison.
	Fl.	Kr.	Per c.	Fl.	Kr.	Per c.	Fl.	Kr.	Per c.	Fl.	Kr.	Per c.
1751–1760.	1	84.74	− 4.70	1	40.85	− 8.87	1	19.61	− 5.18	1	48.40	− 6.16
1761–1770.	1	89.10	+ 2.35	1	36.36	− 3.19	1	08.63	− 9.18	1	45.07	− 2.24
1771–1780.	2	09.70	+10.89	1	57.38	+15.42	1	21.91	+12.22	1	62.99	+12.35
1781–1790.	2	31.12	+10.17	1	79.12	+13.81	1	33.20	+ 9.26	1	81.14	+11.13
1791–1800.	2	54.95	+10.31	1	83.90	+ 2.67	1	48.06	+11.16	1	95.63	+ 7.99
1801–1810.	4	71.61	+84.98	3	53.07	+91.98	3	02.81	+104.53	3	75.82	+92.11
1811–1820.	4	38.17	− 7.09	3	10.60	−12.03	2	53.76	−16.18	3	34.16	−11.08
1821–1830.	2	87.97	−34.28	2	10.83	−32.11	1	62.14	− 36.10	2	20.31	−34.07

It is to be kept in mind, however, that these were articles which would be in particular demand during the Napoleonic wars on the Continent. But the comparison of the average prices for 1781–1790 with those for either the period 1811–1820 or even 1821–1830 shows a marked rise of prices in the later periods. Still this does not furnish very strong proof that the value of gold had not risen relatively to grain, because Dr. Schebek has reduced all the quotations to silver prices. Therefore, there is a probable induction[2] to be made

---

[1] "Collectiv-Ausstellung von Beiträgen zur Geschichte der Preise," Prague (1873), p. 102.

[2] Another table from Dr. Schebek (p. 87) is given herewith, which warrants the same inferences:

PERIODS.	Beer (Lower-Austrian measures), eimer.		Barley (Lower-Aust.), peck.		Hops, cwt.		Wood, cord.	
	Fl.	Kr.	Fl.	Kr.	Fl.	Kr.	Fl.	Kr.
1751–1760.......	1	80	1	12	26		1	64
1761–1770.......	2	18	1	..	35		2	4
1771–1780.......	2	30	1	44	24		1	46
1781–1790.......	2	29	1	28	29		2	10
1791–1800.......	2	25	1	31	38		2	64
1801–1810.......	2	37	2	45	54		3	27
1811–1820.......	3	11	2	98	100		4	92
1821–1830.......	2	71	1	71	44		2	94

from the table, so far as it goes, to the effect that since silver prices had risen, the value of silver had fallen in its purchasing power in grain; for if more silver is needed to purchase grain than before, the value of silver has fallen relatively to grain.

§ 4. The value of either of the precious metals at a given short period is a question of demand and supply; and it can be seriously influenced by cost of production only in the course of long periods, unless the lessened cost of obtaining the supply throws enormous quantities on the market at once, and thus depresses its value in a comparatively few years. The effect on the value, however, takes place through the operation of supply and demand. To determine the causes affecting the value of silver, therefore, we must take into account not only those influences which operate as supply, but also those which operate as demand.

When we discover that Mr. Horton's main position is that the English demand for gold had so important an influence as to alter the relation of gold to other commodities throughout the world, silver included, we find him appealing to demand. But in this question he ignores the question of supply. " How was this rise of gold, or, if it be preferred, this increase of difference between the metals, brought about? Was it due to any alteration in the relative cost of production? So far as I am informed, *history has nothing to say on this subject.*"[1] It is just here that I am compelled to dissent from his position. History has a great deal to say on the subject; and the historical method will serve us excellently well in this investigation. Induction is here our only method. I shall therefore proceed, so far as I am able, to show by the facts what have been the influences affecting the supply of the precious metals relatively to each other.

Inasmuch as the question here involved is one of a relation between the values of gold and silver, and of relative changes in the production and supply of the two metals,

---
[1] " Report of 1878," p. 702.

I have computed from Dr. Soetbeer's tables[1] of the production of the precious metals the following figures, intended to show the annual production of silver relatively to gold (by weight) since the discovery of America:

PERIOD.	Average yearly production of silver in kilogrammes.	Average yearly production of gold in kilogrammes.	Number of times the average yearly production of silver was greater than that of gold.
1493–1520	47,000	5,800	8·1
1521–1544	90,200	7,160	12·6
1545–1560	311,600	8,510	36·6
1561–1580	299,500	6,840	43·7
1581–1600	418,900	7,380	56·8
1601–1620	422,900	8,520	49·6
1621–1640	393,600	8,300	47·4
1641–1660	366,300	8,770	41·7
1661–1680	337,000	9,260	36·4
1681–1700	341,900	10,765	31·7
1701–1720	355,600	12,820	27·7
1721–1740	431,200	19,080	22·6
1741–1760	533,145	24,610	21·6
1761–1780	652,740	20,705	31·5
1781–1800	879,060	17,790	49·4
1801–1810	894,150	17,778	50·2
1811–1820	540,770	11,445	47·2
1821–1830	460,560	14,216	32·4
1831–1840	596,450	20,289	29·4
1841–1850	780,415	54,759	14·2
1851–1855	886,115	197,515	4·4
1856–1860	904,990	206,058	4·4
1861–1865	1,101,150	185,123	5·9
1866–1870	1,339,085	191,900	6·9
1871–1875	1,969,425	170,675	11·5
1876–1880	2,500,575	172,325	14·5

To accompany this table I have constructed Chart IV, which contains two lines—one representing the value of silver[2] relatively to gold, the other the quantity of silver relatively to gold which has been produced annually in the same periods.

The upper line, in the beginning of the chart, shows that, on the discovery of America, about eleven ounces of silver bought one ounce of gold; while silver has changed its relation to gold so much in the intervening time to the present time, that more than eighteen (now even requiring

---

[1] See Appendix I.   [2] For the figures, see Appendix II.

CHART IV.

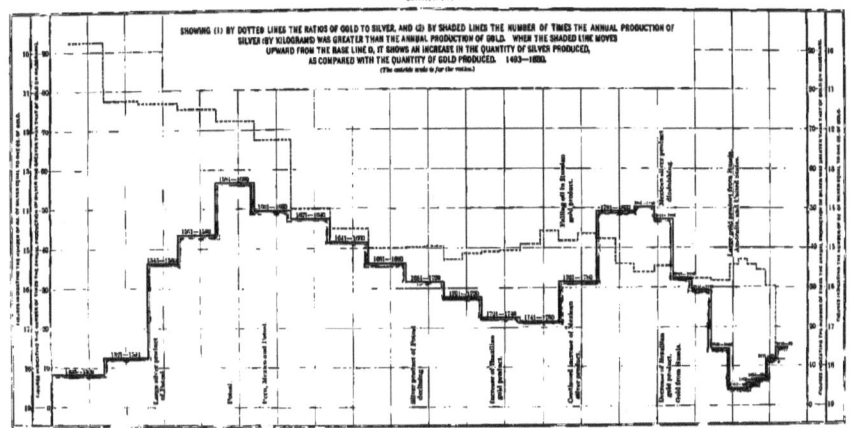

twenty) ounces are now required to buy one ounce of gold. The one exception to this steady downward tendency was in the period from 1710–1780, in which silver showed a tendency to recover its position relatively to gold ; that is, in this period there was an upward movement of the line, which represented an increasing value of silver relatively to gold. This, however, does not of course imply that gold remained stationary in value. For the increased amount of gold produced to within a few years also has lowered its value 300 or 400 per cent relatively to other articles since the discovery of America. Any casual reader of history knows that a given amount of gold in the middle ages had then a much greater purchasing power than it has now.

The other line shows two considerable variations since the discovery of America—one in the period 1545–1680, and another in the period 1781–1820. Inasmuch as this line indicates the relative quantities of the two metals produced in each year, the line will rise whenever more silver than gold is produced, or whenever the gold product falls off (even if the silver product remains the same) ; and the line will decline whenever the silver product falls off relatively to the gold, or whenever the gold product increases (even if no change takes place in the production of silver). The line, therefore, indicates relations, not quantities. For example, the chart shows that 56·8 times as much silver as gold was yielded by the mines annually in 1581–1600, and 50·2 times as much silver in 1801–1810. But still the annual production of both metals was very much larger in this last period than in the former, although the number expressing the relation is less in the second case than in the first; for in 1581–1600 the annual production of silver was 418,900 kilogrammes, and of gold 7,380 kilogrammes ; but in 1801–1810 there was produced annually 894,150 kilogrammes of silver and 17,778 kilogrammes of gold. And yet the line did not rise so high in the last period as in the former.

From the data before us it ought to be possible now to see what effects have been produced by these great movements of gold and silver. The principal event in the history of the precious metals, and which has received the attention of writers on economic history (the very event, in fact, which led to a discovery of the economic laws underlying money and gave birth to political economy), was the enormous production of gold and silver, beginning about 1545, from the mines of Mexico, of Peru, and especially of Potosi. The fact that a disproportionate mass of this production was silver—about forty-five times as much silver as gold—has been generally recognized. The effect on the relative value of gold to silver was extraordinary. By 1660 the enormous supply of silver had reduced the value of silver relatively to gold about 36 per cent. It is not to be understood, however, that this fall of silver indicated an absolute steadiness in the value of gold. The increased production of gold, as already mentioned, has also lowered its value since the discovery of America to a very serious extent. Chevalier estimates the fall[1] of gold as much as 4 to 1. This fall in the value of silver is capable of explanation. The value of a commodity (cost of production apart) at a given time depends upon the relation between the demand and the total available supply then in existence. If the demand remain the same, and the supply be increased, the value will fall. Moreover, the extent of the fall will depend largely on the proportion between the amount of the increased supply and the amount already in existence. At the time of the discovery of America the world's stock of silver was comparatively small, and the influx of vast quantities from the American mines was capable of making a great change in the value of this existing stock. The ratio of gold to silver was changed from 1 : 11 to 1 : 15 by 1660 —a change so sudden and so considerable (since gold itself had fallen) that it could only have been caused by the action of large annual supplies on a small existing stock, unsupported by a proportional demand.

---

[1] Cf. Cairnes's "Essays in Political Economy," p. 124.

It is to be remarked, also, from an examination of Chart IV, that the fall in the value can become generally apparent only after the annual supply, joining with the supply previously existing, has had the effect to increase the total supply, with which alone comparisons of commodities are to be made; so that only as the level of the total supply in existence rises (not the actual amount of the annual supply itself) can the change in value show itself. In other words, the change in relative values (of durable articles, like gold and silver, of which there is always an existing stock) must always follow, not be contemporary with, the change in the relative annual supply. An illustration of these principles can be seen in examining Chart IV. The fall in the value of silver was comparatively slight until 1620, although a large excess of silver over gold had been produced since 1545; and the effect of the silver production does not show its full effect until 1660, and even leaves its mark as late as 1701–1740. The effect of a production of silver, very large in comparison with that of gold, on the relative values of the two metals at this time, therefore, can not be denied, it seems to me, for a moment. The influence was the more considerable because of the disproportion between the large new production of silver and the comparatively small supply of silver then existing.

We are now in a position, at last, to discuss the causes operating to affect the relative values of gold and silver in the later period of 1780–1820, during which it happened that Hamilton was founding a bimetallic system in the United States, and was seeking for a satisfactory ratio. As has been said, a reference to Chart IV will show that the line indicating the relative product of the two metals has made only two great movements upward in the last four centuries. The first one we have just discussed, and history has generally admitted all the results as to the value of silver that have been here attributed to it; but, naturally enough (perhaps because fit materials for study have been wanting until of late), no sufficient account has been taken of the second great movement in the history of the precious metals from 1780 to 1820. Jacob[1] was too close to the events when he wrote to grasp the whole situation. But of this period, as extraordinary in its way as the period of 1560–1660, Horton remarks,[2] "History has nothing to say." In short, the changes in the relative production of silver and gold from 1781–1820 are on so enormous a scale as to be comparable only with the changes which occurred immediately after the discovery of the American silver mines. By changes I mean the immense preponderance of the silver over the gold product. In the earlier period the mass of new silver acted on a comparatively small existing stock, and brought a fall in value of 36 per cent. By 1780, however, the total quantity of both gold and silver in existence was largely increased by the whole annual production during the exceptional period in the sixteenth and seventeenth centuries. Turning to the period from 1780–1820, it is seen that a very great excess of silver over gold was produced. But the situation was a different one from that when a similar occurrence took place in 1560–1660. The existing stock had been enormously increased by 1780, and the annual supply of new silver, therefore, naturally bore a less ratio to the existing stock than did the annual supply to the whole stock in 1560. And even a greater annual production of silver in 1780 would have produced a less effect on the value of silver at that time than the annual supply in 1560 produced on the value of silver in the sixteenth century. Therefore, even if a greater amount of silver was mined in 1780–1820 than in 1560–1660, we must expect to find that it produced a less change in the former, than actually occurred in the latter, period. This is a matter capable of homely illustration. If a pailful of water be

---

[1] "An Historical Inquiry into the Production and Consumption of the Precious Metals" (1831).

[2] Mr. Horton has even quoted the figures of Soetbeer from 1761–1830, and strangely says they show no "change of relative quantity" sufficient to cause a rise in the value of gold due to consumption by the arts ("Report of 1878," p. 702).

CHART V.

Relative Quantities of Gold and Silver produced, 1560—1660.

100 YEARS.

TOTAL QUANTITY OF SILVER PRODUCED,

1560—1660,

43,009,600 KILOGRAMS.

TOTAL QUANTITY OF GOLD PRODUCED, 1560—1660,

932,380 KILOGRAMS.

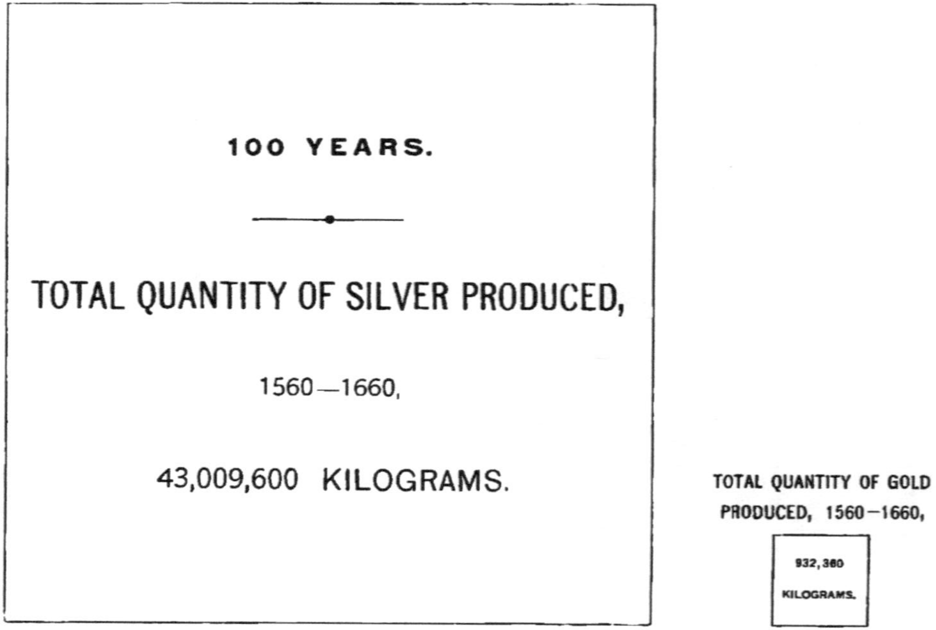

CHART VI.
Relative Quantities of Gold and Silver produced, 1761—1820.

60 YEARS.

TOTAL QUANTITY OF SILVER PRODUCED,

1761—1820,

59,324,400 KILOGRAMS.

TOTAL QUANTITY OF GOLD PRODUCED, 1761—1820,

1,354,360 KILOGRAMS.

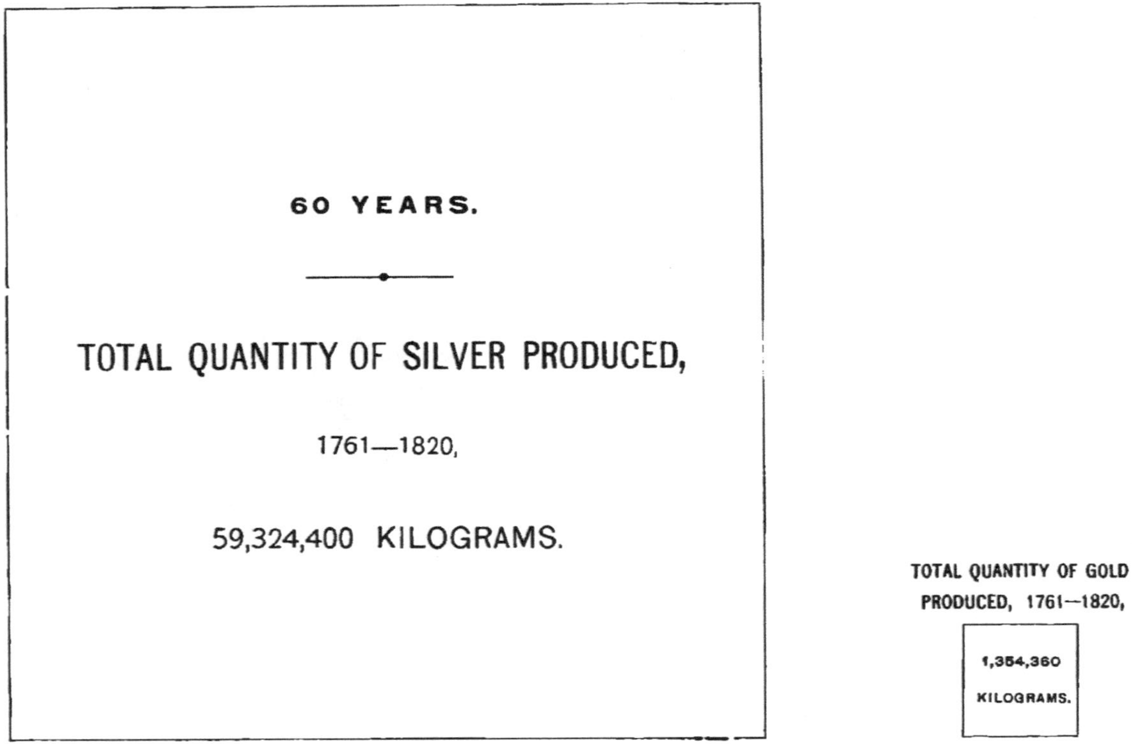

poured into a tub, the surface-level of water will rise on the sides of the tub higher than it would have risen had the pailful been poured into a village pond, because there was a greater quantity of water in the pond to be affected by the new water added. So in respect of silver. There was a greater quantity of silver already in existence by 1780 than in 1560 to be affected by the new supply.

The real influence of the period from 1780–1820 on the precious metals can be appreciated only by a comparison with the well-known period of 1560–1660, when the production of silver relatively to gold was at its highest point. Chart V will show the relative quantities of both gold and silver added to the world's stock in those years. The disproportion between the production of gold and silver is visibly large, and it is not surprising that it caused a change in the relative value of silver to gold of 36 per cent.[1]

With this exposition of the metallic product in 1560–1660 compare the production of silver relatively to gold in 1780–1820, as shown in Chart VI, constructed on the same scale as Chart V; and, although the latter period extends over only sixty years while the former covers one hundred years, it will be seen that the total product in 1780–1820 was much larger for both metals than in 1550–1660, although the relation between the amounts is about the same. In short, this later period is fully as extraordinary for its excessive silver product as the better-known but earlier period. As will be seen by reference to Chart IV, this great increase of silver was chiefly due to the increasing richness of the Mexi-

---

[1] "The entire foreign trade of the greatest commercial nation then in existence [in the sixteenth century] probably did not much exceed that which is now carried on in a single English or American port. The total tonnage of the united galleons which constituted the Spanish mercantile marine only amounted, a century later, as we are informed by Robertson, to 27,500 tons, little more than the tonnage of the Great Eastern steamship. Some of the most populous and wealthy communities of the present day had not yet begun to exist; and the whole quantity of the precious metals then in use was probably less than that which now circulates in some second-rate European kingdoms."—Cairnes's "Essays," p. 111.

can[1] mines. Without doubt, although our statesmen had no knowledge[2] of what was going on, it was this great outflow of silver from Mexico which made silver so abundant in our circulation and filled the West Indies, with which we traded, with the cheapened metal. This was noticed in 1819 by Mr. Lowndes,[3] who says:

"The West Indies, which are probably our most considerable bullion markets, estimate gold in proportion to silver very little, if at all, below an average of one to sixteen. And this is done, although some of the most considerable colonies belong to powers whose laws assign to gold a lower relative value in their European dominions. This estimate, which was forced upon many of the colonies by the necessity of giving for gold *the price which it commanded in their neighborhood, and particularly in the countries which formed the great sources of their supply*, seems to indicate the fair proportion between the metals in the West Indies."

If the preponderance of the silver over the gold production in 1545-1660 caused a change in the relative values of the

---

[1] The mines of Valenciana in 1760, of Catorce in 1773, and the districts of Zacatecas in 1750 and Guanaxuato in 1766, began the movement. "The vein of Biscaina, though it began to be worked at the beginning of the sixteenth century, did not become enormously productive till 1762, though in twelve years from that period the owner of it had gained a profit of more than a million sterling, with part of which he presented to the King of Spain two ships of war, one of them of 120 guns, and besides lent him upward of 200,000 pounds." Jacob, "Precious Metals," pp. 382, 383.

[2] Even Tooke, who is quoted by C. P. White, had little knowledge of what was going on, although he suspects the truth. He "is inclined to doubt the correctness of the opinion that the British demand increased the relative value of gold; and he remarks: 'These circumstances, collectively' (diminution in the export of silver to Asia and the emancipation of Spanish America), 'are likely to have increased the supply of silver, and give reason to expect that *the fall in the price of silver arose from a relative increase of its quantity and consequent diminution of its value rather than from a diminished quantity and increased value of gold.*' He admits, however, that 'all information hitherto accessible relating to the proportion of the supply and demand of the precious metals is vague, and insufficient to build any practical conclusions upon; and the only object of the arguments brought forward is to afford grounds for calling in question the opposite presumption, which, in my opinion, has been much too generally and hastily admitted.'"—"Report No. 278," 1833-1834, p. 42.

[3] Report of January 26, 1819. 3 "Finance," p. 399.

two metals of 36 per cent, it is not merely conceivable, but most natural, that a like preponderance in 1780-1820 should have had a similar effect. The actual change in the later period, however, was about 8 per cent. This fact, then, which I set out to examine, seems to me to be fully explained by the history of the relative production of the precious metals. Indeed, in considering the very great disproportion between the gold and silver mined in 1780-1820 as shown by Chart VI, the wonder is, not that a change in the value of silver should have resulted, but that the change should have been so small as is indicated by 8 per cent. But this, however, according to a well-known principle of value, already given, must be due to the fact that by 1780 the existing stock had been so largely increased since 1500 that an extraordinary production in 1780-1820 was not capable of producing so great an effect as before, because of the greater mass to be affected.

This, then, is the explanation of the downward tendency of the value of silver relatively to gold in 1780-1820, as it appears from the results of my investigation.[1] I have found what I must think is a very substantial cause for the fall of silver, beginning its work in 1780 and reaching very marked

---

[1] Secretary Ingham ("Report on the Relative Value of Gold and Silver," May 4, 1830) makes a point in 1830 that the comparative demand for silver had fallen off, and that this had produced a fall in the value of silver: "(1) That which has the most direct influence upon it is the revolution in the India trade; some of the chief manufactures of that country are no longer consumed in the United States, and England pays for her whole consumption of India fabrics in fabrics of her own manufacture. It was stated by Mr. Huskisson, in 1829, that in the commerce with India the difficulty was not, as formerly, to find precious metals to remit in payment of the balance, but to find returns from India to Europe. (2) The change adopted in the monetary system of England in 1816, by which payments in silver were limited to forty shillings, has also diminished the comparative demand." See also "Report of 1878," pp. 562, 563. There is no ground, I believe, for supposing that from 1780-1820 there was any change in the absorptive power of Eastern nations for silver at all commensurate with the change in the relative values of gold and silver. No such change in the comparative demand mentioned by Secretary Ingham is claimed for the period of 1780-1820. His point, therefore, even if substantial, applies to a period later than we have in view.

results on the relations of the two metals before any measures whatever were taken by England to resume specie payments. In a word, chronology kills Mr. Horton's theory.[1]

§ 5. The foregoing explanation, moreover, is the only one which will clear up other difficulties, and for this reason gives an additional presumption of its truth. The fact has been pointed to that the annual production of silver was falling off after 1810, and yet that it was exactly in the period after 1810 that the fall in the relative value of silver to gold began to be very marked.[2] The inference from this is that it is absurd to suppose that the relative values of the two metals in this period could have been affected by the previous excessive production of silver. There ought to be no difficulty here. It must rain in Abyssinia before the Nile can rise in Egypt. Or, to refer to a former illustration, in showing that the annual supply can not regulate the value of gold or silver, the surface level of a pond is not fixed by the pailful poured in, but by the water already in the pond, together with the new supply—or, in brief, by the total existing supply. So with the value of silver. It was true the produc-

---

[1] For another theory, that paper drove out gold, see chap. iv, § 1.

[2] Mr. Seyd says, in examining Dr. Soetbeer's tables: "Indeed, the objection urged against the concurrent use of gold and silver is based on a mathematical theory, which asserts that as one metal is produced at one time in greater quantity than the other, so it must fall in relative value to that other. *The actual facts utterly contradict this axiom.* . . . It will be admitted that this table does not in any way bear out the theory that the greater supply of the one metal over another causes its decline in relative value. . . . In 1810 the production of silver [relatively to gold] was eleven times as high as in 1851 and 1860, and yet no change [in the relative values] took place. . . . Can anything be more conclusive as to the utter fallacy of the supposed 'mathematical' principle?

"Those in favor of the monometallic system have hitherto contented themselves with *asserting* that the varying supply *must have the effect they suppose*, without *even examining the actual results.* At a meeting of the Statistical Society of the 1st of April, 1879, Prof. Jevons, after using the ordinary platitudes, said: 'The value of silver, of course, falls as the ratio of weight given rises.' Like Dr. Soetbeer, Mr. Jevons belongs to the class of men who violate the rules of supply and demand by their one-sided view respecting them."—"Decline of Prosperity," pp. 81, 82.

tion[1] fell off after 1810. But the extraordinary new supply added since 1780 was only just beginning to show its full force on the previously existing stock. It may have stopped raining in Abyssinia, while the rising tide was still sweeping down the channels of the Nile many thousand miles below. In truth, there was in this movement of the value of silver another illustration of the fact that the effect on the value of money is not contemporary with, but subsequent to, the changes in production. Indeed, the general principles governing the value of the precious metals find in these facts, connected with our history, striking illustrations.

Having thus offered as my explanation of the cause of the divergence in the relations of gold and silver in 1780–1820 the excessive production of silver in Mexico and South America (which can be compared only with the period of 1560–1660), without having found that tables of prices showed any diminution in the purchasing power of gold by 1820 as compared with 1782–1792, I must conclude that the character of the change was that of a fall in the value of silver, and not of a rise in that of gold.

In the following chapter I shall proceed to discuss the means adopted by Congress to meet the inherent difficulty of balancing a double standard on a movable ratio. It is a feat which has never been successfully performed since the world began; but it is a matter of serious concern to find out the lessons of our own experience in the matter. It will be of interest to see whether we have learned anything from the events which overthrew Hamilton's system.

---

[1] After long years of peaceful mining the annual production of silver began to fall off by 1810, owing to the revolutions and intestinal wars in Mexico, New Granada, Peru, and Bolivia. The mines and mints often changed hands, and, as a consequence, the Mexican dollars coined from 1810 to 1829 were of various degrees of fineness, owing to the ignorant haste and carelessness with which the silver was mined and mixed with other substances; and they were accordingly discounted from 15 to 20 per cent. See Jacob, "Precious Metals," chap. xxv.

CHAPTER IV.

CHANGE OF THE LEGAL RATIO BY THE ACT OF 1834.

§ 1. THE condition of the currency of the United States from 1820 to 1830, arising from the disappearance of gold, from the extensive issue of paper money (a large part of it secured only by small reserves), and from the circulation of foreign coins, was confused in the extreme.[1] At the adoption of the Constitution we possessed virtually a metallic currency of scanty amount. The first United States Bank (1791-1811) was conservatively managed, and did not issue its notes excessively, nor in denominations below ten dollars. "Bank-notes were rarely seen south of the Potomac or west of the mountains." After the failure to renew the United States Bank charter in 1811, local banks multiplied and paper issues expanded without limit. The suspension of the banks in 1814, and the continued issue of paper, in denominations "from one sixteenth part of a dollar upward," certainly did not aid in increasing the quantity of the precious metals in the country. The establishment of the second United States Bank (1817-1837) assisted in bringing about specie payments in the United States soon after its re-charter. But the bank reserves were almost entirely of silver.[2] The silver coinage,

---

[1] For a short account, see White's "Report No. 278," 1831, pp. 56, 57.

[2] The Bank of the United States had arranged to import some specie from London through Messrs. Baring and Reed. "Under this contract, gold and silver were to be furnished, if it were practicable, in equal amounts, according to the American relative value of 1 : 15. Upward of $2,000,000 of silver have been accordingly supplied, but not one ounce of gold."—Lowndes, 1819, 3 "Finance," p. 399. "It is ascertained, in one of our principal commercial cities quite in

however, was in a deplorable confusion, and requires some brief description.

There were few United States coins in circulation. The act of 1792 decreed that each dollar should " be of the value of a Spanish milled dollar as the same is now current." In fact, the Spanish milled dollar formed the most important part of our silver currency, and, being heavier than the American dollar piece, commanded a premium. The tendency showed itself, consequently, to coin United States dollar pieces, and hoard foreign dollars. By exporting the lighter American dollars to the West Indies, and to any places where they were received for their face value equally with Spanish dollars, these latter were imported, sent to our Mint, and a profit realized. Foreign dollars, therefore, bore a premium [1] of one quarter to one half per cent over United States dollars. The banks, therefore, paid out United States dollars when called upon for silver for exportation. This process kept the Mint busy, but without the effect of filling the circulation with our own coins. The Mint, therefore, was a useless expense to the nation, but a source of profit to the money-brokers. The coinage of dollar pieces was consequently suspended in 1805 by the President,[2] and none were coined until 1836.

---

the vicinity of the Mint, that the gold coin in an office of discount and deposit of the Bank of the United States there located, in November, 1819, amounted to $165,000, and the silver coin to $118,000; that since that time the silver coin has increased to $700,000, while the gold coin has diminished to the sum of $1,200, one hundred only of which is American."—Report, February 2, 1821, by Whitman, 3 " Finance," p. 660.

[1] C. P. White, " Report No. 278," 1833-1834, pp. 66-72. The foreign dollars contained about 373¼ to 374 grains pure silver. Secretary Crawford said: "Spanish milled dollars compose the great mass of foreign silver coins which circulate in the United States, and generally command a premium when compared with the dollar of the United States."—Quoted by Talbot, January 6, 1819, 3 " Finance," p. 395.

[2] Cf. C. P. White, ibid., p. 85. I find no reason whatever to suppose that this action of President Jefferson was as represented by Mr. Upton ("Money in Politics," p. 199). "He desired that gold should circulate as well as silver, and, *to prevent the expulsion of gold*, he peremptorily ordered the Mint to discontinue the coinage of the silver dollar." He did it to stop the exchange of our dollars for foreign silver dollars.

The legal value of foreign coins in the United States, moreover, was regulated by an act of 1793, and by its terms these foreign coins were made a legal tender. But these enactments were temporary, and ran only for short periods. Congress, however, "ceased to regulate the value of one description of foreign coins after another until finally, in 1827, none were recognized as legal tenders except our ancient money,[1] the 'Spanish milled dollar.'" Now, although the coinage of the United States silver dollar was discontinued in 1805, a profit was still realized by importing Spanish dollars, because two half-dollars served the same purpose as a dollar piece did before, containing, as they did, as much pure silver as the dollar piece. And our silver continued to be coined and exported,[2] while foreign silver continued to flow in. So far had this gone that of $11,000,000 of silver coined in the five years preceding 1831, $8,000,000 had been coined[3] from foreign dollars; and, of the specie in the United States Bank, only $2,000,000 out of $11,000,000 were in our own coins. These foreign coins, however, were now not all "Spanish milled dollars." The Spanish countries of America had before this date established their independence of Spain and assumed new names, so that their coins could no longer strictly be termed "Spanish dollars," and consequently these South American coins, although in circulation, were not thereafter a legal tender. The effect of this condition of affairs was quite considerable, as may be seen by statements of the currency. The amount of the metallic circulation in 1830 is thus estimated:[4]

Total coins in United States..... $23,000,000
Coins issued by United States.... 14,000,000
Spanish dollars and parts of dollars[5] 5,000,000

---

[1] C. P. White, "Report No. 278," 1833–1834, p. 65.

[2] White says the exportation came to be considerable in 1811–1821. Ibid., p. 85. [3] Ibid., p. 72.

[4] Sanford, January 11, 1830, "Sen. Doc. No. 19," 1st session, 21st Congress, p. 11.

[5] In 1836 there were in circulation, of denominations below a dollar, pieces of 6¼ cents, of 12½ cents, of 6d. sterling, pistareens (of 16 cents and 18 cents),

CHANGE OF THE LEGAL RATIO BY THE ACT OF 1834. 55

There had been coined to this date $34,000,000 of silver coins by the United States Mint, of which only $14,000,000 remained in the country. These Spanish coins, which had displaced the American silver, moreover, became much worn and reduced in weight, and, being in practice current with other coins, without regard to weight, naturally acted to drive out our own coins.[1] A memorial[2] of the New York bankers, led by Mr. Gallatin, in 1834, represented

"that the dollar of Spain and the gold and silver coins of the United States constitute, at present, the only legal currency of the country ; and that, from the commercial value of the Spanish dollar, and the intrinsic value of the gold coins of the United States, they have become mere articles of merchandise, and are no longer to be considered as forming any portion of the metallic currency."

The only legal medium being United States silver coins, " of which there is not a sufficient quantity to answer the ordinary purposes of business," commerce was obliged to use foreign coins which were then no longer a legal tender. Since United States silver dollars were no longer coined, and since it was more profitable to send the Spanish dollars to the Mint, not enough dollar pieces remained in circulation. They asked, therefore, that the silver "dollar of Mexico, Colombia, Chili, and Peru, which are equal in weight and fineness to the Spanish dollar, be likewise made a legal tender, if weighing not less than 415 grains." It is clear that, however much some remedy might be needed, this step would only increase the difficulties. The bill would increase the means of driving out United States silver coins. It was enacted into law[3] January 25, 1834, although Mr. Sanford had very

---

English shillings, Spanish quarters, half-crowns, two-and-sixpence sterling, five-franc pieces, etc.

[1] Mr. Jones (Ga.) said, in 1834: "Spanish and South American dollars furnish all our present circulation."—"Cong. Debates," vol. x, Part IV, 1833–1834, p. 4657.

[2] "Report of 1878," pp. 679–683.

[3] January 21, 1834, a law was also passed fixing the value of certain gold coins of Great Britain, Portugal, and Brazil at 94·8 cents per dwt.; those of

properly shown[1] that no foreign coins should be made a legal tender. The enactment, however, had no bad influence, because the coinage act of 1834 soon made it ineffective.

The confused state of the silver coinage as thus described, the absence of gold, and the existence of a paper currency, therefore, complicated the situation. It was thought by some that the disappearance of gold was due to the existence of paper money. "Paper[2] was the antagonist of gold, and, our gold being at present undervalued, the paper had driven it out of circulation." And naturally, during the war on the bank, the scarcity of specie was attributed to the action of this institution. Secretary Ingham,[3] in 1830, reasoning *post hoc ergo hoc*, observed that, "prior to the year 1821, gold and silver generally bore the same relation in the market of the United States which they did in the Mint regulation. . . . But, at no time since the general introduction of bank paper, has gold been found in general circulation." While wrong, of course, as to the ratio, he had yet observed the disappearance of gold about the time of the extension of bank issues. This was probably true;[4] but that the paper was the cause of the disappearance of gold is another question. In driving specie out of circulation, paper has no special hostility to the one metal, gold, and none whatever to the other metal, silver. Large denominations of paper would, of course, act to supersede the more valuable metal used in large transactions; but paper issues would have driven out silver equally well with gold. As a matter of fact, however, the paper had not driven out silver; indeed, the metallic circulation and the reserves be-

---

France at 93·1 cents per dwt.; and those of Spain, Mexico, and Colombia at 80·9 cents per dwt.

[1] "Senate Doc. No. 19," 1st session, 21st Congress, January 11, 1830.
[2] Mr. Gillet, " Cong. Debates," ibid., p. 4659.
[3] " Report of 1878," p. 575.
[4] " We may experiment on our gold coins without fear . . . ; though a legal tender, they have never been a measure of value " (White, " Report No. 278," 1833, 1834, p. 87). " Our gold coins are withdrawn from circulation soon after they are issued from the Mint " (Sanford, 1830, " Senate Doc. No. 19," p. 19.)

hind the paper were in silver. For this use, gold, if in circulation, would have been equally employed. That is, whatever effect the paper had to supersede specie, it would have acted equally against silver or gold; and if only one metal had disappeared and the other had remained, this must unquestionably have been due to a force of a different nature than that supposed, and one which had the effect of leaving only one metal and driving out another. This may be made more clear by anticipating our story somewhat. After 1834, as we shall soon see, gold came into circulation. Why did not the paper drive out the gold after 1834, as it was thought to do before 1834? It certainly did not do it. We can not, therefore, believe that the paper, however much it may have helped in the process, was the cause of the disappearance of gold. What the cause was has been already fully explained.[1]

§ 2. Having seen the condition of our currency after Hamilton's system had been tried twenty-five years, we must admit that this condition was much worse in 1820 than it was in 1800. It was not a cheerful prospect. But we now turn from this picture to see how the country proposed to deal with these difficulties, to see whether the true causes were understood, and whether experience had taught its lessons.

As early as 1818 the United States began to recognize that Hamilton's ratio of 1:15 differed so much from the market ratio between gold and silver, that if it were still designed to maintain a double standard, a new adjustment of the legal relations of the two metals was necessary. While nominally possessing a double standard, the country really had only one, and that a silver standard. Owing to causes beyond the control of a legislature, and which could not have been foreseen, the value of silver was so affected in its relation to gold as to destroy the working of a bimetallic system. Here is to be found the inherent difficulty of such a scheme. Had Agassiz, when measuring the movement of the glaciers in the Alps, attempted to build an observatory resting partly

---

[1] Chapter iii, § 4.

on the bank of solid rock and partly on the surface of the slowly-moving stream of ice, his house might have hung together only on condition that the bank had sympathetically begun to move with the ice, but in no other way. Our Congress, however, did not yet realize the whole situation. Either they must give the double standard another trial at a new ratio corresponding with the change in the market ratio, or choose one of the two metals as a single standard. If they did the former, what assurances were there that, even if the legal ratio then were the same as the market ratio, the country should escape from future changes and not again see the same results as ensued from Hamilton's auspicious experiment? There are evidences[1] that this was distinctly seen by several writers. But there were other ideas as to the remedies.

The first proposition in Congress appeared in a resolution, worthy of Charles V of Spain, to inquire into the expediency of prohibiting the exportation of gold from the United States. The "exportation of specie of every description was rigidly prohibited by law" during the embargo in 1807–1808, and in 1812. But, as Talbot[2] reported, "the Bank of the United States, and some of the State banks, made considerable efforts to import specie. The exportation of it during the same period has, it is believed, been equal, if not greater, than the importation by the banks and by individuals."

A committee, of which Mr. Lowndes was chairman, reported,[3] in 1819, in favor of a new legal[4] ratio of 1 : 15·6,

---

[1] "The very fact that gold and silver have departed from the proportions established by our laws is ample proof that no such laws should ever have been enacted ; and the *certainty* of a future change is equally conclusive against any further legislation on the subject. Even since the date of the report of the committee above referred to a more wide separation between the two metals has taken place ; and had a law been enacted a year ago, agreeably to their suggestion, it might possibly have required an additional one in the present year to give it effect.—Condy Raguet, "Currency and Banking," p. 208, written January 26, 1822.

[2] "Senate Doc. No. 549," 2d session, 15th Congress, 3 "Finance," p. 394.

[3] 3 "Finance," p. 399.

[4] The silver dollar was to be reduced to 356·4 grains pure silver and 399·36

to correspond with the market ratio. The error was perpetuated of a subsidiary coinage containing proportional quantities of silver to the dollar piece; but it was suggested that coins less than half-dollars be limited in their legal-tender power to five dollars.

The most considerable contributions to the discussions on the coinage in the early part of this century were made in the three reports of Mr. Campbell P. White, of New York.[1] In his first report of 1831 he expounds the following doctrine:[2]

"That there are inherent and incurable defects in the system which regulates the standard of value in both gold and silver; its instability as a measure of contracts, and mutability as the practical currency of a particular nation, are serious imperfections; while the impossibility of maintaining both metals in concurrent, simultaneous, or promiscuous circulation appears to be clearly ascertained.

"That the standard being fixed in one metal is the nearest approach to invariableness, and precludes the necessity of further legislative interference."

In the report of 1832 he adds:

"If both metals are preferred, the like relative proportion of the aggregate amount of metallic currency will be possessed, *subject to frequent changes from gold to silver*, and *vice versa*, according to the variations in the relative value of these metals. The committee think that the *desideratum in the monetary system is the standard of uniform value;* they can not ascertain that both metals have ever circulated simultaneously, concurrently, and indiscriminately in any country where there are banks or money-dealers; and they entertain the conviction that the nearest approach to an invariable standard is its establishment *in one metal*, which metal shall compose exclusively the currency for large payments."

The committee, therefore, recommended a single standard

---

grains standard, and the gold eagle was to contain 237·98 grains pure gold and 259·61 grains standard weight. A seigniorage of 14·85 grains of silver was to be exacted on each dollar coined, which would have made the ratio less than 15:1.

[1] "H. R. No. 278," 23d Congress, 1st session, entitled "Gold and Silver Coins," contains all three.

[2] "Report No. 278," 1833–1834, p. 61.

of silver[1] alone. In short, our experience since 1792 had made a deep impression on the minds of the intelligent men of that time. Both Mr. C. P. White and Secretary Ingham[2] began to see that, in the nature of things, a double standard, without constant changes of the legal ratio, could not exist for any length of time. Mr. Ingham saw no safety in bimetallism, because, in his opinion, it was impossible to keep the mint and the market ratios alike. In the best discussion of the subject there was a disposition shown to select a single standard, and that of silver. And, with this general review of the plans proposed, we may now go on to recount the choice of means actually adopted in 1834.

§ 3. When the matter finally came before Congress, the bill first proposed by Mr. White's committee in the House contained a scheme for a double standard at a ratio of 1 : 15·6. But in the selection of a ratio there were various opinions at that time, thus tabulated,[3] as to the weight of the gold coins (leaving the silver dollar unchanged):

	Fine.	Alloy.	Standard.	Proportion of alloy.	Gold to silver.	Advance per cent.
Mint	238¼	23¾	260	$\frac{1}{12}$	1 : 15·777	3$\frac{34}{100}$
Mr. Gallatin[4]	237¾	21½	259½	$\frac{1}{12}$	1 : 15·607	4$\frac{23}{100}$
Mr. Ingham (report)	237$\frac{6}{10}$	21$\frac{6}{10}$	259$\frac{2}{10}$	$\frac{1}{12}$	1 : 15·625	4½
Committee (White)	237$\frac{6}{10}$	26$\frac{6}{10}$	264	$\frac{1}{10}$	1 : 15·625	4½
Mint	234	26	260	$\frac{1}{10}$	1 : 15·865	5$\frac{77}{100}$
Mr. Sanford	233$\frac{26}{33}$	21$\frac{13}{33}$	254$\frac{39}{33}$	$\frac{1}{12}$	1 : 15·900	6

[1] "Silver is the ancient currency of the United States, the metal in which the money unit is exhibited, the money generally used in foreign commerce, and that description of the precious metals in the distribution of which we exercise an extensive agency. The committee, upon due consideration of all attendant circumstances, are of opinion that the standard of value ought to be legally and exclusively, as it is practically, regulated in silver."—"Report of 1878," p. 675, and "Report No. 278," p. 8.

[2] "Report of 1878," p. 568. "The fluctuations in the value of gold and silver can not be controlled ; and even the attempt to conform the Mint to the market values must produce a change in the latter."

[3] By Mr. Moore, Director of the Mint. See "Report No. 278," 1833-1834, p. 79.

[4] See "Report of 1878," p. 682.

CHART VII.

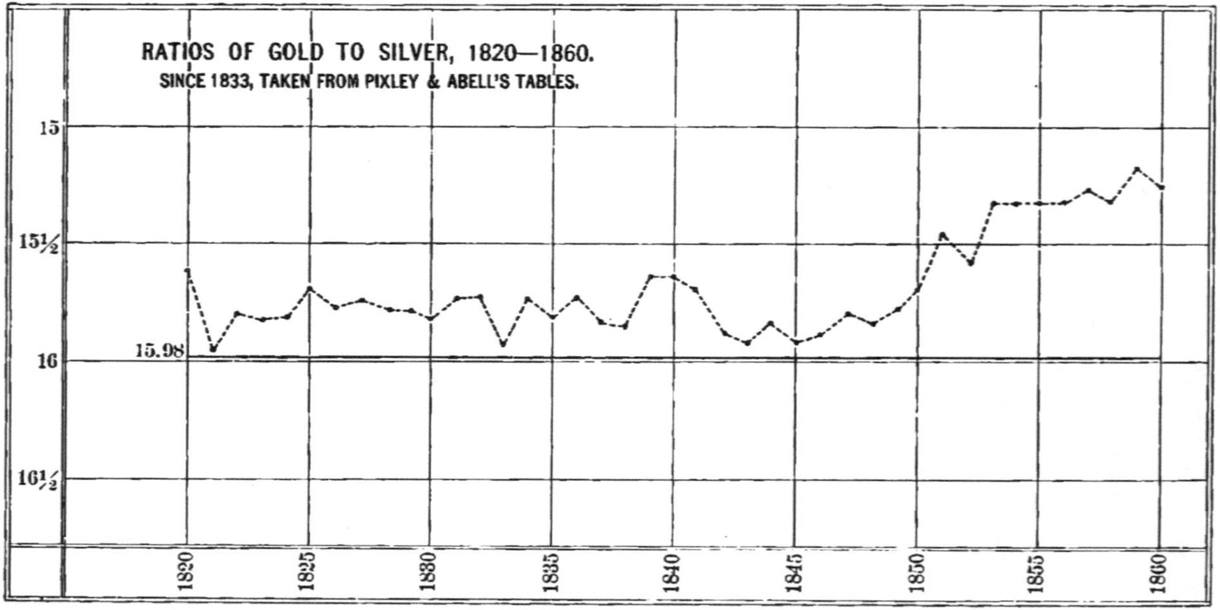

RATIOS OF GOLD TO SILVER, 1820—1860.
SINCE 1833, TAKEN FROM PIXLEY & ABELL'S TABLES.
15
15½
16
16½
15.98
1820
1825
1830
1835
1840
1845
1850
1855
1860

Speaking of the failure of the two metals to circulate concurrently, and of the inaction on that subject since the death of Mr. Lowndes in 1822, Condy Raguet[1] gives a reason for the presentation of this bill in 1834:

"We should possibly have for many years remained in that situation, had it not been for a fresh occurrence by which fancied private interest was brought to bear upon Congress. That occurrence was the discovery of gold in North Carolina and other Southern States. . . . This gradually increasing production of gold at the South engendered precisely the same spirit as the increased production of iron had done at the North. The owners of the gold-mines cried out for legislative protection, as the owners of the iron-mines had previously done, and laws were solicited to enable the former to get more for their gold, or rather for the rent of their land, than they could otherwise have obtained."[2]

Political projects also entered, as we shall soon see, into the passage of this bill and the selection of a ratio. How they worked may be seen first by a reference to the actual ratios of gold to silver in these years. The quotations of silver since 1833 have been authoritatively given in the London tables of Pixley and Abell, and since that date are not disputed. We have consequently an exact knowledge of the market ratios of gold to silver at this time when a new adjustment was being made. Chart VII has been constructed on the basis of these tables, and shows that the average ratio from 1825 to 1835 was a little more than 1 : 15·7. The only action which could be justified by monetary experience, or by the hope of maintaining a double standard, demanded that the United States in 1834 should adopt the market as the legal ratio. Did the statesmen in charge of the bill have a definite knowledge of the market ratio, even if they intended

---

[1] "Currency and Banking," pp. 224, 225, 226.

[2] C. P. White felt the force of this reason in 1832 ("Report No. 278," p. 56): "It may be fairly concluded that the amount of silver annually furnished is not upon the increase, while, on the other hand, we have positive evidence of a rapid increase (as yet, to be sure, not comparatively on a great scale) in our own country, in the production of gold from mines represented to be of great territorial extent, and of encouraging and fruitful appearance."

to follow it? There seems to be no doubt of it. Three of the plans given at the beginning of this section were based on a ratio of 1 : 15·6, which was generally supposed to be the market ratio in the United States (and it was very near the true ratio). The bill of the committee embodying a double standard based on the ratio of 1 : 15·6 was introduced into the House, and had passed through the Committee of the Whole,[1] when it encountered the political breezes and was driven out of its course. Mr. C. P. White changed front, and, although in his previous elaborate reports he had strongly urged[2] the ratio of 1 : 15·6, he himself proposed an amendment altering the ratio in the bill to 1 : 16, which was adopted and finally enacted. The bill proposed by Mr. White's committee became significantly known as the "Gold Bill." This move, which was of course at variance with any attempt to retain a double standard, had probably both a political and a monetary object. It will be remembered that Mr. White, in his reports, opposed a double standard and favored a single standard of silver. In my judgment, he was easily led by his preference for a single standard to join in establishing a ratio between gold and silver which must, in the nature of things, soon bring about a single standard, if not of silver, at least of gold; while, on the other hand, there was a strong political party waging war against the United States Bank, and desirous, as part of their warfare, to make a battle-cry of a gold currency, in distinction to the paper issues of the bank. Under the leadership of Benton, the anti-bank party made support of the "Gold Bill" and the ratio of 1 : 16 a partisan shibboleth.

Benton[3] said that 1 : 15⅜ "was the ratio of nearly all who

---

[1] "Cong. Debates," vol. x, Part IV, 1833–1834, p. 4663.

[2] "The committee are finally of opinion that the rate proposed by the Secretary of the Treasury, of 1 of gold for 15·625 of silver, is the utmost limit to which the value can be raised, with a due regard to the paramount interest; the preservation of our silver as the basis of circulation."—"Report No. 278," p. 56.

[3] "It is true that all who approved the gold bill were not friends of General Jackson, and that all who opposed it were not his foes, but as the vote in Con-

seemed best calculated, from their pursuits, to understand the subject. The thick array of speakers was on that side; and the eighteen banks of the city of New York, with Mr. Gallatin at their head, favored that proportion. The difficulty of adjusting this value, so that neither metal should expel the other, had been the stumbling-block for a great many years; and now this difficulty seemed to be as formidable as ever."

It was urged that Spain, Portugal, Mexico, South America, and the West Indies (except Cuba, which had 17:1) rated silver to gold at 16:1; but it is quite likely that the ratio of 16:1 was favored as much because it gave a slight advantage to gold as that other countries had such a ratio. In the debates in the House, Mr. Cambreleng, of New York, openly admitted[1] the object of the change: "By adopting a higher ratio we shall be more certain of accomplishing our object, which is to secure for our own country the permanent circulation of gold coins." And the political considerations triumphed.[2] Mr. Selden, of New York, moved

---

gress was made, in a great degree, a party vote, the party which so turned it to account are using every effort to reap the fruits of their policy."—Raguet, "Currency and Banking," p. 218.

[1] "Cong. Debates," 1833–1834, vol. x, Part IV, p. 4671. Mr. Jones, of Georgia (where gold had been discovered), held: "If the gentleman is correct in saying our gold coins will return to us again after they have once left us, I can only say this is a consummation most devoutly to be wished. . . . If this ratio (1 : 16) will have the additional effect to bring them [gold coins] back again, it must be considered an additional recommendation to the substitute."—Ibid., p. 4654.

[2] "Mr. White gave up the bill which he had first introduced, and adopted the Spanish ratio. Mr. Clowney, of South Carolina, Mr. Gillet and Mr. Cambreleng, of New York, Mr. Ewing, of Indiana, Mr. McKim, of Maryland, and other speakers gave it a warm support. Mr. John Quincy Adams would vote for it, *though he thought the gold was overvalued;* but if found to be so, the difference could be corrected hereafter. The principal speakers against it and in favor of a lower rate, were Messrs. Gorham, of Massachusetts; Selden, of New York; Binney, of Pennsylvania; and Wilde, of Georgia. And eventually the bill was passed by a large majority—145 to 36. In the Senate it had an easy passage [35 to 7]. Messrs. Calhoun and Webster supported it; Mr. Clay opposed it, and on the final vote there were but seven negatives: Messrs. Chambers, of Maryland; Clay; Knight, of Rhode Island; Alexander Porter, of Louisiana; Silsbee, of Massachusetts; Southard, of New Jersey; Sprague, of Maine."— "Report of 1878," p. 696, chap. cviii, 1834—"Thirty Years' View"; and see

as an amendment the adoption of a ratio of $1:15\frac{5}{8}$, but it was lost by a vote of 52 to 127; and Mr. Gorham's amendment of a ratio of $1:15\cdot825$ was rejected, 69 to 112.[1] In short, the majority were evidently aiming at a single gold standard,[2] through the disguise of a ratio which overvalued gold in the legal proportions. In the market an ounce of gold bought 15·7 ounces of silver bullion; when coined at the Mint it exchanged for sixteen ounces of silver coin. Silver, therefore, could not long stay in circulation.

§ 4. The Coinage Act of 1834,[3] therefore, in contradistinction to the policy of Hamilton in 1792, did not show the result of any attempt to select a mint ratio in accord with that of the market. It was very clearly pointed out in the debates that the ratio of $1:16$ would drive out silver.

Mr. Gorham,[4] of Massachusetts, "warned the House not to bring about, by its hasty legislation, the same state of things

---

"Cong. Debates," p. 2122, vol. x, Part II, 1833–1834. The bill seems to have been little discussed in the Senate.

[1] "Cong. Globe," vol. i, p. 467; John Quincy Adams voted for the bill "reluctantly and in the hope that the ratio would be amended elsewhere. He considered it entirely too high."—"Cong. Debates," vol. x, Part IV, p. 4673.

[2] The Washington "Globe" said with some party rancor: "Contrary to their will, the bank party, even in the Senate, have been obliged to vote for the measures of the Administration, deemed essential to carry out its policy. By public opinion they have been forced to vote for the GOLD BILL, which is a measure of deadly hostility to the interests of the bank, will supersede its notes, and is the harbinger of a *real* SOUND CURRENCY. The people are now enabled to understand the policy of the Administration, and to see that it would give them GOLD instead of PAPER. The great bank attorney, Mr. Clay, was bold enough to vote against this bill; but he could carry only six of the bank Senators with him. The mass of them, although they voted for the bill with the utmost reluctance, dared not to tell the people, '*We will deny you gold, and force you to depend for a general currency on the notes of the mammoth bank.*' Thus were they *forced* to minister to the triumph of the Administration."—Quoted in "Niles's Register," vol. x, fourth series.

[3] See Appendix III for the text of the act.

[4] "Cong. Debates," 1833–1834, vol. x, Part IV, pp. 46, 51, 52: "It was admitted there must be a concurrent circulation of silver and gold. The difficulty of fixing the ratio of their relative value arose from the various causes which concurred perpetually to alter the value of both, and which no one could control.

in relation to silver which had heretofore existed respecting gold. . . . If the law should make gold too cheap, the country would have no silver circulation. . . . We should soon have the same cry about the want of silver coin which there was now about gold. Then the next step would be to tamper with the value of the dollar."

So long as the market ratio was 1 : 15·7 and the Mint ratio 1 : 16, there would certainly be a tendency to the disappearance of silver. But it was urged that, inasmuch as the value of silver relatively to gold had been steadily falling for many years, it was quite likely that it would continue to fall still more in the future. Not knowing the cause of the fall in silver, it was only natural that this error should have arisen. The ratio of 1 : 16 was therefore urged, because, as it was said, it would anticipate [1] the change of the next few years in the market ratio. This, however, did not come, as may be seen by Chart VII.

The effects of the undervaluation of silver, and the overvaluation of gold, in the legal ratio of 1 : 16, as compared with a market ratio of 1 : 15·7, were soon manifest. Gresham's law was brought into play, but its operation in this period was exactly the reverse of that in the preceding period (1792–1834). In the latter, the depreciated silver drove out gold; in the former, the overvalued gold began to drive out silver. It is evident that there would be a gain in putting gold into the form of coin, instead of, as heretofore, regarding it as merchandise. A man could buy for $15,700 an amount of gold bullion, which, when coined for its owner at the United States

---

If the ratio should be fixed to-day, these causes would change it to-morrow." Gorham was one of the earliest to propose that for every payment, beyond a small amount, one half should be paid in gold, and one half in silver. Cf. also Selden, ibid., pp. 44, 46.

[1] "We have seen that there is a continual increase in the value of gold, and if the increase of the legal value cause any increase in the market value, it must be evident that 1 : 16 will, in a short time, be only equal to the increased market value. If we stop short of this [1 : 16], we shall soon be compelled again to increase the value of that metal, or to struggle with the same difficulties which now prevent the circulation of our precious metals."—Jones (Georgia), "Cong. Debates," vol. x, Part IV, 1833–1834, pp. 46, 56.

Mint, possessed a legal tender coin value of $16,000. A debtor, therefore, would gain $300 by paying his creditor in gold, the overvalued metal. And as there was such a premium on the use of gold, so there was a corresponding premium on the disuse of silver. If a debtor had $16,000 of silver coin, he need take of it only $15,700, melt it into bullion, and in the bullion market buy gold bullion, which, when coined at the Mint into gold coins, would have a debt-paying power of $16,000. There was a profit of $300 in not using silver as a medium of exchange, and in treating it as merchandise. The act was passed in June; and in the fall[1] of 1834 gold began to move toward the United States in such quantities that for a time some alarm was created in London as to the amount of reserves in the Bank of England. It then became very difficult to get silver[2] in the United States, and there began a displacement of silver by gold, irrespective of the issues of paper money, which at last culminated, when the discoveries of gold in 1848 had lowered the value of gold, in the entire disappearance of silver. It can not be said, then, that the act of 1834 was properly a part of a bimetallic scheme. For

---

[1] Early in the fall of 1834 (September 6th) it is recorded that 50,000 English sovereigns were imported into the United States, and the statement given that arrangements had been made for the importation of 2,000,000 more ("Niles's Register," fourth series, vol. xi, p. 1). Another record was made of the arrival of 40,000 English sovereigns. In the last week of July 400,000 sovereigns had been shipped from Liverpool (ibid., pp. 20, 21). A large part of this specie, it was said, belonged to the Bank of the United States.

September 13th, the Washington "Globe" reports the presentation of $208,-000 in the form of foreign gold coins at the United States Mint.

In the third quarter of 1834, $2,800,000 in gold coin or bullion was imported into the United States. The movement of gold to the United States was so considerable that it excited alarm in London as to the condition of the Bank of England. The drain, however, soon ceased.

[2] Says the "New York Star": "The keeper of one of our principal hotels sent on Saturday a $100 note to one of the pet banks for silver, but was refused it, only $10 being given, and $90 in gold. He then sent the gold to a broker, who charged ½ per cent. to exchange it for half-dollars." The cashier of an Albany bank said, "My table is literally loaded with applications from the country banks for change."—"Niles's Register," fourth series, vol. xiii, p. 132, October 24, 1835.

certainly we did not long enjoy the use of both metals in our circulation. The very process by which gold began to come in, carried silver out of use.[1] "It would probably be safe to assert that . . . one half of the citizens of our country, born since 1840, had never seen a United States silver dollar. If we should be mistaken in this; if it should be shown that one half of our people had seen a silver dollar some time in their lives, we could still fall back on the well-known historic fact that the dollar in question was rarely used as money after 1840."[2]

It is quite clear, however, that had the ratio of $1:15\cdot6$ been adopted in 1834, instead of a counterfeit bimetallism at a ratio of $1:16$, the same results would have ensued in the former case as in the latter. The gold discoveries so altered the relative value of gold to silver—exactly reversing the situation in 1780-1820—that the system would again have been left on one leg, and that a gold one. A glance at Chart VII will show that after 1850 the ratio of gold to silver moved in the opposite direction, and, instead of approaching $1:15\cdot6$, it fell to between $1:15\frac{1}{2}$ and $1:15$. In short, a purely bimetallic scheme in 1834 could not have succeeded in retaining both metals in concurrent circulation, owing to the impossibility of forecasting the future supplies of the precious metals, to say nothing of anticipating the changes in the future demand for them. In attempting to settle upon a legal ratio which will correspond with the market ratio for any length of time, a problem of the nature of perpetual

---

[1] "The gold coins were so reduced in weight that it was now cheaper to pay debts in them than in silver coins. In consequence, no more silver was coined for circulation, and the amount then in circulation, upward of $50,000,000, at once disappeared, being sent abroad in payment of obligations, or melted down for other uses at home. This sudden contraction of the currency [but it was filled by gold] created considerable distress, and the loss of the small silver pieces caused no little inconvenience. The panic of 1837 followed. Depreciated bank bills, 'shin-plasters,' and a few worn Mexican pieces came into circulation to take the place of full-weight silver pieces, which had been superseded by the cheaper gold coins."—Upton, "Money in Politics," p. 175.

[2] Simon Newcomb, "International Review," March, 1879, p. 310.

motion is encountered. Calculation must be made not merely as to the future value of silver, but also as to the future value of gold. Neither of these things is possible. The value of each metal depends on its own demand and supply; so that for the two metals there are four independent factors to be considered. It is absurd to suppose that, if there should be a change in one of these factors, there should *ipso facto* be changes in the three other factors of such a character as to neutralize the change in one. The situation is like a table resting on four legs. Two of these legs at one end may represent the demand and supply of silver, and the two at the other end the demand and supply of gold. The first two fix the height of the table at one end relatively to the height at the other end; moreover, a change in one leg will cause a destruction of the general level of the table, not to be counterbalanced except by an accommodating change in each of the other three. But it is impossible that these changes should be either in a direction or extent that should exactly offset the effect of an interfering change in but one factor. It is well worth notice, too, that changes of this description were going on in the values of both gold and silver in the years when there was no complaint that discrimination[1] was exercised against one metal or another.

We can see, then, that the ratio of 1 : 16 resulted in a movement of silver out of, and of gold into, the circulation, somewhat earlier than it would have come about had the ratio of 1 : 15·6 been adopted; but the movement, operating with no great force for a few years, received an unexpected momentum from the gold discoveries, which, by lowering the market value of gold toward 1 : 15, made the overvaluation of gold in the legal ratio of 1 : 16 still more evident, and so still further increased the profit in coining gold and melting sil-

---

[1] Except possibly the charge that England "discriminated" against silver by confining it to her subsidiary coinage in 1816, which could have had no effect such as has been described, between 1780–1820, on the fall of silver. And the desire of the Jackson party for gold was not accompanied by any "hatred" of silver, but by only opposition to bank issues.

CHART VIII.

Showing the Coinage of Gold and Silver at the United States Mint, 1834–1860. Ratio, 1 : 15.98. Silver ▬▬▬ Gold ▬▬▬

CHANGE OF THE LEGAL RATIO BY THE ACT OF 1834. 69

ver into bullion. We should expect, therefore, to find a confirmation of this explanation in the movement of gold and silver to the Mint of the United States. In the preceding period of 1780–1834, we saw by Chart II that the coinage of silver, the cheaper metal, preponderated; and now we can see, in Chart VIII, a similar movement, but very much more marked,[1] in the opposite direction. The coinage of the overvalued gold soon preponderated over that of silver. A comparison of Chart VIII with Chart II will show the force and opposing direction of the influences at work in the two periods in a very distinct manner. It will be remembered that the silver coinage was chiefly of denominations below a dollar. Of silver dollar pieces, not a single one was coined from 1806 to 1836, and thereafter only in very small quantities. But, so far as the Mint figures tell the story, a very considerable movement of gold to the Mint did not begin until 1843; for the Russian mines began by that time to sensibly increase the supply of gold.

§ 5. The act of 1834 changed the legal ratio from 1 : 15 to 1 : 16. The readjustment of the weights of the coins in order to meet this change could have been made in two ways: (1) either by increasing the number of grains in the silver dollar until it had reached the value of the gold dollar, and thus restored to it the value it had lost by its depreciation; or (2) by lessening the weight of the gold dollar until it had been accommodated to the fall in the value of the silver dollar. The latter, unfortunately, was the course adopted. It is to be regretted that, in this manner, we laid ourselves open to the charge of debasing our coinage;[2] but it is true. The

---

[1] The lines in Chart VIII, owing to the larger figures, are drawn on a smaller scale than those of Chart II for the earlier period.

[2] Whitman ("Report of 1878," p. 556) recognized this fact in 1821: "It will, of course, be objected that, if we should now render gold four per cent better, we shall thereby put into the hands of its present holders a clear net gain to that amount, provided they hold it with an intent to use it in this country. But it is not perceived how this will injure the public or individuals. And it will not be regretted by the benevolent that individuals should be benefited, if no

amount of pure silver in the dollar was left unchanged at 371·25 grains; but the amount of pure gold in the gold eagle was diminished from 247·5 grains to 232 grains. This debased the gold coins of the United States 6·26 per cent, and to that extent the law gave gold a less legal-tender value than it had possessed before 1834. Not knowing that the Mexican product had lowered the value of silver, and that gold had not risen in value in 1820, our statesmen refused to maintain the unit of unchanged purchasing power represented at that time by gold, and dropped to the level of the cheapened silver standard. By adhering to the dollar of silver, and altering the gold coins to suit it, we had the appearance of retaining "the dollar of our fathers," but we overlooked the essential fact that this silver dollar had fallen seriously in value.

Mr. Ingham took the ground [1] in 1830 that silver should be adopted as the standard of the United States, because all contracts were at that time practically made in terms of silver, and because for many years silver had been the only coin in circulation. This does not seem to me a tenable position. The highest justice is rendered by the state when it exacts from the debtor at the end of a contract the *same purchasing power* which the creditor gave him at the beginning of the contract, no less, no more. The statement of Mr. Ingham does not imply that contracts should be paid in silver, because silver furnished the unit which had varied least in value. His conclusion was, of course, based on no such position; but only on such a supposition could it be

---

one be injured." As if a change of standard could benefit some without at the same time injuring others! He goes on to say: "If, however, individual wealth be a public blessing, all will be benefited. At any rate, this is an incident utterly unavoidable, to a certain extent, in this case. It must be submitted to, as otherwise a positive national evil of great magnitude, as your committee deem it, must be encountered." The national evil he referred to was the disappearance of gold, which was due to a ratio which drove out silver. But he did not think the debasement of the standard should be considered in comparison with the disappearance of gold; without seeming to reflect that gold could have been restored equally well by increasing the weight of the silver dollar, and that thereby we could have escaped the charge of a debasement of the coinage.

[1] "Report of 1878," p. 568.

just. To claim that the amount of silver in a dollar ought not be raised, because all contracts were payable in silver, would have been just only if he had proved that silver had not changed in its purchasing power. Those whose contracts were paid in silver, after that metal had fallen in value, lost an amount of purchasing power equivalent to the depreciation.

It is not certain, also, that after the act of 1834 drove out silver, contracts entered into before 1834 were protected by retaining the original weight of the silver dollar. For example, before 1834 a debt might have been paid either by 100 ounces of pure gold, or 1,500 ounces of pure silver, in coin; after 1834, the debt, owing to the debasement of the gold coins, could be paid by 94 ounces of pure gold in coin, or 1,500 ounces of pure silver in coin. But if silver was practically out of circulation, the creditor, in receiving 94 ounces of gold, would obtain in terms of silver only what silver bullion he could buy with the gold. If the market rate were $1:15\cdot7$, he would have received of silver only $1475\cdot5$ ounces of silver bullion, thus suffering a loss of $24\cdot5$ ounces of silver. On this supposition, contracts were not protected by retaining the monetary unit as fixed in the dollar made of the depreciated silver. Indeed, Mr. Ingham saw the effect, in case of a disappearance of silver, when he said, "Successive changes of this nature must in time subject the policy of this Government to the reproach, which has been so justly cast upon those of the Old World, for the unwarrantable debasement of their coins." And this was exactly what happened.[1] Moreover, full warning[2] of this was given in the debates in Congress.

---

[1] Before 1834 the gold eagle was worth in silver coin $10.66¼. The act of 1834 reduced its value to $10.—"I may remark that the total United States [gold] coin returned to us from the change of standard to the close of this year (1852) is but $1,534,963, showing that, of over twelve millions issued prior to 1834, but a small portion had remained in the country."—G. N. Eckert, Director of the Mint, January 17, 1853.

[2] Mr. Binney said: "If [gold is] overvalued, its effect would be to enable a debtor to pay his present debts with less than he owed; and to that extent, con-

As was to have been expected, the effect of this debasement was not confined to the time in which it occurred. Its evil lived after it, and came up in the form of precedent. It would not be unnatural that it should raise its ugly head, if it is desired in the future to tamper with contracts by altering the standard of payments, since it has already been quoted as a precedent by the Supreme Court of the United States in the second legal-tender decision [1] of 1871. Since

---

sequently, to defraud his creditor; and it would, if it [the overvaluation] is considerable, place silver exactly in the condition in which gold now was, and make it an article of trade instead of currency."—" Cong. Debates," vol. x, Part IV, 1833–1834, p. 4665. Ewing "contended that it would impair existing contracts."
—Ibid., p. 4669. As to the matter of debasement, Webster gave a characteristic reply: "If it had been imagined that there would have been any evil, it would not have been recommended."—" Cong. Debates," vol. x, Part II, 1833–1834, p. 2121.

[1] In discussing the fifth amendment, which forbids taking private property without just compensation or due process of law, the decision reads: "By the act of June 28, 1834, a new regulation of the weight and value of gold coins was adopted, and about 6 per cent taken from the weight of each dollar. The effect of this was that all creditors were subjected to a corresponding loss. The debts then due became solvable with 6 per cent less gold that was required to pay them than before. . . Was the idea ever advanced that the new regulation of gold coin was against the spirit of the fifth amendment? . . . It is said, however, now, that the act of 1834 only brought the legal value of gold coin more nearly into correspondence with its actual value in the market, or its relative value to silver. But we do not see that this varies the case, or diminishes its force as an illustration. The creditor who had a thousand dollars due him on the 31st day of July, 1834 (the day before the act took effect), was entitled to a thousand dollars of coined gold of the weight and fineness of the then existing coinage. The day after he was entitled only to a sum 6 per cent less in weight and in market value, *or to a smaller number of silver dollars.* Yet he would have been a bold man who had asserted that, because of this, the obligation of the contract was impaired, or that private property was taken without compensation or without due process of law."

On the point that the "obligation of a contract to pay money is to pay that which the law shall recognize as money when the payment is to be made," it was laid down: "No one ever doubted that a debt of one thousand dollars, contracted before 1834, could be paid by one hundred eagles coined after that year, though they contained no more gold than ninety-four eagles, such as were coined when the contract was made; and this, not because of the intrinsic value of the coin, but because of its legal value."—" Banker's Magazine," 1871–1872, pp. 765–767.

even monetary irregularities, after being enacted into law, have the sacredness of legal precedent, a legislator may well pause before dealing with such questions as these in haste, or in obedience to party policy.

§ 6. The act of 1834 was supplemented by a law in 1837[1] which changed the proportion of alloy to pure metal in our coins. It will be remembered that Hamilton recommended $\frac{11}{12}$ of the weight to be pure, and $\frac{1}{12}$ to be alloy for both gold and silver coins. This recommendation, however, was carried out only in respect of gold coins in the act of 1792; for silver coins were issued with an alloy[2] of slightly more than $\frac{1}{9}$, or in the proportion of 371.25 grains pure, in 416 grains of standard silver. Therefore, the original silver dollar, as it was coined from 1792 to 1837 (and 100 cents of the subsidiary coinage also), weighed 416 grains, "standard weight"— that is, the pure silver plus the alloy. The 416-grain dollar, of course, contained 371.25 grains of pure silver.

In 1837 a very sensible reform was made by establishing the same proportion of alloy for both gold and silver coins; and by making that proportion $\frac{1}{10}$, which was equivalent to saying that the amount of pure metal in a coin should always be $\frac{9}{10}$ of its standard weight, or 900 thousandths fine. This is our present system, and the amount of pure metal in a coin can now be found by subtracting $\frac{1}{10}$ from its full or standard weight; or the standard weight can be found by adding $\frac{1}{9}$ to the weight of the pure metal. Pure gold and silver is defined as 1,000 thousandths fine.

By the act of 1834, the pure gold in an eagle (no gold dollar pieces were yet coined) was reduced from the weight of 247.5 grains given by act of 1792 to 232 grains, and the standard weight fixed at 258 grains. This, in decimal terms, was equivalent to 899.225 thousandths fine for our gold coinage. The act of 1837, therefore, slightly changed the quantity

---

[1] See act, Appendix III.
[2] That is, the fineness, in the act of 1792, when reduced to decimal terms, was for gold coins 916.66$\frac{2}{3}$, and for silver coins 892.43 thousandths.

of pure gold from 232 grains to 232·2 grains, retaining the standard weight of 258 grains, and thus gave exactly 900 thousandths fine for the eagle, as well as for our other gold coins of less denominations which contained weights proportional to the eagle. This addition of $\frac{2}{10}$ of a grain to the pure gold makes the legal ratio between gold and silver coins 371·25 : 23·22, or 15·98 + to 1; while in the act of 1834 the ratio was almost exactly 16 : 1 (371·25 : 23·2).

In dealing with the weight of the silver dollar, the amount of pure silver in it was left untouched, as it was fixed by the act of 1792, at 371·25 grains. But in order to establish the ratio of alloy at $\frac{1}{10}$, the standard weight, which was fixed at 416 grains in the act of 1792, was changed in 1837 to 412½ grains. This is the origin of the common name of "412½-grain dollar." It dates from 1837; although the quantity of pure silver in it has been unchanged since the act of 1792; 412½ grains is its "standard weight."

CHAPTER V.

THE GOLD DISCOVERIES AND THE ACT OF 1853.

§ 1. THE discoveries of gold in Russia, Australia, and California, by which the gold product reached its highest amount soon after 1851, form an epoch in the monetary history of every modern state with a specie circulation. They have been the most important events in the later history of the precious metals, and their effect upon the relative values of gold and silver has been serious and prolonged. It is not too much to say that almost all the bimetallic discussions of recent years would not have arisen had this unexpected and astonishing stream of gold from the mines of both the Old and the New World never been poured upon the market. From it date almost all our modern problems relating to gold and silver, and, as we shall later see, we can not discuss the silver question of to-day without reference to this extraordinary production of gold.

The figures of annual production, which are elsewhere[1] given, show the extent of the addition which was made to the world's supply already in existence. From an average annual production in 1840–1850 of about $38,000,000, the gold supply increased to a figure beyond $150,000,000 after 1850. The effect of this increase was unquestionably to lower the value of gold; in other words, to diminish its purchasing power over commodities of general consumption.[2] It was one of those unexpected events which no human sagacity

---

[1] See Appendix I.
[2] See Jevons, "A Serious Fall in the Value of Gold ascertained" (1863).

could have foreseen ; and, as it seriously affected the value of one of the two metals in our double standard, it threw a new obstacle in the way of its successful progress. There being a fall in the value of gold this time, instead of a fall in the value of silver as before, the necessity arose of a new adjustment of the legal ratio for our gold and silver coins in order to keep both metals in circulation. That is, if bimetallism was to be continued, the experience of the United States required a constant readjustment of the Mint ratio to the market ratio, because of constant changes in the relative values due to natural, and so to unforeseen, causes. After an experience of sixty years, did the United States propose to continue a nominal double standard after its constant failure to keep both metals in circulation ? We shall confine ourselves to this question in the present chapter, and to the legislation in which the decision on this matter was contained.

The extraordinary change in the annual production of gold is made clear by noticing in Chart IX the rise of the space covered by yellow after 1850, and comparing this with the extent of the space covered by the same color in earlier periods.[1]

Of the general and more important effects ensuing from the increased gold production I shall speak in a later chapter,[2] in connection with its influence on the value of silver.

§ 2. When the value of gold fell under the regular flow of a new and extraordinary supply, as might have been expected, Gresham's law began to work more actively than ever. It has been seen already that the Mint ratio of 1 : 16 began in 1834 the movement which was slowly substituting gold for silver. The fall in the value of gold now aggravated this tendency into a serious evil. The divergence between the legal and the market ratios clearly revealed by 1849, at the latest, a long-standing error in regard to the subsidiary coinage. In 1834 an ounce of gold bought about 15·7 ounces of silver in the bullion market (but 16 ounces

---

[1] Chart IX is taken from Dr. Soetbeer's " Edelmetall-Production," 1879.
[2] See chap. viii.

CHART IX.

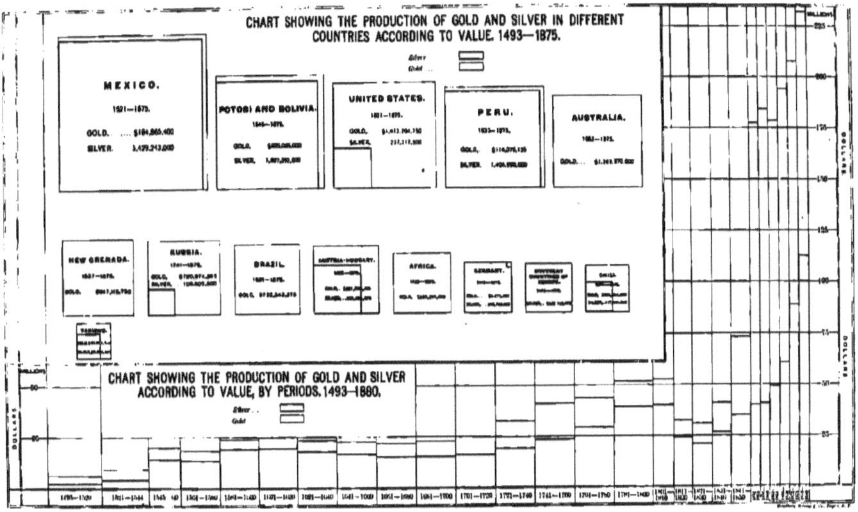
CHART SHOWING THE PRODUCTION OF GOLD AND SILVER IN DIFFERENT COUNTRIES ACCORDING TO VALUE. 1493—1875.
Silver
Gold
MEXICO.
1521—1875.
GOLD.
SILVER.
POTOSI AND BOLIVIA.
GOLD.
SILVER.
UNITED STATES.
GOLD.
SILVER.
PERU.
GOLD.
SILVER.
AUSTRALIA.
GOLD.
NEW GRENADA.
GOLD.
RUSSIA.
GOLD.
SILVER.
BRAZIL.
GOLD.
AUSTRIA-HUNGARY.
AFRICA.
CHART SHOWING THE PRODUCTION OF GOLD AND SILVER ACCORDING TO VALUE, BY PERIODS. 1493—1880.
Silver
Gold
MILLIONS
DOLLARS

in the form of coin). In the period we are now considering, however, since gold had fallen in value, one ounce of gold could buy 15·7 ounces no longer, but a less number, which in 1853 was about 15·4 ounces. It will be seen at once that this widened the difference between the Mint ratio of 1 : 16 and the market ratio, and so offered a greater profit to the watchful money-brokers. Being able to make legal payment of a debt either in silver or gold, a man having 1,600 ounces of silver could take only 1,540 of them to the bullion market, and there buy 100 ounces of gold, which would by law be a legal acquittal of his debt. He would thus gain 60 ounces by paying his debt in gold rather than in silver. When the ratio was 1 : 15·7, he would have gained only 30 ounces. So that the fall in the value of gold acted to increase the speed with which gold drove out silver.

This changed relation is to be found in the quotations of silver coins in gold prices. The amount of pure silver in a dollar, or two halves, four quarters, etc., was 371·25 grains; in a gold dollar, 23·2 grains. The act of 1834 had said that gold was 16 times as valuable as silver, and that 23·2 grains of gold should be equivalent to 371·25 grains of silver; but the market is unaffected by legal decrees, and values are not fixed by any legislature. The market values of the two metals in 1853 having then assumed a relation of about 1 : 15·4, a gold dollar[1] could buy 15·4 times 23·2 grains of silver in the market, or 357¼ grains. This amount was 14 grains less than the legal silver dollar. But if 357¼ grains was the market equivalent of a gold dollar, 371¼ grains would be worth more than a gold dollar in the market; that is, silver dollars were worth about 104 cents of a gold coin in 1853, and even rose to 105 cents in 1859.[2] Taking these figures, it will be seen in another way why it was unprofitable to use a

---

[1] Gold dollar pieces were first coined in 1849. See laws of the United States in Appendix III.

[2] For a table of the value of a silver dollar in gold coin from 1834 to 1876, showing that it had always been above the value of a gold dollar since 1834, see Appendix V.

silver coin as a medium of exchange. If a dollar of silver was worth 104 cents in gold coin, and since gold coin was a legal tender for all payments, no one would, on grounds of self-interest, choose to pay 104 cents when 100 cents would serve the same purpose. Consequently, only the cheaper metal was used, and that was gold, while silver was wholly banished from use as money, and in the United States became an article of merchandise only.

But this went further than ever before. It will be recalled that the subsidiary coinage of silver had since 1792 contained weights of pure silver proportional to the weight of the dollar piece; that is, two halves, four quarters, ten dimes, and twenty half-dimes, contained as much pure silver as a dollar piece, or $371\frac{1}{4}$ grains. Consequently, if a dollar piece of silver had become worth 104 cents in gold, two halves, four quarters, etc., would have become worth the same sum in gold; therefore the profit in exchanging gold for subsidiary silver was such that it was also driven from use. A half-eagle exchanged for ten half-dollars gave the same profit as when exchanged for five separate dollar pieces. In this way all the silver used for small "change," the subsidiary coinage, disappeared from circulation. Through the operation of Gresham's law even the coins needed for small retail transactions had been reached, and the business of the country became seriously embarrassed by the want of small coins.[1] "We have had but a single standard for the last three or four years," said Mr. Dunham[2] in behalf of the Committee of Ways and

---

[1] "There is, then, a constant stimulant to gather up every silver coin and send it to market as bullion to be exchanged for gold, and the result is the country is almost devoid of small change for the ordinary small business transactions, and what we have is of a depreciated character. This does not injure your Wall Street brokers, who deal by thousands. They are making a profit by it; but it is a serious injury to the laboring millions of the country who deal in small sums."—C. L. Dunham, "Congressional Globe," Appendix, 2d session, 32d Congress, p. 190, February 1, 1853.

[2] Ibid., p. 190. Mr. Skelton (New Jersey) remarked: "Gold is the only standard of value by which all property is now measured; it is virtually the only currency of the country."—"Congressional Globe," vol. xxvi, 2d session, 32d Congress, p. 629. "The expense of coining a given value of silver into

Means in 1850; "that has been and now is gold." In short, by 1850 the people of the United States found themselves with a single standard of gold, but without enough silver to serve for necessary exchanges in retail transactions. The balancing plank in this vacillating system had now tipped quite in the other direction, for before 1834 the silver end was up. Now it was the gold end. How soon would it be the silver end again, if we adhered to such a system?

This, then, was the situation produced by the gold discoveries in connection with the act of 1834, establishing the ratio of 1 : 16. It now remains for me to recount the remedy which Congress was again forced to apply to the situation as a corrective. As we shall see, the difficulties were met much more intelligently than ever before.

§ 3. The act of 1853 was a practical abandonment of the double standard in the United States. There was virtually no opposition to the bill, even though its real purpose was openly avowed in the clearest way in the House by Mr. Dunham, who had the measure in charge and who showed an admirable knowledge of the questions involved :[1]

"Another objection urged against this proposed change is that it gives us a standard of gold only. . . . What advantage is to be obtained by a standard of the two metals, which is not as well, if not much better, attained by a single standard, I am unable to perceive ; while there are very great disadvantages resulting from it, as the experience of every nation which has attempted to maintain it has proved. . . . Indeed, it is utterly impossible that you should long at a time maintain a double standard. . . . Gentlemen talk about a double standard of gold and silver as a thing that exists, and that we propose to change. *We have had but a single standard for the last three*

---

the smaller coins is much greater than into the large, and when coined the great demand for them gives them a higher currency value than that assigned by law. As a proof of this, the demand for silver for exportation has not operated as yet upon these smaller coins ; that is to say, the dime and half-dime (the quarter, too, has been partially exempted), while it has swept the silver dollar and half-dollar from the country."—Hunter, Chairman Fin. Com. of Sen., " Report No. 104," 1st session, 32d Congress, p. 11.

[1] " Congressional Globe," Appendix, 2d session, 32d Congress, p. 190.

or four years. That has been, and now is, gold. We propose to let it remain so, and to adapt silver to it, to regulate it by it."

In answer to another plan, the same speaker[1] said :

"We would thereby still continue the double standard of gold and silver, a thing the committee desire to obviate. *They desire to have the standard currency to consist of gold only*, and that these silver coins shall be entirely subservient to it, and that they shall be used rather as tokens than as standard currency."

We have heard a great deal in later years about the surreptitious demonetization of silver in 1873. There was, however, vastly too much criticism wasted on the act of 1873; for the real demonetization of silver in the United States was accomplished in 1853. It was not the result of accident; it was a carefully considered plan, deliberately carried into legislation in 1853, twenty years before its nominal demonetization by the act of 1873. The act of 1853 tried and condemned the criminal; and, after twenty years of waiting for a reprieve, the execution only took place in 1873. It was in 1853 that Congress, judging from our own past experience and that of other countries, came to the conclusion that a double standard was an impossibility for any length of time.

It can not be said, however, that this conclusion was reached wholly through unselfish reasons. The underlying prejudice in favor of gold, if gold can be had, which we are sure to find deeply seated in the desires of our business community whenever occasion gives it an opportunity for display, was here manifesting itself. The country found itself with a single metal in circulation. Had that metal been silver, we should have had to chronicle again the grumbling dissertations on the disappearance of gold which characterized the period preceding 1834. But in 1853 the single standard was gold. This was a situation which no one rebelled against. Indeed, no one seemed to regard it as any-

---

[1] "Congressional Globe," Appendix, 2d session, 32d Congress, p. 190.

thing else than good fortune (except so far as the subsidiary coins had disappeared). It was very much as if a ranchman, starting with one hundred good cattle and one hundred inferior ones, had found, when branding-time came, that, by virtue of exchange with his neighbors, the two hundred cattle assigned to him were, in his judgment, all good ones, and none inferior. From a selfish point of view, he had no reason to complain. It would have been a very different story had the two hundred cattle all been inferior.

In the debates it was proposed [1] that, as the cause of the change in the relative values of gold and silver was the increased product of gold, the proper remedy should be to increase the quantity of gold in the gold coins. This was exactly the kind of treatment which should have been adopted in regard to silver in 1834, and it seems quite reasonable that this should have been the only true and just policy in 1853. Certainly it was, if it was intended to bring the Mint ratio into accord with the market ratio, and try again the experiment of a double standard. But this was exactly what Congress chose to abandon. There was no discussion as to how a readjustment of the ratio between the two metals might be reached, for it was already decided that only one metal was to be retained. This decision, consequently, carried us to a point where a ratio between the two metals was not of the slightest concern. And so it remained. The United States had no thought about the ratios between gold and silver thereafter until the extraordinary fall in the value of silver in 1876. The policy of the United States in retaining gold, once that it was in circulation, was only doing a little earlier what France did in later years. When the cheapened gold, after 1850, had filled the channels of circulation in France, and had driven out silver, France made no objections; but when a subsequent change in silver tended to drive out the gold, France quietly held on to her gold. The United States, as well as France, again showed the unconscious preference for gold of which Hamilton spoke in 1792.

---

[1] By Mr. Jones (Tennessee).

§ 4. In the provisions of the act[1] of 1853 nothing whatever was said as to the silver dollar-piece. It had entirely disappeared from circulation years before, and acquiescence in its absence was everywhere found. No attempt whatever was thereafter made to change the legal ratio, in order that both metals might again be brought into concurrent circulation. Having enough gold, the country did not care for silver. At the existing and only nominal Mint ratio of 1 : 16, the silver dollar could not circulate, and no attempt was made in the act to bring it into circulation. It is, therefore, to be kept distinctly in mind that in 1853 the actual use of silver as an unlimited legal tender equally with gold was decisively abandoned. Under any conditions then existing a double standard was publicly admitted to be hopeless. The main animus of the act, therefore, is to be found in what is not included in it, that is, in the omission to insert any provision which would bring the silver dollar again into circulation.

As the act stands on the statute-books, it is practically nothing more than a regulation of the subsidiary silver coinage,[2] and its study is but a lesson in the proper principles which should regulate that part of a metallic currency. Hitherto 100 cents of fractional silver coin had contained 371¼ grains of pure silver; and, as has been seen, whenever anything happened to drive out the silver dollar-piece, the subsidiary coins disappeared equally with the dollar. The recognition of this fact led to the adoption of the first correct rule for such money. The act reduced the number of grains of pure silver in 100 cents from 371·25 to 345·6 (the standard weight being changed from 412½ to 384 grains), equivalent to a reduction of 6·91 per cent from the former basis. This was

---

[1] For the act, see Appendix III.

[2] "The main object of the bill is to supply small silver change, half-dollars, quarter-dollars, dimes, and half-dimes. . . . The bill does not propose to change the value of the gold currency; it does not propose to disturb the standard of value now in existence throughout the country. Gold is the only standard of value by which all property is now measured; it is virtually the only currency of the country."—Skelton (New Jersey), "Congressional Globe," vol. xxvi, p. 629.

more than the difference between the value of the gold dollar and the silver dollar (which was worth about 104 cents in gold). In short, it was intended[1] to reduce silver to the position of a subsidiary metal. The reason for the reduction of weight, so that 100 cents of the small coins should be worth even less than the value of the gold dollar, is substantiated by the experience of many countries. It protects the subsidiary coin from disturbance, even if changes in the relative values of gold and silver drive out one or the other metal which is coined in larger pieces. There were only 345·6 grains of pure silver in 100 cents of this coin; a dollar of gold (23·2 grains) would buy 357¼ grains of silver bullion (at a market ratio of 1 : 15·4). If a person should melt the new silver coins (345·6), he would fall considerably short of having enough (357¼) to buy a gold dollar; and, there being no profit, there would be no motive in melting the silver, or withdrawing them from circulation. The first step, therefore, was gained by lowering their weight so that the market value of the pure silver in the subsidiary coins was worth less than the gold dollar.[2] The silver was given a face value in that form greater than as bullion, and there could be no reason to withdraw them from use.

Far from there being any fear of their disappearance, the next question was, how to prevent silver from flowing to the Mint and seeking the form in which it would be more highly rated than as bullion. In fact, if the weight of the subsidiary coinage were too far reduced, it would offer a premium to counterfeiters, even if as much silver were used in the false, as in the United States, coin. But the second principle to be ob-

---

[1] "We propose, so far as these coins are concerned, to make the silver subservient to the gold coin of the country. . . . We mean to make the gold the standard coin, and to make these new silver coins applicable and convenient, not for large but for small transactions."—Dunham, ibid., p. 190. The only silver coins in circulation were three-cent pieces and Spanish coins ("fips," 12½-cent pieces, and quarters): 100 cents of the former contained only 83⅓ cents of intrinsic value; and the latter were so abraded that they contained intriusically from 6 per cent to 20 per cent of silver below their nominal or face value.

[2] I can now speak of the gold dollar, since the Mint began to coin it in 1849.

served prevented too great a quantity of silver from flowing to the Mint. This was the withdrawal of "free coinage" of subsidiary currency, and a limitation of the supply by leaving its amount to the discretion of the Secretary of the Treasury.[1] The limitation of the supply to the amount actually needed for the use of the public would keep subsidiary coins current at their face value; because of the necessity of having such pieces for small transactions. Of course, the complete theory demands that the Government should redeem them at their tale value, in order to prevent redundancy; but this was not carried out in the act of 1853. These coins could be purchased[2] only from the Mint, and naturally, with gold, at their face value; they would, therefore, get into circulation at first only at par. Consequently, no more would get out than those who offered a full gold value for them believed were needed, or no more than they could pass at their face value. In the original bill, as proposed by Mr. Dunham's committee, it was intended to make these coins receivable for debts due to the Government of the United States. This, of course, was a partial means of redemption; but it was not[3] then adopted by Congress. In practice, however, such a pro-

---

[1] "Sec. 5. That no deposits for coinage into the half-dollar [etc.] shall hereafter be received, other than those made by the Treasurer of the Mint, as herein authorized, and upon account of the United States."

[2] Strangely enough, this law was evaded in actual practice. "All other governments pay the expense of minting by the difference between the intrinsic value of subsidiary coins and the value at which they circulate, and at which the government redeems them. And such was the law in this country until, by a ruling of Mr. Guthrie when he was Secretary of the Treasury, the Mint was ordered to receive silver from private individuals and coin it."—Mr. Kelley, "Congressional Globe," Part III, 2d session, 41st Congress, p. 2311. In 1870, John Jay Knox, in his Report accompanying the bill which became the act of 1873, said: "The practice at the Mint for many years [written 1870] has been to purchase *all silver bullion offered* at about $1.22¼ per ounce, which is above the market price, paying therefor in silver coin. . . . The effect of the Mint practice has been to put in circulation silver coins, without regard to the amount required for purposes of 'change,' creating a discount upon silver coin."—"Sen. Misc. Doc., No. 132," 2d session, 41st Congress, p. 10.

[3] June 9, 1879, however, an act was passed (see Appendix III) redeeming subsidiary silver coins in sums of twenty dollars.

vision has not proved necessary in order to keep the coins at par. Almost the only serious opposition to the bill was made by Andrew Johnson, of Tennessee, who seemed to be unable to grasp the foregoing principle :[1]

"Congress can not regulate the value of the coin. . . . If we can, then, by law, reduce the present standard seven per cent, and make the value of the reduced standard equal to the other, I ask the House and the country if the philosopher's stone has not been discovered ? . . . The commercial world will take the coins for what they are intrinsically worth, and not for what the legal stamp represents them to be worth."[2]

The third principle applicable to a system of subsidiary coinage, and which was followed in the act of 1853, was that which limited its legal-tender power to a small sum. The difference between the intrinsic and face value, if there were free coinage, would enable a large payment to be made in a very inconvenient form by means of large sums of small coins. This, however, could be avoided by such a provision as was included in this act, which limited the amount of subsidiary coins to be offered in payment of debts to a sum not exceeding five dollars.[3] But this difficulty was also checked by the absence of free coinage. Even in this case, however, the limitation of legal-tender power would prevent a possible annoyance in business transactions.

The bill, which originated in the Senate, passed the House without any practical alteration. A motion to lay the bill on the table was twice lost, by votes of 54 to 109, and of 65 to 111. It was passed in the House with 94 ayes, the noes not counted.[4]

---

[1] He was afterward President of the United States.

[2] "Congressional Globe," vol. xxvi, 2d session, 32d Congress, p. 476. He did not believe, moreover, that the great production of gold had lowered its value : " I assume here, and I defy successful refutation of it, that the quantity of gold may be increased upon that of silver without changing the relative commercial value of the metals."—Ibid., p. 490. He also said : " So far as coin is concerned, the changing of our standard of gold and silver has no more effect upon the gold and silver coinage of the United States than a change in the standard of weights and measures would have upon the price of our cotton or wheat."—Ibid., p. 491.

[3] June 9, 1879, the amount to which silver coins in denominations below one dollar are a legal tender was raised to ten dollars.

[4] "Congressional Globe," ibid., pp. 629, 630.

CHAPTER VI.

THE GOLD STANDARD, 1853-1873.

§ 1. At no time after the act of 1853 until the Civil War was the silver dollar of 412½ grains equal to less than 103 or 104 cents of our gold coins, and, consequently, it was never seen in circulation. The country had willingly acquiesced in the practical adoption of the single gold standard, and so well did the situation satisfy all demands that the question of gold and silver dropped out of the public mind. The subsidiary coinage of silver introduced by the act of 1853 served its purpose admirably. With gold as the medium of exchange for large payments, and an overvalued silver coinage for small payments, the business interests of the country were fully content, and no trouble need have arisen to this day from any disturbances in our system of metallic currency had we been saved from the evils of our Civil War. Until the passage of the Legal-Tender Act early in 1862 (specie payments were suspended December 31, 1861) our currency continued to be what it was intended it should be in 1853—a gold currency. Paper money, issued by the State banks, was, of course, in circulation; but I do not propose here to include the history of paper issues. Paper money acts to drive out either metal which is in use; and so its existence does not alter conclusions which are concerned only with the two metals. We can say, without hesitation, that our coinage system from 1853 to the Civil War worked admirably. There were evidently no longings to use the silver dollar piece when it was worth 3 or 4 per cent premium.

§ 2. The act of February 25, 1862, issued the first installment of United States legal-tender notes to the amount of $150,000,000. A similar amount was authorized by a second act passed July 11, 1862, but which was going through the preliminary stages of enactment in June. The result of the depreciation of the paper money which became manifest by a premium on gold in June to the extent of 5 per cent, and in July of 20 per cent, naturally brought Gresham's law into operation, by which the cheaper paper was substituted for the more valuable gold. Gold disappeared before the depreciating paper, and it was not until January 1, 1879, that it again appeared.

The displacing paper did even more than this. It drove out the subsidiary coinage in 1862. As early as July 2d the newspapers noted the disappearance of small coin, and its accompanying inconveniences. But in Congress there was very little conception of the causes at work. While the second legal-tender bill was under discussion in June, members seemed to be utterly unconscious of what was going on. On June 17th an amendment was introduced into Section 1 of the bill in regard to the small denominations of paper to this effect:

"*Provided*, That no note shall be issued for the fractional part of a dollar, and not more than thirty-five millions shall be of lower denominations than five dollars."

This measure was evidently intended to protect the small coins in circulation. It was believed, no doubt, that, if paper of small denominations were not issued, subsidiary coins would remain in circulation. The discussion and probable passage of an act authorizing this second issue of paper so depreciated its value that, before the five-dollar notes could have been issued from the printing-press, and even before the passage of this bill, the disappearance of the small coins was remarked upon (July 2d). This showed distinctly that ten-dollar notes, if depreciated, could drive out silver coins of denominations less than one dollar. There was, in truth, only a greater profit in dealing with larger sums. A large quantity of silver coins collected together and sold for depreciated legal-tender paper of large denominations gave the same proportional profit as if small notes had been used in the process.[1]

The subsidiary silver, containing 345·6 grains of pure metal, circulated at its face value in exchange for gold coins; but, if a 412½-grain dollar, containing 371·25 grains of pure silver, were counted as par, 345·6 grains of subsidiary coinage would be worth relatively, so far as regards the pure silver it contained, only 93·09 cents (although its legal value in small payments was 100 cents). The market value of a dollar containing 371·25 grains, in 1862, however, was 104·16 cents of our gold coins. But, inasmuch as the subsidiary coins would be melted, or exported, only on estimates of their intrinsic value, the market price of 345·6 grains of silver would be 96·96 cents of our gold coins. As soon, therefore, as the paper money depreciated below 96·96 cents, as compared with our gold coins, the movement of subsidiary silver out of circulation would begin. The operation can be easily seen by the adjoined diagram. As soon as the United States notes depreciated below 100, or par, there would be a profit in withdrawing our gold coins from use, according to Gresham's law. And when the depreciation had reached a point below 96·96, the silver coins must of necessity disappear. By June 1, 1862, the premium on gold was 5 per cent, which showed a depreciation of the United States notes to 95·23 cents in a dollar; by the 1st of July the premium on gold was about 18 per cent, showing a depreciation to 84·7 cents in a dollar. In short, the subsidiary coins must have been withdrawn

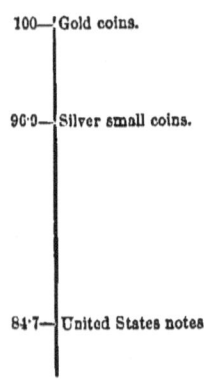

---
[1] There had been good authority for the belief that coin would continue to circulate provided no paper of a corresponding denomination were issued. See J. S. Mill's "Political Economy" (Laughlin's edition), p. 348.

very soon after any effect on the gold coins was apparent. The paper money at 84·7 cents would very rapidly dislodge both kinds of coins.

Although, on the 17th of June, in the second legal-tender act, any paper issues of denominations less than a dollar had been forbidden, Congress was forced, by the events we have just described, to pass a bill authorizing the issue of a paper fractional currency on July 17, 1862. The absence of small silver had brought into existence tokens, tickets, checks, and substitutes of every description, issued by merchants and shopkeepers; and Congress was obliged hastily to authorize a currency, originally based on the likeness of postage-stamps, but which finally resulted in simple exercise of the function of note-issues for small denominations. Congress was unwilling to admit the necessity for such issues of paper, and the first act was entitled "An Act to authorize payments in stamps."[1]

§ 3. The paper-money period continued until the resumption of specie payments, January 1, 1879. Meanwhile no gold was in circulation. The fractional paper notes continued in use in spite of an ill-judged and ridiculous attempt of the Secretary[2] of the Treasury to redeem them, with but a small reserve of silver, in October, 1873. This incident is an evidence of extraordinary ignorance in a finance minister. Very soon after the commercial crisis of September, 1873, the exceptional condition of the exchanges and the arrival of gold caused a fall in the premium on gold in October from 11 to 6 per cent. But with a gold dollar worth 106 cents in paper, the paper was worth only about 94 cents in gold, while, as it will be remembered, the 345·6 grains of silver in the subsidiary coinage were equivalent to 96·9 cents in gold.[3] Not until gold had fallen to 104, at least, could it be hoped

---

[1] Sec. 12, "Statutes at Large," 592. The twenty-five cent note, for example, contained a copy of five five-cent postage-stamps.   [2] Secretary Richardson.

[3] Cf. also a broker's table giving purchasing prices of silver coins in paper for exportation, in the "Financial and Commercial Chronicle," November 1, 1873, p. 590.

that silver would remain in circulation. But Secretary Richardson announced that *silver* had fallen so low that he proposed to resume payments in that metal. He had in the Treasury not more than half a million[1] in silver; gold was selling at not less than 106, and a profit still existed in exchanging paper for subsidiary silver. On the 27th of October, 1873, " Secretary Richardson issued a circular letter to the several sub-treasury officers, directing them to pay out silver coin to public creditors, should they desire it, in sums not to exceed five dollars in any one payment."[2] In practice, the silver was paid out in sums of a few hundred dollars a day, for, of course, every creditor demanded his share of silver. The silver was not given in exchange for paper currency. The silver, when paid out, disappeared, and would have done so had the Secretary issued millions, instead of hundreds, of dollars of it.[3]

While discussing the subject of subsidiary coinage, it may be best to anticipate our story slightly and narrate here the means by which resumption of silver payments was finally achieved in 1877–1878. The Resumption Act, passed January 14, 1875, enacted (Sec. 1):

" That the Secretary of the Treasury is hereby authorized and required, as rapidly as practicable, to cause to be coined at the mints of the United States silver coins of the denominations of ten, twenty-five, and fifty cents, of standard value, and to issue them in redemption of an equal number and amount of fractional currency of similar denominations ; or, at his discretion, he may issue such silver coins through the mints, the sub-treasuries, public depositaries, and post-offices of the United States ; and upon such issue he is hereby authorized and required to redeem an equal amount of such fractional currency until the whole amount of such fractional currency outstanding shall be redeemed."

Not until 1877, however, did the premium on gold fall so low that, by the corresponding rise in the value of paper, it

---

[1] Upton, "Money in Politics," p. 146, says he had " only a few thousands."
[2] Upton, ibid., p. 146.
[3] The Secretary said he could have resumed silver payments if the newspapers had not discovered his plan and discussed it!

warranted an attempt at resumption of silver payments. The following table [1] will show the value of a paper dollar in gold since 1865:

Secretary Bristow felt some doubts [2] as to his authority to pay out silver coins for notes under the provision of the Resumption Act just quoted, and a subsequent bill [3] was passed April 17, 1876. The amount of fractional currency outstanding was about $42,000,000, and the pressure for redemption at first was very strong.[4] All but $16,000,000 of the fractional paper notes had at once come in for redemption; but since then about $1,000,000 more have been redeemed, leaving $15,000,000 yet outstanding, or, more probably, destroyed. After the first severe pressure due to the redemption of the fractional paper-money had ceased, the demand for silver coins at the Mint still continued in order to satisfy the needs of trade; whereon Congress permitted an additional issue of $10,000,000 in exchange for legal-tender notes.[5]

Year ending June 30th.	Coin value of one dollar of paper.
1865	·71
1866	·66
1867	·71
1868	·70
1869	·73
1870	·85
1871	·89
1872	·87½
1873	·86¼
1874	·91
1875	·87
1876	·89
1877	·95
1878	·99½
Jan. 1, 1879	1·00

---

[1] Taken from Upton, "Money in Politics," p. 145.
[2] Upton, ibid., p. 148. [3] See Appendix III, A, ix.
[4] Secretary Bristow sold $17,594,150 of 5-per-cent bonds to aid in purchasing the silver bullion for the subsidiary coinage, which was subsequently met out of the surplus revenue.
[5] See Appendix III, A, x, July 22, 1876.

CHAPTER VII.

THE DEMONETIZATION OF SILVER.

§ 1. In 1873 we find a simple legal recognition of that which had been the immediate result of the act of 1853, and which had been an admitted fact in the history of our coinage during the preceding twenty years. In 1853 it had been agreed to accept the situation by which we had come to have gold for large payments, and to relegate silver to a limited service in the subsidiary coins. The act of 1873, however, dropped the dollar piece out of the list of silver coins. In discontinuing the coinage of the silver dollar, the act of 1873 thereby simply recognized a fact which had been obvious to everybody since 1849. It did not introduce anything new, or begin a new policy. Whatever is to be said about the demonetization of silver as a fact must center in the act of 1853. Silver was not driven out of circulation by the act of 1873, which omitted the dollar of 412½ grains, since it had not been in circulation for more than twenty-five years. In 1853 Congress advisedly continued in motion the machinery which kept the silver dollar out of circulation, and, as we have seen, avowed its intention to create a single gold standard. This, then, was the act which really excluded silver dollars from our currency. A vast deal of rhetoric has been wasted on the act of 1873, but its importance is greatly overrated. A law which merely recognized existing conditions can not be compared with the law which had for its object to establish those conditions; and this states the relative force of the act of 1853 and that of 1873.

The act of February 12, 1873,[1] is known as the act which demonetized the silver dollar. Important consequences have been attached to it, and it has even been absurdly charged that the law was the cause[2] of the commercial crisis of September, 1873. As if a law which made no changes in the actual metallic standard in use, and which had been in use thus for more than twenty years, had produced a financial disaster in seven months! To any one who knows of the influence of credit and speculation, or who has followed the course of our foreign trade since the Civil War, such a theory is too absurd to receive more than passing mention. To the year 1873 there had been coined of 412½-grain dollars for purposes of circulation only $1,439,457, and these were coined before 1806.

But while the act of 1873 had little importance in changing existing conditions, it had an influence of a kind which at the present time can scarcely be overestimated. We are now, in the course of our story, approaching the year 1876, in which occurred the phenomenal fall in the value of silver. Had the demonetization of the silver dollar not been accomplished in 1873 and 1874, we should have found ourselves in 1876 with a single silver standard, and the resumption of specie payments on January 1, 1879, would have been in silver, not in gold; and 15 per cent of all our contracts and existing obligations would have been repudiated. The act of 1873 was a piece of good fortune, which saved our financial credit and protected the honor of the State. It is a work of legislation for which we can not now be too thankful.

§ 2. It is, moreover, possible that the silver dollar was not "demonetized" in 1873, in spite of the prevailing impression to that effect. The *legal-tender power* of the silver dollar was not taken away by this measure. The coinage laws had not been revised since 1837, and in the act of 1873

---

[1] See Appendix III.
[2] "Report of the United States Silver Commission," 1877, vol. i, p. 125.
[3] Upton, "Money in Politics," p. 201.

occasion was taken to drop out the silver dollar from the list of coins which were thereafter to be issued from the Mint.[1]

"SEC. 15. That the silver coins of the United States shall be a trade-dollar; a half-dollar, or fifty-cent piece; a quarter-dollar, or twenty-five-cent piece; a dime, or ten-cent piece; and the weight of the trade-dollar shall be 420 grains troy; the weight of the half-dollar shall be 12 grams (grammes) and one half of a gram (gramme); the quarter-dollar and the dime shall be, respectively, one half and one fifth of the weight of said half-dollar; and said coins shall be a legal tender at their nominal value for any amount not exceeding five dollars in any one payment.

"SEC. 17. That no coins, either of gold, silver, or minor coinage, shall hereafter be issued from the Mint other than those of the denominations, standards, and weights herein set forth."

It will be noticed that the dollar of $412\frac{1}{2}$ grains is omitted from the list of silver coins which were in the future to be issued by the Mint, and of this list it is said that they shall be a legal tender to the amount of five dollars; but nothing is said which *takes away* the legal-tender quality of a coin already in existence, but of which no mention was made. Whatever silver dollars there were in existence were still a legal tender to any amount after the act was passed, although no more could be coined. The silver dollar, however, was demonetized; but not by the act of 1873. The revision of the Statutes of the United States, previously authorized, was adopted as the law of the land in June, 1874. In the Revised Statutes[2] the legal-tender power of *all* silver coins is thus limited:

Act of June, 1874 : "§ 3586. The silver coins of the United States shall be a legal tender at their nominal value for any amount not exceeding five dollars in any one payment."

This statement, it will be noticed, is a general one, and applies to any silver coins of the United States whatever, while the act of 1873 predicated a limited legal-tender power of only a specified list of silver coins. The legal enactment, therefore, which really took away the legal-tender quality of

---

[1] See act of 1873 in Appendix III, Sec. 15 and 17.   [2] See Appendix III.

the silver dollar of 412½ grains, was passed June 22, 1874. The act of 1873 only discontinued its coinage; the provision of the Revised Statutes took away its debt-paying power for sums beyond five dollars.[1]

The act of 1873 also made a change in the charge for seigniorage. Until 1853 the expense of changing bullion into coin was borne by the Government; but the act of 1853 inserted a charge of one half of one per cent. on all but subsidiary silver coins. No seigniorage, of course, was charged for subsidiary coins, because there was no "free coinage" of them by individuals. The act of 1873 now reduced the charge from one half to one fifth of one per cent.[2]

§ 3. The act of 1873 has been the subject of a curious controversy. After the fall of silver in 1876, and the subsequent rise of bimetallic discussions, severe denunciations of the act of 1873 were heard. It was asserted that the demonetization of silver was secretly carried out without any knowledge of it by the general public, or even by financial experts. In the silver discussion of 1878 it was charged[3] that the silver

---

[1] Cf. Upton, "Money in Politics," p. 207. This matter was quite thoroughly discussed in January, 1878, in the debates in the Senate. See, for example, the "Globe," p. 262, vol. vii, Part I, 2d session, 45th Congress.

[2] The charge for seigniorage, however, was repealed by the Resumption Act in 1875; so that, like England, the United States now makes no charge for manufacturing its coin.

[3] The following examples, out of many, may be cited: Senator Hereford (West Virginia) charged the fraudulent passage of the act of 1873, on May 27, 1872, on the House, because Mr. Hooper, in charge of the bill, reported a substitute, and moved to suspend the rules and pass the substitute; and because Mr. Hooper said, in answer to an inquiry concerning coins of small denomination: "This bill makes no change in the existing law in that regard. It does not require the recoinage of the *small coins*." The charge is made that the substitute was not read before it was passed.—" Globe," vol. vii, Part I, 2d session, 45th Congress, p. 205.

Mr. Bright (Tennessee) said in the House: "It was passed by fraud in the House, never having been printed in advance, being a substitute for the printed bill; never having been read at the Clerk's desk, the reading having been dispensed with by an impression that the bill made no material alteration in the coinage laws; it was passed without discussion, debate being cut off by operation of the previous question. It was passed, to my certain information, under such

dollar had been demonetized surreptitiously in 1873. The probable ground for this belief arose from the form of the bill, which, as we have seen, made a list of the silver coins, and from this list simply omitted the silver dollar without calling attention in the enactment itself to its discontinuance. An enactment, however, does not usually describe what has been omitted; its affirmations are positive. The discontinuance of the silver dollar, moreover, was not kept a secret during the time of more than two years when the bill was before Congress. Mr. W. D. Kelly, chairman of the Committee of Coinage, Weights, and Measures of the House, and reported the bill January 9, 1872, in the following words,[1] with the recommendation that it pass:

"It was referred to the Committee on Coinage, Weights, and Measures, and received as careful attention as I have ever known a committee to bestow on any measure. . . . The committee proceeded with great deliberation to go over the bill, not only section by section, but line by line and word by word." [This applied to the previous session.]

"I wish to ask the gentleman who has just spoken if he knows of any government in the world which makes its subsidiary coinage of full value. The silver coin of England is 10 per cent below the value of gold coin, and, acting under the advice of the experts of this country and of England and of France, Japan has made her silver coinage within the last year 12 per cent below the value of gold coin, and for this reason: *It is impossible to retain the double standard.* The values of gold and silver continually fluctuate. You can not determine this year what will be the relative values of gold and silver next year. They were 15 to 1 a short time ago; they are 16 to 1 now."

Far from having been accomplished surreptitiously, the discontinuance of the silver dollar was very well known

---

circumstances that the fraud escaped the attention of some of the most watchful as well as the ablest statesmen in Congress at the time. It was passed near the closing days of the session, when, in the bustle and precipitate rush of business, it was most favorable for the concealment of fraud. . . . Ay, sir, it was a fraud that smells to heaven. It was a fraud that will stink in the nose of posterity, and for which some persons must give account in the day of retribution." —"Globe," vol. vii, Part I, 2d session, 45th Congress, p. 584.

[1] "Congressional Globe," Part I, 2d session, 42d Congress, p. 322.

through the attention given it by the Secretary of the Treasury in his reports for 1870, 1871, and 1872. The bill,[1] substantially as passed, was the work of John Jay Knox, and was transmitted by Secretary Boutwell to Senator Sherman, chairman of the Senate Finance Committee, April 25, 1870; the bill was sent out for criticism and suggestions to no less than thirty persons familiar with the Mint and with coinage operations; it was printed thirteen times by order of Congress; it was considered during five different sessions of the Senate and House; the debates on the bill in the Senate occupy 66, and in the House 78, columns of the "Congressional Globe," and it was not finally passed until February 12, 1873.

---

[1] It is to be remembered, however, that the bill dealt with many more matters, and those of a technical nature, than the omission of the silver dollar in itself. The originator of the bill, Mr. Knox, thus explains in his report (p. 2) how it was prepared: "The method adopted in the preparation of the bill was first to arrange in as concise a form as possible the laws now in existence upon these subjects [Mint, assay-offices, and coinage], with such additional sections and suggestions as seemed valuable. Having accomplished this, the bill, as thus prepared, was printed upon paper with wide margin, and in this form transmitted to the different mints and assay-offices, to the First Comptroller, the Treasurer, the Solicitor, the First Auditor, and to such other gentlemen as are known to be intelligent upon metallurgical and numismatical subjects, with the request that the printed bill should be returned, with such notes and suggestions as experience and education should dictate. In this way the views of more than thirty gentlemen who are conversant with the manipulation of metals, the manufacture of coinage, the execution of the present laws relative thereto, the method of keeping accounts and of making returns to the department, have been obtained, with but little expense to the department and little inconvenience to correspondents. Having received these suggestions, the present bill has been framed, and is believed to comprise within the compass of eight or ten pages of the Revised Statutes every important provision contained in more than sixty different exactments upon the Mint, assay-offices, and coinage of the United States, which are the result of nearly eighty years of legislation upon these subjects." Mr. Knox's report accompanied the bill to Congress, and gives a clear idea of its full character, with comparative tables of the existing and proposed coinage.—"Letter of the Secretary of the Treasury to the Chairman of the Committee on Finance, communicating a report of John Jay Knox, in relation to a revision of the laws pertaining to the Mint and coinage of the United States," May 2, 1870; "Sen. Misc. Doc. No. 132," 2d session, 41st Congress.

The following table[1] will show the slow process by which the bill finally became a law:

PROCEEDINGS.	Senate.	House.
Submitted by Secretary of Treasury............	Apr. 25, 1870	
Referred to Senate Finance Committee........	Apr. 28, 1870	
Five hundred copies printed................	May 2, 1870	
Submitted to House........................		June 25, 1870
Reported, amended, and ordered printed......	Dec. 19, 1870	
Debated...................................	Jan. 9, 1871	
Passed, by vote of 36–14...................	Jan. 10, 1871	
Senate bill ordered printed		Jan. 13, 1871
Bill reported with substitute, and recommitted		Feb. 25, 1871
Original bill reintroduced and printed........		Mar. 9, 1871
Reported and debated......................		Jan. 9, 1872
Recommitted..............................		Jan. 10, 1872
Reported back, amended, and printed........		Feb. 13, 1872
Debated...................................		Apr. 9, 1872
Amended, and passed by vote of 110–13......		May 27, 1872
Printed in Senate...........................	May 29, 1872	
Reported, amended, and printed.............	Dec. 16, 1872	
Reported, amended, and printed.............	Jan. 7, 1873	
Passed Senate.............................	Jan. 17, 1873	
Printed with amendments...................		Jan. 21, 1873
Conference Committee[2] appointed...........		
Became a law, February 12, 1873............		

Although it was in reality a codification of laws relating to all questions connected with details of the Mint, assay-offices, and coinage, the intention of the bill in regard to the omission of the silver dollar is unmistakable. In the original bill, as sent out by Mr. Knox for suggestions, a silver dollar of 384 standard grains was proposed, or one on the basis of the existing subsidiary coinage. In this provision there was not only no intention of retaining the dollar of 412½ grains (at the old ratio of 1 : 15·98), but it was intended to insert in its place one containing 25·65 grains less of pure silver. The discontinuance of the old silver dollar by the bill was mentioned by Mr. Knox in his report to the Secretary of the

---

[1] A brief history of the passage of the bill can be found in the "Report of Comptroller of the Currency," 1876, p. 170.

[2] Sherman, Bayard, Scott, and Hooper, Houghton, McNeely.

Treasury accompanying the bill[1] when laid before Congress. The experts, moreover, to whom the bill was sent for suggestion, noticed this change in our policy:

"The bill proposes the discontinuance of the silver dollar, and the report which accompanies the bill suggests the substitution, for the existing standard silver dollar, of a trade-coin of intrinsic value equivalent to the Mexican silver piaster or dollar.

"If the existing standard silver dollar is to be discontinued and a trade-coin of different weight substituted, I would suggest the desirableness of conforming to the Spanish-Mexican silver pillared piaster of 1704. . . . The coins most in demand for Oriental commerce were for many years the pillared Spanish-Mexican piasters; and such was their popularity that they continued to be preferred long after their intrinsic value had been considerably reduced by wear in use. The restoration, as a trade-coin, of a silver dollar approximating to the old standard—to wit, one containing 25 grammes of pure silver—is a subject which would seem to demand favorable consideration."[2]

"The silver dollar, half-dime, and three-cent piece are dispensed with by this amendment. Gold becomes the standard money, of which the gold dollar is the unit. Silver is subsidiary."[3]

"Sec. 11 reduces the weight of the silver dollar from

---

[1] "The coinage of the silver dollar piece . . . is discontinued in the proposed bill. It is by law the dollar unit, and, assuming the value of gold to be fifteen and a half times that of silver, being about the mean ratio for the past six years, is worth in gold a premium of about 3 per cent (its value being $1·0312), and intrinsically more than 7 per cent premium in other silver coins, its value thus being $1·0742. The present laws consequently authorize both a gold-dollar unit and a silver-dollar unit, differing from each other in intrinsic value. The present gold dollar piece is made the dollar unit in the proposed bill, and the silver dollar piece is discontinued. If, however, such a coin is authorized, it should be issued only as a *commercial dollar*, not as a standard unit of account, and of the exact value of the Mexican dollar, which is the favorite for circulation in China and Japan and other Oriental countries "—" Sen. Mis. Doc. No. 132," 2d session, 41st Congress, p. 11.

[2] E. B. Elliott (now Government Actuary), "Letter of the Secretary of the Treasury to the Speaker of the House of Representatives, communicating a report of John Jay Knox, Deputy Comptroller of the Currency, giving the correspondence of the department relative to the revision of the Mint and coinage laws of the United States, H. R. Exec. Doc. No. 307," 2d session, 41st Congress, June 29, 1870, p. 70.

[3] Robert Patterson, ibid., p. 19.

412½ to 384 grains. I can see no good reason for the proposed reduction in the weight of this coin. It would be better, in my opinion, to discontinue its issue altogether. The gold dollar is really the legal unit of and measure of value."[1]

"I see that it is proposed to demonetize the silver dollar."[2]

All this testimony is important because it affords corroborative proof to show beyond cavil that, in 1873, bimetallism was considered an impossibility for the United States. The contrast between the state of mind in 1873 and after the remarkable fall of silver in 1876 is, therefore, very striking, and demands some special explanation in later chapters.

When the bill came before Congress for discussion there was no opposition whatever to the omission of the silver dollar of 412½ grains from the list of authorized coins. The Senate occupied its time chiefly on questions of seigniorage[3] and abrasion,[4] and the House on a question of the salaries of the officials.[5] The chief debate was in the House, when the bill was in charge of Mr. Hooper (Massachusetts), on April 9, 1872. He explained the bill to the House section by section,[6] during the course of which he said:

"It declares the gold dollar of 25 and eight tenths grains of standard gold to be the unit of value, gold practically having been in this country for many years the standard or measure of value, as it is legally in Great Britain and most of the European countries. The silver dollar, which by law is now the legally declared unit of value, does not bear a correct relative proportion to the gold dollar. Being worth intrinsically about one dollar and three cents in gold, it can not circulate concurrently with the gold coins. . . . The committee, *after careful consideration, concluded that twenty-five and eight tenths grains of standard gold* constituting the gold dollar *should be declared the money unit* or metallic representative of the dollar of account.

"Sec. 16 re-enacts the provisions of the existing laws defining the silver coins and their weights, respectively, *except in relation to the silver dollar*, which is reduced in weight from 412½ grains to 384 grains, thus making it a subsidiary coin in

---

[1] Dr. Linderman, late Director of the Mint, ibid., p. 30.
[2] J. R. Snowdon, formerly Director of the Mint, ibid., p. 38.
[3] January 9, 1871.   [4] January 17, 1873.   [5] January 9, 1872.
[6] "Congressional Globe," Part III, 2d session, 42d Congress, pp. 2305, 2306.

harmony with the silver coins of less denominations, to secure its concurrent circulation with them. The silver dollar of 412½ grains, by reason of its bullion or intrinsic value being greater than its nominal value, long since ceased to be a coin of circulation, and is melted by manufacturers of silverware. It does not circulate now in commercial transactions with any country, and the convenience of these manufacturers in this respect can better be met by supplying small stamped bars of the same standard, avoiding the useless expense of coining the dollar for that purpose."

To this position no objection was taken except that, as we had no gold or silver then in circulation, it was profitless to legislate on such questions.[1] The opposition to the bill concerned itself with seigniorage, abrasion, or salaries, and the apparently self-evident policy of omitting the silver dollar was so generally accepted that it was used by Mr. Kelly (Pennsylvania) as a means to silence other objections:

"All experience has shown that you must have one standard coin which shall be a legal tender for all others, and then you may promote your domestic convenience by having a subsidiary coinage of silver, which shall circulate in all parts of your country as legal tender for a limited amount and be redeemable at its face value by your Government. But, sir, I again call the attention of the House to the fact that the gentlemen who oppose this bill insist upon maintaining a silver dollar worth three and a half cents more than the gold dollar, and worth seven cents more than two half-dollars, and that, so long as these provisions remain, you can not keep silver coin in the country."[2]

What the animus of Congress was in respect of the question of bimetallism is perfectly clear, and was as well epitomized as in any other words by the following remarks:

"Aside from the three-dollar gold piece ... the only change in the present law is in more clearly specifying *the gold dollar as the unit of value.* ... Gold is practically the standard of value among all civilized nations, and the time has come

---

[1] "This bill provides for the making of changes in the legal-tender coin of the country, and for substituting as legal tender coin of only one metal instead, as heretofore, of two. I think myself this would be a wise provision, and that legal-tender coins, except subsidiary coin, should be of gold alone; but why should we legislate on this now, when we are not using either of those metals as a circulating medium?"—Mr. Potter, ibid., p. 2310.

[2] "Congressional Globe," Part III, 2d session, 42d Congress, p. 2316.

in this country when the gold dollar should be distinctly declared to be the coin representative of the money unit." [1]

In the act of 1792 our "unit" had been declared (Sec. 9) to be a silver dollar; in the act of 1873, on the other hand, it was enacted (Sec. 14): "That the gold coins of the United States shall be a one-dollar piece, which, at the standard weight of twenty-five and eight tenths grains, shall be the unit of value," etc.

§ 4. The act of 1873 authorized the coinage of a piece known as the trade-dollar, whose subsequent history proved a mystery to many people, and which afforded to speculators an opportunity for profit. Its existence was not due to the demand for ordinary coins at home, and had a different origin.

It is a well-known fact that Oriental nations have a peculiar power of absorbing [2] silver in great quantities. To such an extent is this true that merchants in the China trade require silver as the best means of purchasing goods from that country. Naturally enough, of the various coins of a certain general kind, the coin which contained the most pure silver, and which also passed at the same tale value, was preferred by Eastern nations. The Spanish silver dollar was the coin originally used in this Oriental trade, but later gave place to the Mexican dollar. And within recent years, until 1873, because it was in highest favor with the Chinese, the Mexican dollar was systematically bought and sold by the banks in the United States to supply merchants who had payments to make in the East. The reason for this is to be seen by comparing the quantities [3] of pure silver in the various coins circulating in Chinese ports (with the trade-dollar also included):

COIN.	Standard Weight.	Fineness.	Pure Silver.
	Grains troy.		Grains troy.
Mexican dollar	417$\frac{4}{7}$	902$\frac{1}{2}$	377$\frac{1}{4}$
Japanese yen	416	900	374$\frac{1}{10}$
American dollar	412$\frac{1}{2}$	900	371$\frac{1}{4}$
Trade dollar	420	900	378

[1] Mr. Stoughton (Michigan), ibid., p. 2308.
[2] See chap. ix, "India and the East."
[3] Linderman, "Money and Legal Tender," p. 54.

By this table it may be seen that a coin like the trade-dollar, which contained more pure silver than the Mexican dollar, might supersede it in the favor of the Chinese, and thereby afford a new market for the silver of the United States—which, as early as 1873, began to feel the effects of an increasing production. It was therefore proposed by Dr. Linderman,[1] later Director of the Mint, to the Treasury that the Mint should coin silver bullion into the form which should meet this Eastern demand and better serve the wants of our merchants. The plan was proposed to Congress by the Secretary of the Treasury, and was incorporated into the revision of the Mint laws which formed the main object of the act of 1873. As was seen in the preceding section of this chapter, it was first proposed to coin a silver dollar of only 384 grains standard coin; but the Senate struck out this provision, and, to serve the wishes of those who proposed a new market for silver, the trade-dollar of 420 grains was authorized instead. It was not intended to issue a silver dollar which should circulate in the United States, but merely to lend the authority of the Government stamp to silver bullion in order to aid in finding a market for silver in the East, and at the same time to relieve merchants from paying the high premium exacted for the Mexican dollars, sometimes amounting to from 11 to 22 per cent.[2]

---

[1] Linderman, "Money and Legal Tender," pp. 47–59.

[2] "I don't know what we should do with the bulk of silver if it was not disposed of in some such way. I am very well aware that before the coinage of the trade-dollar the rate of exchange with China, owing to the scarcity of Mexican dollars, had caused them to change 7 per cent here within a week.

"*Q.* Always commanding at that time a premium? *A.* Yes, sir. There was an extra duty on them from Mexico which gave them a premium at once; and an additional premium was created by the demand for them for shipment to China. I have paid 22 per cent premium for Mexican coin for shipment to China, and for many years the range was from 11 to 16 per cent."—Testimony of General La Grange before the United States Treasury Commission, "Report of Director of Mint," 1877, p. 52.

"*Q.* Which do you like best to ship, trade-dollars or Mexican dollars? *A.* At present trade-dollars are better, because we get about 2 per cent more premium on them in China."—Fung Chung, ibid., p. 53.

This object was very successfully carried out, and the trade-dollar, authorized by the act of 1873, was extensively shipped to China, where it was generally received in the southern ports.[1] Inasmuch as a dollar of 371¼ grains bore a premium in gold until 1874, a trade-dollar containing 378 grains of pure silver would be worth still more in gold than the other dollar, and there could be no reason for its circulation in the United States.

The trade-dollar was in reality an ingot, shaped like a dollar piece, but with different devices than those on the dollar of 412½ grains; it weighed 420 grains standard weight (that is, 900 fine), and, consequently, contained 378 grains of pure silver. The cost of manufacturing the coin at the various mints was charged upon the owner of the bullion presented for coinage; so that the expense of melting, refining, assaying the silver, and the expense of making the dollar,[2] was borne entirely by the owners of bullion, and not by the United States.

As was said, the trade-dollar was not intended to circulate in the United States. Not having been considered a legal coin, it was not intended to give it any legal-tender quality whatever. It will be remembered, however, that the act of 1873 presented a list of coins to which was given a legal-tender power in sums not exceeding five dollars. By inadvertence, and without any intent, the trade-dollar was

---

[1] "Trade-dollars are current by count at Singapore, Penang, Bangkok, and Saigon; they are current by weight at Swatow, Amoy, Foochow, and Canton. In Hong-Kong they are not a legal tender, and the banks will only take them from each other by special arrangement; but the Chinese take them freely in Hong-Kong when they want coin of any description, which is very seldom, as they prefer bank-notes, and only take coin from the banks when they require to export it from the colony. In the south of China, the Straits, and Cochin China the trade-dollar is well known and passes without comment along with the clean Mexican dollars, but in Shanghai and the northern ports it is unknown, and it is not likely to be current for a length of time."—" Report of the Hong-Kong and Shanghai Banking Corporation, and the Oriental Bank," January 30 and 31, 1877, in "Report of Director of Mint," 1878, p. 10.

[2] This was one and a quarter per cent at the Philadelphia Mint, and one and a half at the San Francisco Mint, on the tale value.

included in this list, and became possessed of a legal-tender power equally with subsidiary coins to the limit of five dollars. When this was discovered, the error was corrected by an act of July 22, 1876, which took away any legal-tender quality from the trade-dollar.[1] Of its subsequent history and the closing of its career I shall speak in another chapter.

In our story we have now reached another unexpected and unforeseen incident, the extraordinary fall in the value of silver in 1876 and later years. To this event I shall devote the following chapters in Part II, treating of the Indian demand, the demonetization of silver by Germany, the action of France and the Latin Union, and the causes of the fall in the value of silver in 1876. Thus prepared, we can then intelligently study the history of bimetallism in the United States subsequent to that date.

---

[1] See Appendix III, act of July 22, 1876, Sec. 2.

PART II.

THE LATE FALL IN THE VALUE OF SILVER.

PART II.

THE LATE FALL IN THE VALUE OF SILVER.

CHAPTER VIII.

THE PRODUCTION OF GOLD SINCE 1850.

§ 1. The reason for making so considerable a digression in our story of the bimetallic experiences of the United States as to discuss the action of France, Germany, India, and the Latin Union in the chapters of Part II, is to make it possible to get a rational view of events in the United States in the period subsequent to 1873. There came into the monetary world, beginning in 1872 and amounting to a panic in July, 1876, a most unusual disturbance in the silver market. Nor did silver recover itself after 1876. The depreciation brought with it frequent fluctuations in value, which have ended in a generally lower level; and, in September, 1885, the fall was almost, if not quite, as low as in July, 1876. So far as it has become a matter of public discussion, bimetallism dates from this monetary event. In our country the fall of silver introduced the declining metal into politics; in Europe it has excited great discussion, and led to the meeting of two International Monetary Conferences—one in 1878, another in 1881. It becomes highly essential to the history of bimetallism in the United States,— if we are to understand its movements with some show of insight,—to know what the facts were which affected the value of silver in Europe and the East, and to try to reach some conclusion as to the probable cause of the extraordinary fall. We could then know better how to judge the actions of the United States in the field of its monetary policy.

§ 2. In a preceding chapter, while discussing the act of 1853, we had occasion to speak of the gold discoveries in the United States and Australia. The importance of these discoveries, and their social and economic influences, are now well recognized; but our nearness to the events has concealed, perhaps, some of their effects, or at least public attention has not been called to them. The economic influences have been discussed by the ablest writers.[1] The effect upon contracts and obligations of long standing of an enormous production of gold has been fully considered. Mr. Cairnes has, in a series of remarkable essays, explained the process by which the new wealth was distributed from the gold-producing countries over the remainder of the world, and has given an exposition of the social and economic changes which were produced by this action. Mr. Jevons demonstrated beyond any reasonable doubt that the increase of the gold production had resulted in a fall of its purchasing power of at least 9 per cent, and probably of 15 per cent. It will not now be questioned, I think, that a change was produced in the value or purchasing power of gold; in other words, that it bought less of other goods than before 1850. That is, gold prices rose, without implying an increase in the cost of production of articles for which the gold was exchanged.

, There is no sacredness about the value of gold. Even though some persons think its value is absolutely stable, this belief must have been destroyed by the events which have happened since 1848. It is true people in general do not think gold changes in value, or at least they think it changes very little. And there is no doubt whatever that it is the least changeable of the two metals. It must, however, be

---

[1] Levasseur, "La Question d'Or"; Jevons, "A Serious Fall in the Value of Gold Ascertained"; Chevalier, "On the Probable Fall in the Value of Gold"; Stirling, "Gold Discoveries and their Probable Consequences"; McCulloch, "Precious Metals" in the "Encyclopædia Britannica"; and, above all, Cairnes, "Essays in Political Economy," the first four chapters.

frankly admitted that both the precious metals have within thirty years shown that, like other commodities, they are affected by ordinary forces, and vary in their normal value under the same laws which control the value of other things. In short, when it is admitted that both gold and silver are capable of a change in value, due to unforeseen but natural causes, a step forward has been made in the discussion of bimetallism. Without doubt silver has changed in value more easily than gold. And, if either gold or silver change in value because of natural forces, it makes it impossible to keep both of the metals at such a permanent relation to each other as will maintain an invariable ratio. The events of 1848 and subsequent years are cumulative proof of this position. Moreover, as we shall soon see, the change in the value of one metal produces, *ipso facto*, a change in the other. The intimate connection of the two metals causes reflex changes upon each other; yet the action of silver upon gold is not the same as the action of gold upon silver.

In this chapter I shall confine myself to stating the actual facts of the gold production; to marking the influence of this production on the relative values of the two metals; and, later, to discussing their effect upon our question of bimetallism in the United States. We have already seen one effect in the establishment in 1853 of a single gold currency in this country. Silver was driven out, and we gladly accepted gold in its place. In brief, the United States was the first country of the world to take advantage of the new production, and from its surplus treasures to secure for itself a gold currency. We shall soon see how the same thing was accomplished in other countries.

§ 3. The magnitude of the gold production since 1850 is the marked characteristic of this period. The annual yield of gold in past centuries has been insignificant in comparison with the annual production in the years following the discoveries in Australia and California. Some years before, the Russian mines had been increasing the supply; but from a production of about $15,000,000 a year in 1840, the supply rose to more than $150,000,000 a year soon after 1850. This phenomenon, moreover, was accompanied by an increase in the production of silver of from 25 to 50 per cent a year. The comparative extent of the new gold production may be seen by Chart IX, previously mentioned, which gives the yield from the mines in the years since the discovery of America. The sudden and remarkable ascent of the gold product on the chart after 1850 is all the more noticeable because of the comparison with previous years. In fact, the gold production is the striking feature in this portion of our monetary history.

The figures which have been collected at length in Appendix I give information only as to the annual supply. No confidence is to be placed in guesses as to the amount of the precious metals actually in existence in 1848, or in any other period. In the nature of things we can not know how much has been irretrievably lost, consumed in the arts, or for ever withdrawn from money uses. The estimates made are worthless as statistics from which generalizations can be drawn in regard to the effects of the new supply upon the value of the two metals. The statistics of the annual supply are more trustworthy, although even these vary with every authority. No two persons agree even in regard to the annual supply. In the period[1] preceding 1850 I have used the figures prepared by the distinguished German economist, Dr. Adolf Soetbeer. In regard to the annual production since 1850, I have carefully collated all the tables which have been compiled by leading authorities in Germany, England, France, and the United States, and placed them in parallel columns for comparison. It will be noticed that Soetbeer's figures are larger than those of any other authority, and yet I am inclined to think that they are not far from the truth. In considering the total production of gold and silver in the years between 1850 and 1876, it will be found that there is a rough correspondence in the totals. That the figures are

---

[1] Some figures have been given by Mr. Del Mar for this period, in the "Report of the United States Silver Commission, 1877," but they do not inspire confidence.

approximately correct there can be little doubt, and they will, therefore, serve our general purpose. The reader will consequently have in these tables all the necessary data for a knowledge of the extraordinary gold production since the middle of the present century. It is the third great increase in the production of the precious metals, of which the first occurred soon after the discovery of America, and the second at the close of the last century. The first two lowered the value of silver relatively to other articles, including gold; the last lowered the value of gold relatively to other articles, including silver; but, then, later it had another effect on silver itself.

§ 4. Inasmuch as gold and silver are known to have changed in value, like other commodities, under the influence of a lowered cost of production, which has increased the supply and so the total quantity in existence, we are led at once to discuss briefly the reasons which give gold and silver value as money. Any commodity has value which is limited in quantity and yet satisfies some human desire. Apart from their power to please as ornaments and for uses in the arts, gold and silver satisfy certain desires arising from the need of a medium of exchange. The inconveniences of barter gave rise to desires for money. The metals which have best satisfied these desires are gold and silver.[1] The business world desires as money a metal which is as stable in value as possible, and which remains in this condition for as long a time as possible; one which has considerable value in small bulk, especially where transactions are large; and which possesses the other accepted qualities, such as homogeneity, divisibility, cognizability, etc.

Steadiness of value, as we saw in Hamilton's report, is popularly supposed to belong to gold. Moreover, in great centers of commerce and trade, where the total of transactions rose to great sums, gold was preferred to silver because of its smaller bulk. Then, as credit devices grew and ex-

---

[1] Cf. Mill's chapters on Money, and Jevons's "Money and Mechanism of Exchange," chap. iii, for an explanation of the functions of money and the proper qualities possessed by a metal used as a medium of exchange.

tended, the actual handling of the metal was saved by the use of banks of deposit. The business world began to shun a cumbrous medium, and at the same time to cling to what was believed to be most stable in value. Without now asserting that one metal is more stable than the other in value, what I do assert is that monetary history reveals in every modern commercial country a prejudice in favor of gold as against silver. Granted that it is only a prejudice, yet, whatever it may be termed, it exists. The world of commerce, whatever the reason may be, *believes* in gold. Nor will we say whether this belief is fortunate or not. It is our endeavor only to ascertain the fact. But it is a fact which must be taken into account in discussing the influence of the gold discoveries on the values of gold and silver. The proof of it will be found as we go on with our story. It has already been displayed in the legislation which gave the United States a gold currency in 1853. In brief, gold satisfies the desires of men for a medium of exchange better than silver. This is not a theoretical proposition. It is simply a fact to be ascertained by a historical inquiry.

If, then, it be true that men in trade have a greater desire for gold than for silver as money, this is the cause of a demand for gold; since demand is a desire for a commodity coupled with purchasing power. This desire for gold is the desire for it as a medium of exchange.[1] That is, if men of business are left to seek the metal they naturally prefer, gold will be chosen. Now, however, the law of a land, which fixes a legal-tender value of a given amount upon one or the other metal, can, through the operation of Gresham's law, bring into circulation the cheapest metal, whether the community has a preference for it or not. But whenever the state follows the wishes of its people, if it is a commercial state, it will be found that there is a very strong tendency among its population to the adoption of gold in preference to silver. In other words, although law can override popular wishes in this respect and decide that the cheapest metal

---

[1] We here pass by the question of its consumption in the arts.

shall be used, the natural forces governing demand still exist, and will, sooner or later, make themselves felt. It is quite unlikely, therefore, that there will be any falling off in the demand for gold for money uses. The only question, as all must admit, is rather, whether the supply will be sufficient or not. Law can create a demand for the metal, which would not naturally be chosen, only by overvaluing it in its legal ratio, and thus making it profitable to drive the preferred metal from use. The gain of the money-changer can be absolutely depended upon to bring this about. But if both metals were put upon an equal basis at the Mint—if such a thing is possible for any time—it will be found that gold is preferred in large payments and silver for small payments. The natural convenience of a trading population demands this. A comparison of the countries which use silver—China, India, and semi-civilized countries—with the important commercial states—England, Germany, and the United States—which use gold, affords a striking illustration of this proposition.

§ 5. Setting before us as an object to discover the reasons for the fall in the value of silver in 1876—which has been the beginning of modern bimetallic discussions—we shall confine ourselves to the effect which the great production of gold has had upon the value of silver. And to this end we must bear in mind what has been said in the last section in regard to the prejudice for gold. Then there must be taken with this preference for gold the possibility of satisfying the demand. The amount of gold produced, therefore, is an important part of our problem. We should then proceed to get some idea of this amount.

We find ourselves, in the period following 1850, confronted with an enormously increased production of gold. How enormous it was I do not think has been generally recognized in our monetary discussions, particularly of late in those dealing with the appreciation of gold. It seems almost incredible to say that, in the 25 years following 1850, as much gold was given forth by the mines as had been produced to that time since the discovery of America by Columbus. And yet it is literally true:

	Gold.	Silver.
1493-1850	$3,314,553,000	$7,358,450,000
1851-1875	3,317,625,000	1,395,125,000

The facts may be more conveniently seen in their proper relations in Chart X, which represents, first, by square areas, the total quantities of gold and silver[1] produced since the discovery of America down to 1850. During this time of 357 years it will be seen that more than twice as much silver as gold, in respect to value, was produced. And we have already seen that in this period there occurred two great falls in the value of silver, or at least an almost continuous fall of silver (see Chart IV). But what is remarkable is that—while gold to an amount so much more than enough for the ordinary uses of commerce was produced from 1493 to 1850 that it fell in its purchasing power—in the 25 years succeeding 1850 an amount equal to the product of the previous 357 years was suddenly added to the existing stock of the world. This was an amount far more than was necessary for the growth of trade and population in those 25 years, and, as Prof. Jevons has shown, it resulted in a loss of its purchasing power of from 9 to 15 per cent. The wonder is that its value did not fall more; and it would have fallen more if it had not been for the influences which, as we shall later see, widened the field for its use. Chart X, in the second place, shows an area for the period since 1850 as great for gold as in the previous period; but, while in the previous period the area for silver was twice as large as that of gold, in the later and short period of 25 years the silver product is less than one half as much as that of gold, and about one fifth of the silver product from 1493 to 1850.

§ 6. Now what was the effect upon the relative values of the two metals of suddenly doubling the quantity of gold, without anything like a proportional increase of silver? First of all, gold fell in value, both in regard to silver and to

---

[1] I have here used Dr. Soetbeer's figures. See Appendix I, Tables A and B.

CHART X.

Relative Production of Gold and Silver in 1493–1850 and in 1851–1875, shown by relative areas.

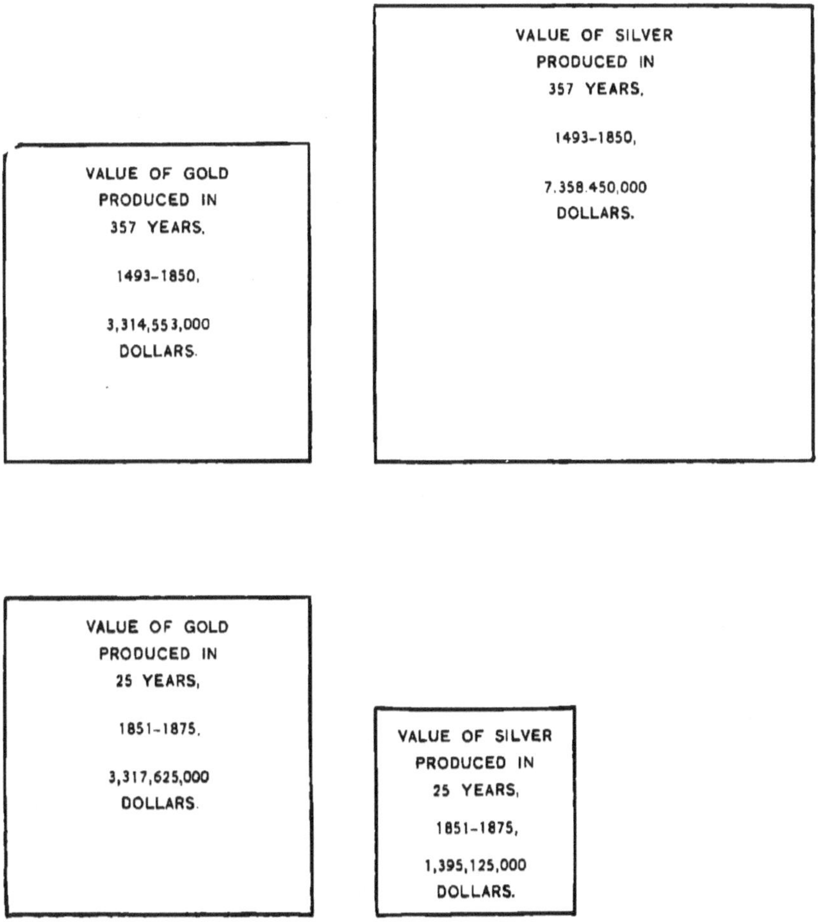

	VALUE OF SILVER PRODUCED IN 357 YEARS, 1493–1850, 7,358,450,000 DOLLARS.
VALUE OF GOLD PRODUCED IN 357 YEARS, 1493–1850, 3,314,553,000 DOLLARS.	

VALUE OF GOLD PRODUCED IN 25 YEARS, 1851–1875, 3,317,625,000 DOLLARS.	VALUE OF SILVER PRODUCED IN 25 YEARS, 1851–1875, 1,395,125,000 DOLLARS.

all commodities. The ratio between gold and silver, which had risen from 1 : 15 to 1 : 16, now showed the effect of the cheapening in gold by dropping to 1 : 15·3 for a time. This was the first effect. But a second effect soon became visible. The cheapened gold began to drive out silver from the currencies of the United States and Europe, because, at former ratios fixed before the gold discoveries, gold was overvalued at the mints, and so by Gresham's law came into circulation as the sole medium of exchange. But the matter worthy of most attention is that this exchange of gold for silver was seen and watched, not only without opposition, but even with satisfaction. Had there been a similar flow of silver into the place of gold, there would have been no such complacency. Here, again, is the preference for gold which we find so constantly present. The effect of this movement was, of course, to prevent gold from falling in value as much as it would otherwise have done; and to withdraw the previously existing demand from silver for use as a medium of exchange in Western commercial nations. The very cheapness and abundance of gold increased the demand for it for use as a medium of exchange, and *ipso facto* diminished the demand for silver. The world could choose between the two. There was silver enough; but, as soon as gold became plentiful, there was no doubt for a moment which metal was preferred. It was in the same spirit in which the modern world made choice between the railway and the stage-coach as a means of transportation. Wherever choice was possible, the best and most convenient means of locomotion was taken. The same idea has been expressed by Mr. Cairnes[1] in the following words:

"If anything unfits one commodity for measuring the value of another, it is the circumstance that they may both be applied to common purposes. No one would think of measuring the fluctuations in wheat by comparing it with oats, because, both grains being employed for the same or similar purposes, any change in the value of one is sure to extend to the other. When, *e. g.*, the wheat crop is in excess while the oat crop is an average one, it always happens that a portion of the con-

---

[1] "Essays in Political Economy," p. 141.

sumption, which in ordinary years falls upon oats, is thrown upon wheat, the effect of which is at once to check the fall in the price of the more abundant grain, while, by diminishing the need for the other, it causes it to participate in the decline. The influence of the increased abundance of one commodity is thus distributed over both, the fall in price being less intense in degree in proportion as it is wider in extent. Now this is precisely what is happening in the relations of gold and silver. The crop of gold has been unusually large; the increase in the supply has caused a fall in its value; the fall in its value has led to its being substituted for silver; a mass of silver has thus been disengaged from purposes which it was formerly employed to serve, and the result has been that both metals have fallen in value together, the depth of the fall being diminished as the surface over which it has taken place has been enlarged. The scene on which this interchange of gold and silver has hitherto been exhibited on the largest scale is the currency of France, in which, owing to the existence of a double standard, . . . one or the other metal is employed according as its worth in the markets of the world happens to vary in relation to its valuation at the French Mint."

In succeeding chapters we shall find abundant evidence of this interchange of gold and silver, which was begun by the United States in 1853. At the present we shall go on to narrate how France followed this example; and subsequently we shall see how Germany did the same. Then it will remain to show how the Latin Union was forced to follow practically the same course.

§ 7. The first marked effect of the new gold on the currencies of Europe was seen in France, furnishing again a very striking illustration of Gresham's law.

Since 1803 a legal ratio of $1 : 15\frac{1}{2}$ had been maintained by France without change. Inasmuch as the market ratio had never been as low as $1 : 15\frac{1}{2}$ between 1820 and 1850, but rather nearer $1 : 16$, the French legal ratio gave gold a less value in the form of coin than it possessed in the form of bullion, while silver was given a greater value in coin than it possessed as bullion. As a natural consequence, gold disappeared from circulation and silver took its place; so that by 1850 the main part of the circulation in France consisted of silver.

CHART XI.

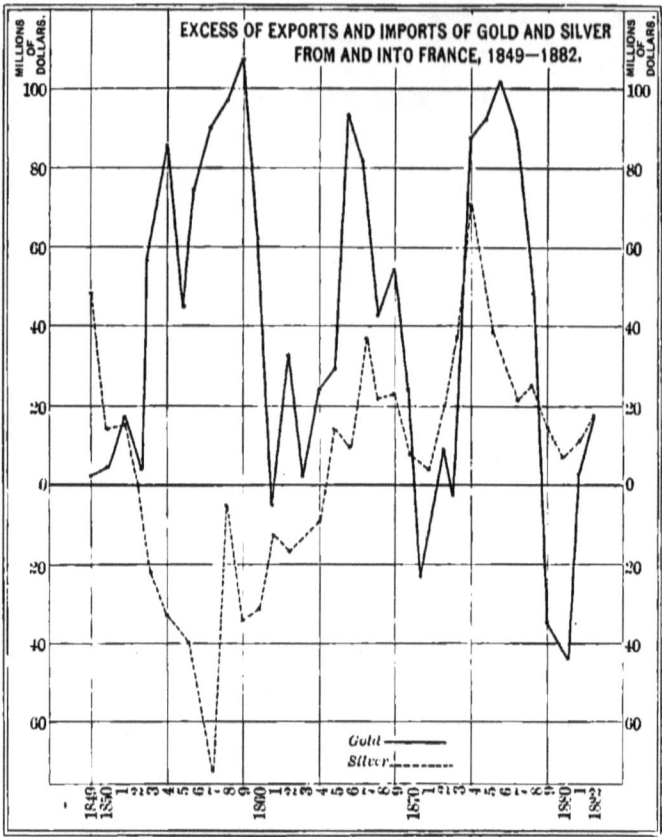

NOTE: When imports exceed exports the line moves above the base-line at 0; when exports exceed imports, the line moves below the base-line.

The discoveries of gold exactly reversed this situation. Gold fell in value; its relation to silver changed so that the ratio remained below 15½ until 1867 (see Chart XIII). Under these conditions, consequently, a revolution took place in the French currency between 1853 and 1865. As things then stood, the ratio at the Mint was still 1 : 15½, while in the market it was lower than that, or somewhat nearer 1 : 15. As a consequence of this, money-changers quickly saw that an ounce of gold exchanged for 15½ ounces of silver in the shape of coin, but for less than 15½ ounces of silver in the shape of bullion. That is, gold was now overvalued by the legal ratio (as silver had been before); and in the form of bullion silver bought more of gold than it did in the form of coin. Consequently, as long as this state of affairs continued, and since "free coinage" existed, there was a stream of gold flowing to the French Mint for coinage, while the silver rapidly disappeared from circulation, and even left the country. How this process went on may be seen by the following table (accompanying Chart XI), which gives in millions of dollars the excess of exports and imports from and into France [1] after 1849:

YEARS.	GOLD.		SILVER.	
	Excess of imports.	Excess of exports.	Excess of imports.	Excess of exports.
1849	1·2	....	48·8	....
1850	3·4	....	14·6	....
1851	17·0	....	15·6	....
1852	3·4	....	....	0·6
1853	57·8	....	....	23·4
1854	83·2	....	....	32·8
1855	43·6	....	....	39·4
1856	75·0	....	....	56·8
1857	89·2	....	....	72·0
1858	97·6	....	....	3·0
1859	107·8	....	....	34·2
1860	62·2	....	....	31·4
1861	....	4·8	....	12·4
1862	33·0	....	....	17·2
1863	2·4	....	....	13·6

[1] Report to H. C. on "Depreciation of Silver," 1876, Appendix, pp. 86, 87, continued since 1875 from the "British Statistical Abstract."

THE LATE FALL IN THE VALUE OF SILVER.

YEARS.	GOLD.		SILVER.	
	Excess of imports.	Excess of exports.	Excess of imports.	Excess of exports.
1864	25·0	....	....	8·4
1865	30·0	....	14·4	....
1866	93·0	....	9·0	....
1867	81·8	....	37·8	....
1868	42·4	....	21·8	....
1869	55·0	....	22·4	....
1870	23·8	....	7·0	....
1871	....	42·8	3·0	....
1872	....	10·6	20·4	....
1873	....	21·6	36·2	....
1874	86·2	....	72·0	....
1875	90·8	....	38·8	....
1876	100·6	....	29·8	....
1877	87·2	....	20·8	....
1878	47·2	....	23·8	....
1879	....	35·0	15·2	....
1880	....	42·6	7·8	....
1881	2·2	....	10·2	....
1882	18·4	....	18·2	....

During the years from 1852 to 1864 France absorbed through direct imports about $680,000,000 of gold, and ejected about $345,000,000 of silver. The French mints were actively engaged in coining this gold into the form in which its legal value was greater than as bullion.

The effect of this great absorption of gold by France on the value of silver is thus fully noticed by Mr. Cairnes[1] while the movement was going on in 1860 :

"Until a recent period the metal which formed the staple of the French currency was silver, but, owing to the fall in the value of gold, consequent upon the discoveries, gold is now [1860] rapidly taking its place and becoming the principal medium of circulation. Up to the year 1852 the importation of silver into France was always largely in excess of its exportation ; but in that year the tide turned, and has since continued flowing outward with increasing volume. M. Chevalier states that by the end of 1857 France had parted with 45,000,000*l.* sterling of silver. On the other hand, during this time she had coined more than 100,000,000*l.* sterling of gold. The currency of France has thus, to borrow the curious but not unapt figure of our author, played toward gold the part of a parachute to

---

[1] "Essays in Political Economy," p. 142.

moderate its descent. But in proportion as gold has thus found a market, silver has been deprived of one ; and the 45,000,000*l.* of silver liberated from the currency of France is as much an addition to the disposable supply in the world, and tends as effectually to lower its value, as if it had been raised immediately from the mines. The fall in the value of gold has thus, up to the present time, been at once checked and concealed—checked by being substituted for silver, and concealed by being compared with it."

CHAPTER IX.

INDIA AND THE EAST.

§ 1. THE discarded silver of France found a home in the East. As early as 1860 Mr. Cairnes wrote[1] of the substitution of gold for silver:

"Australia and California have, during the last eight or ten years [1860], sent into general circulation some two hundred millions sterling of gold. Of this vast sum portions have penetrated to the most remote quarters of the world; but the bulk of it has been received into the currencies of Europe and the United States, from which it has largely displaced the silver formerly circulating, the latter metal, as it has become free, flowing off into Asia, where it is permanently absorbed."

France and the United States saved gold from depreciation to a certain extent by absorbing a vast quantity of the new supply; this process, however, displaced a great amount of silver. India, on the other hand, now saved silver from depreciation to a certain extent by its absorption of the heavier metal no longer in use by Europe. This power of India and the East to absorb apparently an unlimited amount of silver is, and has been, one of the chief factors in the question of the relative values of the two precious metals, and requires some further notice.

The demand of Oriental nations for the precious metals, and especially for silver, is a natural consequence of their barbaric taste for ornaments and their want of civilized methods of exchange.

The passion for ornaments seems to be a source of demand for silver which is likely to continue until the race

---

[1] "Essays in Political Economy," p. 79.

outgrows its barbaric conditions. Once given the passion for ornament, that one of the precious metals will be most in demand which is cheapest, and consequently within the reach of an indigent population. This is the reason why silver is so much desired by Eastern merchants for purchases. Although the people of India are very poor, and are miserably housed, yet they place their little all in the form of ornaments, when the peasantry of England would have added to their stock of utensils or of furniture. The silver rupees coined by the Indian Government and circulated in India suffer from a very considerable melting down by the natives to satisfy this demand for decoration. "In every large village there is a silversmith, or some one who works in silver, and as soon as a man gets a few rupees he employs a silversmith to come to his house and make the ornaments there, who brings his little implements required for manufacturing it, and there the rupees are made into ornaments."[1] "The natives never invest their money in the way in which civilized nations look upon an investment. A native, when he realizes a little money, puts it into the form of ornaments on the females of his family, and in times of scarcity these ornaments are taken to the bankers and sold."[2] "Some of the records of the old Benares Mint show that, in times of scarcity, the greater part of the silver brought to that Mint to be coined was in the shape of ornaments."[3] That this condition of affairs still prevails may be seen by the events of the last few years. During the recent famine in India, from 1877 to 1880, the following amounts[4] of silver ornaments were brought to the mints for coinage:

```
1877-1878 ............. 124 lacs (100,000) of rupees.
1878-1879 ............. 116   "       "       "
1879-1880 .............  92   "       "       "
   Total ............. 332   "       "       "   ($16,000,000).
```

The desire for decoration is not confined in its effects to silver alone. The poorest can only expect to have brass or

---

[1] "H. C. Report of 1876," Q. 1,046.   [2] Ibid., Q. 947.
[3] Ibid., Q. 1,010.   [4] "French Report on Conference of 1881," i, p. 63.

clay, but those who can afford it have silver or gold.[1] It is a matter of pride at great festivals that the children should make a display of ornaments, and they vie with each other in showing the greatest number. In this process they have as eager a demand for gold as for silver, provided they can obtain gold. "When a man (in India) gets a considerable amount of silver ornaments, he will sell these for the purpose of converting them into one gold ornament; because it adds to his prestige in the village if one individual of his family has a large gold armlet, or other ornament."[2] Indeed, the demand of India for gold is of considerable importance,[3] as may be seen by the tables giving the imports of both gold and silver into British India in Appendix VI. More than $450,000,000 of gold was retained by India between 1855 and 1880. The demand for gold is only one form of expression of the insatiate passion for ornament, since gold is not a legal tender, and is not used as a medium of exchange in India to any extent. But as silver is the cheaper of the two metals, both of which are desired for this purpose of ornament, the heaviest demand of a population of about 237,000,000 of people, which is by no means rich, falls upon silver.

§ 2. The second cause of a demand for silver in the East, so soon as the need of money is appreciated, is for its use as a medium of exchange. Throughout a large extent of territory in India, transactions are still carried on by barter.[4] In the interior of Bengal, some years ago, exchanges were effected chiefly by copper coins and cowry-shells, while but very little of silver was in circulation, and whatever appeared was either hoarded or manufactured into ornaments. But silver will be the best natural medium of exchange for the

---

[1] "H. C. Report of 1876," Q. 1,047.
[2] Ibid., Q. 1,050. Mr. Cairnes also quotes Mr. Alexander Forbes: "It has often been said that the natives (of India) hoard silver; now my experience is that they do not hoard silver; they hoard gold; and that the silver is actually required for the commerce of the country."—"Essays in Political Economy," p. 94, note.
[3] Ibid., Q. 938. Gold "is turned into ornaments, used in manufactures, and is hoarded." [4] Ibid., Q. 913 and 1,041.

greater part of India, because the mass of the people are poor, and consequently the transactions are on a scale so small that they can be settled only by the use of the cheaper metal. There being much value in a small bulk of gold, it is needed only in comparatively large transactions. This is the explanation why silver is the usual currency of semi-civilized countries. India, however, is in a condition to use more silver money. Not only can the scanty circulation in districts where the advantages of a medium of exchange are already recognized be profitably enlarged, but the districts where little, if any, money is in use must, as they come under the influence of civilized habits and business customs, some day feel the need of silver as an escape from the inconveniences of barter. The capacity, therefore, of Eastern nations like India to absorb a very large amount of silver as a medium of exchange is very great. But, coupled with their extraordinary passion for gold and silver ornaments, we can see why it is that it has been generally believed that the East has a practically unlimited demand for silver. (We have already seen how the United States tried to take advantage of this characteristic in the coinage of the trade-dollar.) So that whenever the Eastern demand for silver falls off it is a matter of surprise, and some explanation is to be sought in exceptional causes.

§ 3. As Europe and the United States preferred gold to silver when the former metal could be had, the market for the displaced silver in the East was naturally of essential importance to the relative values of the two precious metals. We have seen that France (Chart XI) had expelled about $345,000,000 of silver by 1864, while there had been exported to the East from Europe no less than $764,000,000 in the same period; and from 1852 to 1875 at least $1,000,000,000 of silver had been shipped from England and Mediterranean ports to India and the East, while the total production of silver in the same years from the mines had not been very much more than that amount.[1] The general movement

---
[1] See Appendix VI, and Appendix I, Table B.

of silver into British India since 1852 may be seen by consulting Chart XII. Before 1855 the net imports of silver into India averaged only about $9,000,000, while the annual production of silver averaged about $30,000,000 a year.

From 1855 to 1862 the imports of silver increased. During this period occurred the Sepoy mutiny,[1] the transfer of the Indian Government from the East India Company to the Crown, the borrowing[2] of large sums of money for India in England, and the extensive building of public works. These events rendered necessary large remittances to India, and a demand was therefore felt for silver for shipment.

These conditions were materially affected by the "cotton famine" in England, which began after the cessation of cotton shipments to Europe from the United States during our Civil War. India was pushed to supply the demand for cotton in these years, and this created an abnormal excess of payments to India in the international exchanges, which of course led to larger shipments of silver than ever. This effect lasted from 1861 to 1866. Large exports of gold were made from London to the Continent in order to purchase the silver which English merchants needed for Indian remittances; and silver was also shipped directly from France to the East in large sums.

In 1867 a diminution was clearly marked in the flow of silver to the East, which continued at a less sum until 1876.[3] This was due to the use of bills of exchange sold by the India Council, the Government of India residing in London, and called "council bills." India had been borrowing on a large scale. The departments in India were required to raise funds there with which to pay the interest on her debt, on railway loans, pensions, etc., to a sum which in 1876 amounted to about $75,000,000 a year. Now, if this sum was due from India to the India Council in London, the

---

[1] Broke out May 4, 1857, and ended July, 1859.

[2] Between 1850 and 1873 India borrowed 164¼ millions sterling, which must be repaid in gold. The interest also must be paid in gold. This is the chief difficulty of India, arising from the fall of silver, since more silver is required to pay the same amount as before in gold.

[3] The increase in 1868 was due to payments for the Abyssinian War.

CHART XII.

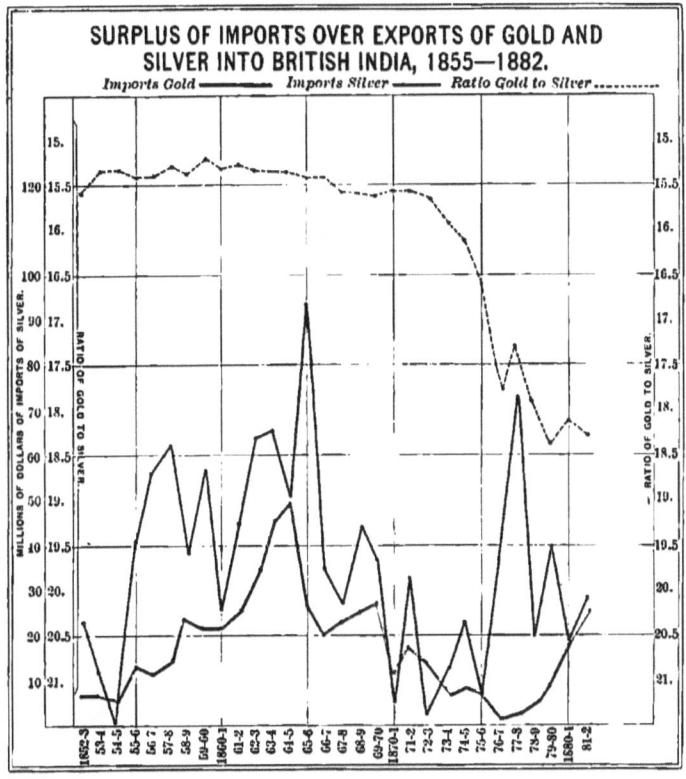

latter would sell their claims to this money in India by going into the London market with bills of exchange drawn on Calcutta or Bombay. Inasmuch as the Indian presidencies collect all their revenues in silver, these bills of exchange were claims only to certain sums of silver, and would naturally be bought by any one wishing to make payments in silver in India for goods brought from that country. It must be apparent, therefore, that just as the expenses of the Indian Government rose, and just in proportion to the number of council bills which were offered for sale in London, would the exportation of silver to India be saved. The amount of silver due from India counterbalanced an equal amount due to India; and the two sums were offset against each other by the use of bills of exchange. The number of council bills rapidly increased about 1872,[1] as may be seen by the following figures:

	Treasure.	Bills.
1868–1869 to 1871–1872............	$200,000,000	$147,500,000
1872–1873 to 1875–1876.............	82,500,000	252,500,000
Annual average, first period...........	50,000,000	37,000,000
" " second period.........	20,500,000	63,000,000
In 1875–1876......................	15,500,000	62,000,000

The fall, therefore, in the line of Chart XII from 1871 to 1876, showing a decline in shipments of silver to India, is due to the increase of payments from India to London as manifested in the form of an increased supply of council bills on the London market. A merchant having a debt to pay in India would buy either silver or a council bill, according as he could buy one or the other cheapest.

The rise in the imports of silver into India in 1876 was thus explained by Mr. Bagehot:[2] "A merchant in London, who is thinking of importing goods from the East, looks at the price-current in Calcutta, and he sees the price quoted in rupees. The merchant in London is in possession of sovereigns in London; therefore he has two operations: first, he

---

[1] "H. C. Report of 1876," p. 33. [2] "H. C. Report of 1876," Q. 1,368.

has to buy his rupees in India; next, with those rupees he has to buy the article which he saw in the price-current. The question of profit and loss to him is compounded of the result of these two operations; if, therefore, he can buy his rupees in Calcutta on more favorable terms, he will find it to his interest to go into a speculation which would not otherwise be profitable. If he can get rupees at 1s. 8d. instead of 2s., and he can buy his goods in Calcutta with the same number of rupees, that is so much extra gain to him. Conversely, the English exporter of goods to the East will receive payment in rupees, and he will have to sell those rupees; and if he sells them for a less amount of sovereigns, he will suffer a loss, and that is a discouragement to exporting from this country to India. The result of these two operations—of the encouragement of exports from India to this country, and the discouragement of exports hence to India—necessarily is an increase of the balance which this country has to pay to India, and consequently a flow of silver to the East." The increasing exports of silver in 1876–1878, therefore, were a consequence of the fall in silver.

§ 4. The conclusions reached by the Government of India in regard to this movement of silver are as follows:[1]

"The large imports of treasure into India since 1850 are due to abnormal circumstances, as follows:

"(1) The Crimean War transferred to India large demands for produce heretofore obtained from Russia.

"(2) The American Civil War exaggerated temporarily the value of Indian cotton.

"(3) Great sums of money have been borrowed for:
    (a) The suppression of the mutiny;
    (b) The construction of railroads (guaranteed and state) and canals;
    (c) The Bengal famine.

"It would be altogether misleading to treat the great imports of treasure in the last twenty-five years as normal, or to expect that they will or can continue. There is, therefore, no reason to expect that silver will be poured into India, although,

---

[1] Dated September 22, 1876, and issued in the form of a resolution upon the suggestions of the Bengal Chamber of Commerce and the Calcutta Trades Association. See "Report of 1878," pp. 411, 412.

of course, if it falls in value a greater weight of it must come to represent the same value."

In an earlier part of the chapter we have seen that two strong reasons existed for the continuance of the Indian demand for silver: the passion for ornament, and the need of an adequate medium of exchange for a population of 237,000,000. With respect to the former it is clear that any change must necessarily be slow, and that the desire for decoration can be subdued only by the gradual progress of the race in civilization.

"The same passion for ornaments [as in savage races] is a powerful instinct amongst the native races of Hindostan, with whom they serve at once as a mode of investment and a means of decoration; but as civilization makes progress, tastes of a different order are developed. Vanity, perhaps, loses nothing of its power, but it exhibits itself under a different guise and is directed to different objects. Luxury, in its modes of display, as in other respects, undergoes refinement, and mankind seeks enjoyment less in the gratification of external sense and more in the cultivation of the higher faculties. The superfluous expenditure of a nation advancing in civilization is accordingly devoted less and less to objects which absorb mere masses of gold and silver and more and more to purposes of a higher order—to the beautifying of its domains, the embellishing of its houses, the general cultivation of its tastes; and parks and mansions, pictures, sculpture, and books take the place of accumulations of plate and collections of jewelry."[1]

For a long time to come, however, we must believe that silver and gold will be used by the people of Hindostan for ornaments.

In regard to the second reason—the need of a medium of exchange—all information leads us to suppose that comparatively little silver is in use as money, that conditions of barter still exist over great areas, and that the districts where money is used can employ a much greater amount. Yet even in this matter the economizing expedients of Western nations must aid in preventing the whole demand for money from falling on gold and silver alone.

"In India, though more than a century under British rule, the advantages of credit as a medium of exchange are only be-

---

[1] Cairnes, "Essays in Political Economy," p. 133.

ginning to be understood. The circulation of bank-notes is exceedingly limited, and is still confined to some of the Presidency towns. Checks, by which so large a portion of the business of this country is carried on, are but slightly used, and the great mass of transactions is effected by a transfer of rupees bodily in every sale. The magnitude of the transactions conducted in this manner may be estimated by the fact stated by Sir Charles Napier, that the escort of treasure constituted one of the severest duties of the late Bengal army, from 20,000 to 30,000 men being constantly occupied in this manner. The quantity of the precious metals employed in thus carrying on the internal traffic of India has been variously estimated between 150,000,000*l*. and 300,000,000*l*. sterling; but this state of things is evidently not destined to be of long continuance. Mr. Wilson's recent minute gives grounds for believing that the Indian Government are alive to this subject, and that India will soon enjoy the advantages of an effective paper system. Such an event can not fail to be attended with important consequences on the trade and industry of that country; and among these consequences we may expect this: that, instead of requiring, as now, continuous large additions to her present enormous stock of metallic money, she will not only be enabled to dispense with these, but will find it for her interest to part with a large portion of what she now employs."[1]

A system of paper money was inaugurated March 1, 1862, and it is quite likely that, in proportion as banking accommodations are extended in India, there will be some check to the absorption of silver,—but of that sum only which would have been used as a medium of exchange and not for ornament. The reserve of more than 50 per cent of the circulation is, of course, largely of silver; but the extent to which bank-notes are already in use may be seen from the annexed table:[2]

Year.	Notes in circulation.	Year.	Notes in circulation.
1863	§22·5	1873	§64·3
1864	25·5	4	54·5
1865	37·3	5	55·4
1866	36·9	6	56·0
1867	49·7	7	59·8
1868	51·5	8	75·2
1869	51·4	9	63·4
1870	56·5	1880	68·9
1871	51·7	1	71·6
1872	54·3		

§ 5. If we eliminate the exceptional period of 1861-1866, during the cotton famine, we shall find that there is a proba-

---

[1] Cairnes, ibid., pp. 127, 128.
[2] "French Report of Mon. Conf. of 1881," ii, p. 205.

bility of continued imports of silver into India so long as the demand for ornaments, and the evident need of a medium of exchange, exists. It would seem to me that for a very considerable time banking devices will not much offset the need of silver for money in common circulation. For some time to come India will require much more silver than she now has for her currency. The progress of banking facilities, moreover, implies also that kind of growth in comprehending the uses of money which is likely to bring with it a change from barter to civilized methods of exchange in remoter districts, and thus to increase the need of silver for circulation, as much or more than credit devices will diminish it.

In addition to all this it must be remembered that at present India is a poor country, and that its vast resources have not yet been advantageously worked. If India begins to grow more wheat for exportation to European markets; if, with the growth of civilization, new methods of production come into vogue, and more products which India can send abroad are brought to market; or if she should furnish herself with substitutes for goods now imported—then India would, in the terms of international exchange, have due to her additional sums of treasure which would be liquidated by silver. But the flow of specie from Europe will, on the other hand, be effectually prevented by any means which will offset this indebtedness of Europe to India. One offset has had an influence already, and drawn considerable attention—it is the debt owed by India to Europe, owing to the increased expenses of government, the sums due England for interest on her debt, and other expenditures. This influence is chiefly apparent by the amounts of India council bills placed on the London market. The following table will show how great this force has been in the past, and the extent of its growth to 1880. The column containing these figures might be otherwise defined as "sums obtained for bills drawn by the Court of Directors, or Secretary of State, on the several governments of India." The column giving the excess of exports of merchandise gives the means of knowing how India pays for her silver, and shows to what extent she has drawn for silver beyond the amounts of the council bills (which serve as an offset to the sum of exports in striking the international balance). Should her exports continue to increase as they have in the past—and they have increased from an average of about $125,000,000 in 1856 to about $300,000,000 in 1880—India will be enabled to buy more silver and continue her absorption of the cheaper metal. [Sums are given in millions.]

YEARS.	Excess of exports of merchandise over imports.	Council bills sold.	Net imports of silver.	Net imports of gold.
1855–1856.......	$45·5	$7·4	$41·0	$12·5
1856–1857.......	56·0	14·1	55·4	10·5
1857–1858.......	61·0	3·1	61·1	13·9
1858–1859.......	40·5	·1	38 6	22·1
1859–1860.......	18·5	·02	55·7	21·5
1860–1861.......	47·5	·004	26·6	21·2
1861–1862.......	70·0	5·9	45·4	25 9
1862–1863.......	126·0	33·2	62·7	34·2
1863–1864.......	192·0	44·9	63·9	44·5
1864–1865.......	199·5	34·0	50·4	49·2
1865–1866.......	179·5	35·0	93·3	28·6
1866–1867.......	64·0	28·1	34·8	19·2
1867–1868.......	76·0	20·7	27·9	23·1
1868–1869.......	85·5	18·5	43·0	25·8
1869–1870.......	98·0	34·9	36·6	28·0
1870–1871.......	104·5	42·2	4·7	11·4
1871–1872.......	155·5	51·6	32·5	17·8
1872–1873	117·0	69·7	3·5	12·7
1873–1874.......	106·0	66·4	12·2	6·9
1874–1875.......	100·5	54·2	23·2	9·4
1875–1876.......	96·0	61·9	7·7	7·7
1876–1877.......	117·5	63·5	36·0	1·0
1877–1878.......	118·5	50·7	73·4	2 5
1878–1879.......	115·5	69·7	19·8	4·5
1879–1880.......	130·0	76·3	39·3	8·7
1880–1881.......	....	....	19·4	18·3
1881–1882.......	....	....	26·9	24·2
	$2520·5	$886·3	$1035·0	$505·3

In considering the effects of the Indian demand on the value of silver, an examination of Chart XII reveals the fact that the value of silver relatively to gold did not show any immediate sensitiveness to a falling off in the export of silver to the East. From 1870 to 1875 there had been a marked decline in the net imports of silver into India; but it was not until 1872–1873 that a slight downward movement in the value of silver was apparent, while it was not until 1876 that the very considerable break in the value of silver manifested itself. In looking forward to our object in Part II, which is to study the causes affecting the late fall in the value of silver, I can not think that the decline of the Indian demand has been so strong an influence in depressing the value of silver as it has been supposed to be by many writers. A temporary withdrawal of the usual demand at a critical time for the value of silver no doubt had a greater effect than it could have had at other times. An increased demand from India, to the extent to which it permanently absorbs a greater quantity of silver, would, of course, help to lighten the influences which are weighing down the value of this metal; but I am not inclined to believe that the flow of silver to the East has been the principal factor in our problem.[1] What makes me think that the Indian demand [2] is not a very potent

---

[1] Writing in 1860, Mr. Cairnes said: "We are aware it has been maintained that the value of silver, so far from having fallen, has really risen during the last few years, in proof of which we are referred to the increased demand for it for Oriental remittance. That silver has risen in its *gold*-price owing to this circumstance we admit, but we deny that this is a proof of a rise in its *value*, any more than a rise in the gold-price of any other commodity would prove a rise in its value at a time when the supply of gold was rapidly increasing. During the last two years (1858 and 1859) the demand for silver in the East has been affected a good deal by requirements connected with the Indian Mutiny; but, if we investigate the causes of the extraordinary demand which has characterized the last four or five years, we shall find that they are in a principal degree traceable to the increased production of gold, operating through the expenditure of enlarged money incomes in England and the United States on Oriental productions; and that thus the increased demand for silver, which is alleged as a proof that silver has risen in value, *is in reality a consequence of the large amount of gold available for its purchase*."—"Essays," pp. 142, 143. Mr. Cairnes was thus of the opinion that the imports of silver after 1850 were abnormal, and, by inference, would decline gradually with the absorption of the new gold.

[2] The coinage of silver in India was, in

1877	$31,355,000
1878	80,900,000
1879	36,050,000
1880 (estimated)	50,000,000
	$198,305,000

See speech of Sir Louis Mallet, "French Report of Conf. of 1881," i, p. 173.

influence in maintaining the general value of silver is the slight influence of its increased demand from 1877–1879 in raising the value.

The total production of gold from 1850 to 1876 was about $3,000,000,000; of silver, about $1,200,000,000. Thus far we have seen that France added about $350,000,000 of silver to the supply, and that India took somewhat more than $1,000,000,000. Of the new gold, France in the same time coined about $1,160,000,000, and India imported $440,000,-000, leaving about $1,400,000,000 of gold to be accounted for. Not all the excess of the production of gold over the former average production was absorbed by the action of France and India. Making large allowances for consumption in the arts, and for increase in their currencies by gold-using countries, a very large part of this $1,400,000,000 of gold remains as a potent, and, to my mind, the chief factor in bringing about a disturbance in the relative values of gold and silver. The absorption of gold by France from 1853 to 1865 limited the demand for silver in its function as a medium of exchange. If the still remaining quantity of gold tempts some other country to take advantage of the abundant gold supply to improve its currency by taking the better medium instead of the poorer—that is, the gold instead of the silver (we are speaking of the preference for gold whenever choice between gold and silver is possible)—then we shall see the field for the employment of silver still further contracted, and the demand for silver withdrawn, because the needs of the community are better served by the other metal which the prodigality of nature has poured upon the world since 1850. In the next chapter we shall see how, in consonance with this supposition, the new gold usurped the place of silver in another country, and left the latter to find a sale in a market already somewhat sated by a full supply.

CHAPTER X.

GERMANY DISPLACES SILVER WITH GOLD.

§ 1. THE movement inaugurated by the United States and France—both of which countries accepted with complacency the substitution of gold for silver—was assisted by Germany. Seeing the great commercial nations of the West taking heed of the opportunity to provide themselves with gold, Germany was shrewd enough to seize her opportunity before it was too late. Had she not done so, she would have but offered to her rival, France, the occasion to do the same thing—the thing which France would to-day most willingly do if it were possible for her to do it. As we have seen, France and India had not absorbed more than about one half of the new gold. Probably $1,500,000,000 of the gold produced from 1850 to 1876 was yet to find a demand either in the arts or in the currencies of other nations. It was from this source that Germany proposed to help herself before it was too late, and thereby array herself in the rank of commercial states which, having large transactions, chose gold, not merely as the most stable in value of the two metals, but as the best medium of exchange for large payments. Here, again, we meet with the undoubted preference for gold over silver. No matter what the cause is, the simple historical fact is undeniable that among commercial nations most men concur in believing gold to be the most stable in value, and the most convenient and trustworthy of the two metals as a medium of exchange. We will not say that this is an unmixed good; but so it is, as a fact of modern history. If any modern commercial country were placed in a position where it could choose on even terms (or even at some sacrifice) between gold and silver, there is no more doubt that gold would be preferred than there is that of two pieces of land a farmer would select for cultivation the one which (other things being equal) was the more fertile and accessible.

Germany, consequently, saw an opportunity to secure gold instead of silver, and was far-sighted enough to understand that, if other countries were permitted to anticipate her in the course of monetary progress, the acquisition of gold necessary to the up-building of a great commercial state with large transactions might later on possibly become a more costly proceeding. At the close of the Franco-Prussian war the new German Empire found the opportunity referred to in the plan for the establishment of a uniform coinage throughout its numerous small states, and was essentially aided in its plan at this time by the receipt of the enormous war-indemnity from France, of which $54,600,000 was paid to Germany in French gold coin.[1] Besides this, Germany received from France bills of exchange in payment of the indemnity which gave Germany the title to gold in places, such as London, on which the bills were drawn. Gold in this way left London for Berlin. With a large stock of gold on hand, Germany began a series of measures to change her circulation from silver to gold. Her circulation in 1870, before the change was made, was composed substantially of silver and paper money, with no more than 4 per cent of the whole circulation in gold, as may be seen by the following statement:[2]

Domestic gold coins............	91,000,000 marks.	4·0 per cent.
Silver coins[3].................	1,500,000,000 "	65·7 "
Subsidiary coins...............	85,000,000 "	3·7 "

[1] See Léon Say's "Rapport fait au nom de la commission du budget de 1875 sur le payement de l'indemnité de guerre."

[2] Dr. A. Soetbeer, "Gegenwärtiger Stand der Währungsfrage und die Zukunft des Silbers" (April, 1885), p. 36; also in "Viertjahrs. für Volkswirt.," xxii, Heft ii.

[3] This item includes 90,000,000 marks of the Prussian War Treasure and the

Foreign coins	40,000,000	marks.	1·8	per cent.
Hamburg bank-funds	36,000,000	"	1·6	"
	1,752,000,000	"	76·8	"
State paper-money	171,000,000	"	7·5	"
Uncovered bank-notes	359,000,000	"	15·7	"
Total	2,282,000,000	"	100·0	"

By this it will be seen that in 1870 Germany had but $22,750,000 of gold in circulation, and as much as $375,000,000 of silver possessing full legal-tender power. The sales of silver by Germany were generally believed to have been responsible for the fall in the value of silver in 1876. I do not think that this can be substantiated by a study of the chronological order of events affecting the value of silver, which will be made in another place.[1] But for the present, it will be well first to describe the measures by which Germany carried through the reform of her coinage.

§ 2. The substitution of gold instead of silver in a country like Germany which had a single silver medium was carried out by a path which led first to temporary bimetallism and later to gold monometallism. And for this purpose the preparatory measures [2] were passed December 4, 1871:

"SEC. 1. There shall be coined an imperial gold coin, 139½ pieces of which shall contain one pound of pure gold.

"SEC. 2. The tenth of this gold coin shall be called a 'mark,' and shall be divided into one hundred 'pfennige.'

"SEC. 3. Besides the imperial gold coin of 10 marks (Sec. 1), there shall be coined imperial gold coins of 20 marks, of which 69¾ pieces shall contain one pound of pure gold.

"SEC. 4. The alloy of the imperial gold coins shall consist of 900 thousandths parts gold and 100 thousandths parts copper. Therefore 125·55 pieces of 10 marks, 62·775 pieces of 20 marks, shall each weigh one pound.

"SEC. 6. *Until the enactment of a law for the redemption of the large silver coins*, the making of the gold coins shall be conducted at the expense of the Empire. . . .

Austrian thalers current in Germany. The item does not include the coins of Alsace and Lorraine.

[1] Chapter xii, § 3.

[2] For the full text of these laws, as well as for the French law, see Appendix III, C.

"Sec. 8. All payments which are by law to be made, or which may be made, in silver coins of the thaler system, of the South German system, of the Lubec or Hamburg current system, or in gold thalers of the Bremen system, can be made in imperial gold coins (Secs. 1 and 3) in such manner as to count the 10-mark piece equal in value to $3\frac{1}{3}$ thalers, or 5 florins 50 kreutzers of the South German system, 8 marks $5\frac{1}{3}$ schillings of the Lubec or Hamburg current system, $3\frac{1}{13}$ gold thalers of the Bremen system. . . .

"Sec. 10. No coinage of gold coins other than those established by this law, *nor of large silver coins*, the coinage of medals excepted, shall take place until further action."

This law of 1871 created new gold coins, current equally with existing silver coins, at rates of exchange which were based on a ratio [1] between the gold and silver coins of $1:15\frac{1}{2}$. The silver coins were not demonetized by this law; their coinage was for the present only discontinued; but there was no doubt as to the intention of the Government in the future, since in Section 6 reference was distinctly made to further action looking to the withdrawal and permanent retirement of large silver pieces. Therefore, so far as Germany had had an annual demand for silver hitherto to replenish her currency, that demand ceased with the end of the year 1871. Existing silver coins still remained a legal tender equally with gold in a bimetallic system based on a ratio of $1:15\frac{1}{2}$.

The next and decisive step toward a single gold standard was taken by the act of July 9, 1873:

"Sec. 1. In place of the various local standards now current in Germany, a national gold standard will be established. Its monetary unit is the 'mark,' as established in Sec. 2 of the law dated December 4, 1871. . . . [Five-mark gold coins were authorized, in addition to gold coins authorized by the act of 1871.]

"Sec. 3. There shall be issued in addition to the national gold coins: 1. As silver coins, five-mark pieces, two-mark pieces, one-mark pieces, fifty-pfennig pieces, and twenty-pfennig pieces. [Copper and nickel coins were also established.]

"P. 1. The pound of fine silver shall produce at coinage

---

[1] The price of silver in 1871 in London was $60\frac{1}{4}d.$, equal to a ratio of $1:15\cdot58$.

twenty five-mark pieces, fifty two-mark pieces, etc. . . . The proportion of alloy is 100 parts of copper to 900 parts of silver, so that 90 marks in silver coin shall weigh one pound. . . .

"SEC. 4. The aggregate issue of silver coins shall, until further orders, not exceed ten marks for each inhabitant of the Empire. At each issue of these coins a quantity of the present silver coins equal in value to the new issue must be withdrawn from circulation, and first those of the 'thirty-thaler' standard.[1]

"SEC. 9. No person shall be compelled to take in payment national silver coins to a larger amount than twenty marks, and nickel and copper coins to a larger amount than one mark. The Federal Council will designate such depositories as will disburse national gold coins in exchange for silver coins in amounts of at least 200 marks, and of nickel and copper coins in amounts of at least 50 marks, upon demand.

"SEC. 14. P. 1. All payments to be made up to that time [the introduction of the national standard] in coins now current, or in foreign coins lawfully equalized with such domestic coins, are then to be made in national coins. . . .

"SEC. 18. By January 1, 1876, all bank-notes not issued according to the national standard must be withdrawn.

"From that date only bank-notes issued according to the national standard, and in denominations of not less than 100 marks, may be emitted and kept in circulation. These provisions also apply to bills hitherto issued by corporations." . . .

By this measure gold was established as the monetary standard of the country, with the "mark" as the unit, and silver was used, as in the United States in 1853, in a subsidiary service. Before this change, when silver was coined at its full weight, 90 marks were coined from one pound of fine silver. By the law of 1873, 100 marks were coined from one pound of fine silver. One hundred coins having been issued where 90 had been before, there was an overvaluation of $\frac{1}{9}$ in the new imperial silver currency, or, in other words, silver coins were issued $\frac{1}{9}$ below their nominal value, or 11$\frac{1}{9}$ per cent. The subsidiary coinage, as in the United States, contains less silver than its nominal or tale value expresses; but its legal-tender value was limited to 20 marks (five dollars), and it was redeemable at govern-

---

[1] By the treaty between Austria and the German States in 1857, a pound of fine silver was coined into 30 thalers.

ment depositories. The silver coin, therefore, was regulated by the usual principles governing subsidiary coinage, Germany thus following in the steps of the United States and of England.

The act also limited the amount of the overvalued silver to ten marks for each inhabitant of the Empire, a comparatively low figure. It will be evident that this fact is to be kept in mind in considering the total amount of silver liberated by Germany, since the amount of the new silver coined and issued was an offset to the total amount withdrawn; that is, not all the silver drawn in was sold, since some of it was recoined and issued in the new form.

The reform in the gold and silver coinage was accompanied by measures affecting the bank-notes and paper money in circulation. The issues of the various small states were withdrawn and a new paper money issued, distributed according to population among the various states, and redeemable in the new imperial currency. The inconvenience of the heavy silver in use in Germany had formerly stimulated the use of substitutes for specie in the form of bank-notes. The act of 1873 regulated the issues of the banks, and banknotes of a denomination less than 100 marks ($25) were forbidden. This was an important measure, because it opened a new demand for silver to take the place of the prohibited bank-notes. If no notes were issued under 100 marks, more coin would be needed to fill the vacancy caused by their retirement.

§ 3. Under the terms of this legislation Germany began to withdraw her old silver coinage, and to sell as bullion whatever silver was not recoined into the new subsidiary currency. The following table[1] will show the amounts of silver sold in the open market by Germany, and the price at which it was sold, until the end of May, 1879, when sales were suspended:

---

[1] "French Report of Mon. Conf. of 1881," i, p. 16. Marks are reduced at the rate of four marks to one dollar.

GERMANY DISPLACES SILVER WITH GOLD.

YEARS.	Pounds fine silver.	Price per Eng. standard oz. at which sold.	Proceeds of sale.
1873	105·9 thousands.	59$\frac{5}{6}$ d.	$2,324,171
1874	703·6 "	58$\frac{3}{4}$ "	15,283,918
1875	214·9 "	57$\frac{1}{4}$ "	4,552,112
1876	1,211·8 "	52$\frac{3}{4}$ "	23,484,120
1877	2,868·1 "	54$\frac{5}{16}$ "	57,606,060
1878	1,622·7 "	52$\frac{11}{16}$ "	31,550,963
1879 (May)	377·7 "	50 "	6,983,604
Total	7,104·8 thousands.	53$\frac{13}{16}$ "	$141,784,948

The silver withdrawn by the end of the year 1880 was 7,474,644 pounds of fine silver[1]; of this it is stated that, at the end of 1880, there remained unsold in the hands of the German Government 339,353 pounds of fine silver. Germany was interrupted in her sales of silver by the decline in the value of silver in 1874, and particularly in 1876; but she adopted the policy of stopping her sales when the price of silver was low, and again selling when the price rose. It will be seen by the table given above that the largest sales were made in the year 1877, when the price of silver was much higher than it had been in 1876. In May, 1879, however, the Government suspended all further sales of silver, and has not resumed them to the present time.

It has been thought by many that the sales of silver by Germany, to the extent of the new supply of silver which was thrown on the market, had been the cause of the extraordinary fall in the value of silver in 1876. It was, therefore, held that if the sales of silver were suspended, the price should recover something of its former height. It was this opinion which led the managers of the Imperial Bank of Germany, in whose vaults a large amount of the old thalers had collected and had not yet been redeemed, to advise the cessa-

---

[1] 1,080,486,138 marks of silver coins were withdrawn; 382,648,841 marks were used in the recoinage; the remainder, 697,797,069 marks, divided by 90 (the number of marks to a pound under the old system), give 7,474,644 pounds. It will be noticed, however, that these figures, taken from the "French Report of Mon. Conf. of 1881," i, p. 16, do not exactly prove. The figures in this "Report," already referred to, are unfortunately marred by many errors.

tion of further sales in 1879. Their advice was taken; but the price of silver did not show the expected buoyancy after sales were suspended. It can hardly be thought now that the fall of silver, which has continued to the present day, was due to the sales of Germany which ceased in 1879.

The later status of the reform in the gold and silver coinage will make our statements in regard to 1876 somewhat clearer. We have the advantage of ten years later information[1] than that which was accessible in 1876 to either the German Government, or to the Committee of the House of Commons, which investigated the causes of the depreciation of silver in that year:

By 1880 old silver coins withdrawn............	$270,000,000
By 1880 new " " coined................	106,000,000
Silver to be disposed of......................	164,000,000
Silver sold to May, 1879....	141,000,000
Supposed amount unsold, 1880................	23,000,000
Old silver coins current in 1870..............	$375,000,000
" " " withdrawn by 1880............	270,000,000
" " " (thalers) outstanding by 1885....	105,000,000

The population by 1880 had increased to 45,194,172, making the amount of fractional silver which can legally be issued 450,000,000 marks, or about $113,000,000. This would absorb $7,000,000 of old silver coin outstanding and yet to be withdrawn. It is quite likely, moreover, that ten marks per head will not prove a sufficient allowance for the silver medium. A rate of twelve marks per head is already discussed. Then it is to be remembered that the thaler pieces yet out must be replaced by other coinage.

Now, adding to $164,000,000 (which was the amount actually to be sold as the result of withdrawals less recoinage to 1880) the sum of thalers yet outstanding, $105,000,000, we get as a maximum about $270,000,000 as the total amount

---

[1] "French Report of Mon. Conf. of 1881," i, p. 16; and Dr. Soetbeer's various writings, particularly the one already referred to, "Währungsfrage."

of silver which Germany could throw upon the market as the result of her policy of displacing silver with gold.[1] I think this is a very liberal estimate, and yet it is not a sum in itself to which a very extraordinary revolution in the price of silver can be attributed; the less so because, between 1873 and 1885, or in twelve years, only $141,000,000 of Germany's silver have actually been put upon the market.

But inasmuch as our object in Part II is to arrive at an explanation of the causes which affected the price of silver in 1876 and subsequent years, it will be necessary to discover what effect German demonetization had had by 1876. By that year Germany had sold in the open market only from $30,000,000 to $35,000,000. That sum represented the actual and visible addition to the supply of silver caused by the German act of 1873. But dealers in silver bullion must always take into consideration more than the actual sales; they must consider also the potential supply. The proper theory of market value has regard not merely to the actual visible supply present and offered for sale, but also to the amount of the prospective supply, the amount which, although not actually present, is capable of being brought at once to market. The potential supply, therefore, was naturally taken into account by dealers in silver, and estimates as to its amount had an important influence upon the price of silver. But, as given above, the total supply of silver which Germany could by all her operations put upon the market was about $270,000,000. Subtracting $30,000,000, the amount actually sold by 1876, the potential supply was about $240,000,000. In 1876, however, the German Government underrated the quantity of the old silver still to be withdrawn. To that date $110,000,000 had been withdrawn, leaving about $265,000,000 still outstanding. In 1876 the estimates on this sum varied from $40,000,000 to $150,000,000. One of the best authorities[2] believed that the face value of the coin to be with-

---

[1] The amount withdrawn from 1880 to 1885, however, must be added to this sum.

[2] Mr. G. Pietsch, manager of the sales of silver for Germany in London. See

drawn was $195,000,000, which Dr. Soetbeer now assures us was $375,000,000 in 1870.

§ 4. At the same time that Germany was liberating silver she was absorbing gold in her new coinage. In order that a comparison may be made between the condition of the currency in Germany under the old silver *régime* and the present condition under the new coinage system, I take[1] from Dr. Soetbeer a table, corresponding to that of 1870 before given, which will show the progress made toward a gold standard by 1885 :

Imperial gold coins...............	1,500,000,000 marks	} 51·6 %
Gold in bars and foreign coins.....	72,000,000 "	
Silver thalers (including Austrian)..	450,000,000 "	14·7 "
Imperial silver coins.............	442,000,000 "	14·5 "
Nickel and copper coins..........	40,000,000 "	1·3 "
	2,504,000,000 "	82·1 "
Imperial treasury-notes..........	145,000,000 "	4·8 "
Uncovered bank-notes............	401,000,000 "	13·1 "
	3,050,000,000 "	100·0 "

It will be seen by comparison with the previous statement for 1870 that the amounts of gold and silver coins in 1885 are almost exactly reversed. In 1870 there were 1,500,000,000 marks of silver ; in 1885, 1,500,000,000 marks of gold coin. But the substitution of the new for the old silver coins has not yet been finished, since 450,000,000 marks of silver thalers are yet to be withdrawn.

The coinage[2] of gold in Germany from 1873 to the end of 1880 is as follows:

20-mark pieces...........................	$317·6	millions.
10-mark pieces...........................	112·2	"
5-mark pieces...........................	7·0	"
Total...........................	$436·8	"

"H. C. Report of 1876," Questions 739–760. The estimate of one third for disappearance on the amount of the original coinage was found in fact to be, on an average, only 21 per cent for three kinds of coin.

[1] Ibid., p. 37.
[2] "French Report Conf. of 1881," i, p. 15.

The old gold coinage of about $23,000,000 previously in circulation is to be subtracted from the total coinage of $437,000,000, leaving $414,000,000 as the probable demand of Germany on the gold stock of the world.[1] The German demand on the new gold which resulted from the discoveries in California and Australia then amounted to $414,000,000 to a date as late as 1880. With the $1,160,000,000 coined by France, and the $440,000,000 imported by India, this makes a total of about $2,000,000,000 taken out of the new supplies of gold by what was practically a new demand in these three countries. I include in Germany's demand the sums absorbed as late as 1880, that there may be no danger of undervaluing the demand for gold, although our immediate purpose confines us properly to the period ending in 1876. There is thus left about $1,000,000,000 of the production of gold from 1850 to 1876 to be accounted for.

Following in the lead of Germany, Denmark, Norway, and Sweden changed their silver circulation to gold, but threw upon the market[2] only about $9,000,000 of silver.

---

[1] From 1871 to 1876 gold to the amount of $119,930,000 was purchased by the German Government in London ("H. C. Report of 1876," Q. 325); $50,000,000 of gold came from France in the War Indemnity; and other amounts came from France, Belgium, and Russia.

[2] See "H. C. Report," p. 30.

CHAPTER XI.

FRANCE AND THE LATIN UNION.

§ 1. The gold discoveries of California and Australia were directly the cause of the Latin Union. It will be remembered that in 1853, when the subsidiary silver of the United States had disappeared before the cheapened gold, we reduced the quantity of silver in the small coins sufficiently to keep them dollar for dollar below the value of gold. Switzerland followed this example of the United States in her law of January 31, 1860; but, instead of distinctly reducing the weight of pure silver in her small coins, she accomplished the same end by lowering the fineness of standard for these coins to 800 thousandths fine. This, of course, only amounted to the same thing as a reduction of weight; since if, without altering the standard weight of a coin, more alloy is used (as, in this case, introducing $\frac{2}{10}$ instead of $\frac{1}{10}$ alloy), there will be less pure silver in the coin than before. Like the United States, Switzerland was forced—by the fall in the value of gold, or the corresponding rise in the value of silver relatively to gold—to reduce the amount of silver in her small coins in order to keep them in circulation. The fall in the value of gold affected countries differently according as they had, or had not, a unit of low value in their coinage. Where countries, like France, had the franc as a unit, it is easy to see that a fall in the ratio of silver to gold should have driven out silver, and so removed from circulation in these states the silver currency in which a unit of low value was necessarily established. Such changes were very serious to the convenience of the people in ordinary payments. In order to keep such a unit in such a metal, they would be obliged to alter the weight of their small coins, and so to change the character of their common unit of account. To meet this difficulty, Switzerland, when she found that her silver coins were fast being exported, made the five-franc piece (instead of the franc) her monetary unit,[1] which was maintained at its former weight and fineness (900); but she lowered the value of her silver pieces of two francs, of one franc, and of fifty centimes, to the position of subsidiary coins, at 800 thousandths fine.

Meanwhile France [2] and Italy had a higher standard for their coins than Switzerland, and as the neighboring states, which had the franc system of coinage in common, found each other's coins in circulation within their own limits, it was clear that the cheaper Swiss coins, according to Gresham's law, must drive out the dearer French and Italian coins, which contained more pure silver, but which passed current at the same nominal value. The Swiss coins of 800 thousandths fine began to pass the French frontier and to displace the French coins of a similar denomination; and the French coins were exported, melted, and recoined in Switzerland at a profit. This, of course, brought forth a decree in France (April 14, 1864) which prohibited the receipt of these Swiss coins at the public offices of France, the customs-offices, etc., and they were consequently refused in common trade among individuals.

Belgium also, as well as Switzerland, began to think it necessary to deal with the questions affecting her silver small coins, which were leaving that country for the same reason that they were leaving Switzerland. Belgium then

---

[1] After 1850 "the five-franc silver began first to disappear; and soon the fractional coins were displaced in their turn; so that the necessary quantity of subsidiary coin was thus diminished to the great injury of small transactions." —"Message of the Federal Council of Switzerland," February 2, 1866.

[2] By the law of May 25, 1864, the coinage of fifty and twenty centimes at a fineness of $\frac{835}{1000}$ was authorized to the amount of thirty millions of francs; which was only about one franc *per capita* of subsidiary coinage. See "Report of 1878," pp. 782, 783.

undertook to make overtures to France,[1] in order that some concerted action might be undertaken by the four countries using the franc system—Italy, Belgium, France, and Switzerland—to remedy the evil to which all were exposed by the disappearance of their silver coin needed in every-day transactions. The discoveries of gold had forced a reconsideration of their coinage systems. In consequence of these overtures, a conference of delegates representing the Latin states just mentioned assembled in Paris, November 20, 1865, and, passing from the immediate question of the subsidiary coins, they advanced to the discussion of the general metallic circulation of the four countries. Belgium, Switzerland, and Italy strongly urged the adoption of a single gold standard, retaining silver in a subsidiary office for coins of denominations below five francs. This was defeated by the action of the French delegates, under influences said[2] to come from the Bank of France and the Rothschilds. But the Conference, fully realizing the effects of the fall of gold in driving out their silver coins, agreed to establish a uniform coinage in the four countries, on the essential principles adopted by the United States in 1853. They lowered the silver pieces of two francs, one franc, fifty centimes, and twenty centimes from a standard of 900 thousandths fine to a uniform fineness of 835 thousandths, reducing these coins to the position of a subsidiary currency. They retained for the countries of the Latin Union, however, the system of bimetallism. Gold pieces of one hundred, fifty, twenty, ten, and five francs were to be coined, together with five-franc pieces of silver, and all at a standard of 900 thousandths fine. Free coinage, at a ratio of $15\frac{1}{2} : 1$, was thereby granted to any holder of either gold or silver bullion who wanted silver coins of five francs, or gold coins from five francs and upward. Each coin, although stamped by either of the four countries with the distinctive devices of the issu-

---

[1] See "Report of 1878," pp. 781–789; and also "H. C. Report of 1876," Appendix, pp. 104–108. The latter reference gives valuable information.

[2] Dr. Soetbeer, "Währungsfrage," p. 29.

ing country upon it, was to be of uniform weight, fineness, diameter, and tolerance, as may be learned from the treaty signed December 23, 1865, which is elsewhere given.[1] The subsidiary silver coins (below five francs) were made a legal tender between individuals of the state which coined them to the amount of fifty francs; and the issuing state agreed to receive them from their own citizens in any amount. The quantity of coin outstanding was to be limited to a quota of six francs *per capita*, as follows:

France	239,000,000 fr.
Belgium	32,000,000 "
Italy	141,000,000 "
Switzerland	17,000,000 "

As regards five-franc silver pieces, however, there was unlimited free coinage to any individual in the Latin Union at the old ratio of $15\frac{1}{2} : 1$.

The treaty was ratified, and went into effect[2] August 1, 1866, to continue until January 1, 1880, or about fifteen years, as decreed by Article 14: "The present convention shall remain in force until January 1, 1880. If not dissolved a year before the expiration of this term, it shall remain in full force for a new period of fifteen years, and so on, fifteen years at a time, if not dissolved."

The Latin Union, while due primarily to the disturbances caused by the new gold, was aided in its formation by the growing disposition in enlightened minds to demand a uniform international coinage; by the natural wish of countries having the same monetary unit to prevent as much as possible all friction in trade across their frontiers; and largely, no doubt, by political considerations which led the French Empire to strengthen its dominant position over its smaller neighbors.[3]

---

[1] See Appendix III, D, for the text in full.

[2] April 10–22, 1867, Greece entered the Union; April 14, 1867, Roumania; June 18, 1866, the States of the Church.

[3] This last was the opinion of Mr. Bagehot. See "H. C. Report of 1876," Q. 1,426.

§ 2. The ratio of 15½ : 1 retained by the Latin Union had been adopted by France in 1803[1] (An XI), at the beginning of her bimetallic legislation. We saw, in the course of our story,[2] that the United States had established a double standard in 1792, but that, owing to the fall in the value of silver, it soon resulted in a single standard of silver. It will be recalled that, in that discussion, it had been claimed that silver had not fallen, but that gold had risen, in value. Moreover, it had been asserted that the reason why gold left the United States in that period was the existence of a ratio in France of 15½ : 1, different from ours; which, by offering half an ounce more of silver in exchange for gold than was secured by the ratio of 15 : 1 in the United States, led to the exportation of silver to France.[3] Unfortunately for this theory, the facts are against it, for M. Chevalier has told[4] us that soon after the year 1803 there occurred the first of three great movements which have disarranged the French coinage from that time to this. He assures us that soon after the law of 1803 was passed the relative values of gold and silver in France changed so considerably, in comparison with what they had been before, that the market rate no longer coincided with the Mint ratio of 15½ : 1; that the market ratio in France rose beyond 15½ : 1; so that an ounce of gold bought more silver in the bullion market than it did at the

---

[1] " When the value of gold relatively to silver increased, the state decreased the weight of gold forming the monetary unit; when it was the value of silver which increased, the state decreased the weight of silver. Thus, in the course of centuries, the weight of the coin was constantly diminished and reduced; it is true, the name remained the same; the monetary unit was always called the livre until the time when its name was changed by law in the year XI to that of franc; but the livre was no longer a pound; it decreased and decreased until it was reduced to a very small part of the original pound. This was profitable to the government who coined the money; it was profitable to debtors who were freed from their debts by a weight of gold or silver less than that which had been agreed upon; but all these profits were made at the expense of the whole people."—M. Burkhardt-Bischoff, " French Report Mon. Conf. of 1881," i, p. 132. For the text of the law of 1803, see Appendix III.

[2] See Chap. ii, § 5.

[3] H. C. Burchard, article " Coinage," in Lalor's " Cyclopædia."

[4] " Journal des Économistes," June, 1876, p. 443.

Mint. As a consequence, gold was bought and sold only as merchandise. Now this was exactly the process which we found going on in the United States at the same time; and, to my mind, there can not be a moment's doubt that the events in the two countries were due to the same cause —the enormous production of Mexican silver after 1780. And, moreover, if gold was being withdrawn from the French circulation, it is difficult to understand how it could have gone from the United States to France, attracted by the French Mint ratio of $15\frac{1}{2}:1$, when gold was not being coined there. In fact, the simultaneous withdrawal of gold in two widely separated countries, so soon as the market ratio diverged from the Mint ratio, starts the presumption that a cause was at work of greater fundamental importance than the difference between the legal ratios of two countries, which acted the one upon the other. France, however, did not modify her ratio, as did the United States in 1834, but remained content with a circulation which, as M. Chevalier states, was composed almost exclusively of silver. This state of affairs continued with some interruptions until 1848, during which the market ratio sometimes approached more nearly to $15\frac{1}{2}:1$, because the production of gold from the Russian mines had largely increased by the year 1841. To 1848, consequently, and during the greater part of the period since 1803, France had virtually but a single standard of silver; although by law she had a double standard of both gold and silver.

The second experience of France with her coinage began with the discoveries of gold in California and Australia. In comparing the beginning of the century with 1864 it appears that the production of gold had increased fourteen or fifteen times, while the production of silver had increased only one third. The consequent effects of this enormous production of gold on the French coinage after 1850 I have already described.[1] The circulation of France underwent a complete change,[2] in spite of the frequent representations

---

[1] Chap. viii, § 6.
[2] Chevalier says that under Louis Philippe there was coined of gold 216,000,-

that the ratio established in 1803 had kept the relative value of gold and silver within such limits as to preserve the concurrent circulation of the two metals. In such questions more satisfaction is to be derived from facts than from vague declamations. After 1850, not only five-franc silver pieces, but the small coins employed in the retail transactions of every-day use, began to disappear. The absence of small silver led, as we have seen in the last section, to the events which brought about the convention of the Latin Union in 1865. But the appearance of gold was hailed by the public of France with that evident satisfaction which, as has been referred to many times before, always results from the universal preference of mankind in commercial and civilized countries for gold over silver. In the years preceding 1848 international commerce with France had been but little developed,[1] and there had been little need for the transportation abroad of very large sums of specie. After 1850, however, commercial conditions began to change, and the use of gold in large payments was naturally a great convenience. The state of mind in France is thus described by M. Chevalier, from whom I again quote:[2]

"The public applauded this introduction of gold into the place of silver for the same reasons which had earlier attracted the English people—viz., gold pieces are more easily handled, a certain amount can be carried more conveniently, and counting takes less time."

Such was the condition of monetary affairs in France at the time of the creation of the Latin Union in 1865. Since 1803 she had first lost her gold and taken an alternative standard of silver instead; and then, reversing the process, because she still maintained the legal ratio of $15\frac{1}{2} : 1$, she lost her silver and took an alternative standard of gold. This last operation undoubtedly acted as a "parachute" to lessen the fall which otherwise gold must have suffered.

---

000 francs, of silver 1,757,000,000 francs; but under the Second Empire 6,152,000,000 francs of gold, and only 625,000,000 of silver.

[1] See "Histoire du système monétaire Français," by L. Pauliat, "Journ. des Économistes," June, 1881, p. 428.

[2] "Journal des Économistes," June, 1876, p. 444.

The whole of this history is a striking commentary on the fact that an increase in the production of silver does not lead to an additional employment of it by the civilized world as a medium of exchange; but that an increase in the production of gold, so long as human nature remains what it now is, does lead inevitably to a more extended use of it as a medium of exchange in modern commercial countries; and just to the extent of its increase does gold push out of use the silver it displaces, as an inferior instrument of exchange, thus contracting the monetary field in which silver can be used, and lessening the demand for it. An increased production of gold has caused a depreciation in silver which forms a part of the movement by which mankind is furnishing itself with better instead of inferior tools in all the departments of commerce and industry. When new and lighter plows come into competition with the heavy and cumbrous machines of the last century, the latter will go out of use and decline in value. So it will be with the heavier and more cumbrous of the precious metals.

§ 3. The International Monetary Conference of 1867, which assembled in Paris with the original motive of bringing about a uniform system of coins throughout the world, was led to ask, Of what metal shall the uniform coins be struck? The almost unanimous verdict of this conference was that the single standard of gold should be recommended. Such was the state of public opinion in the chief commercial nations in 1867. Several elaborate monetary reports were made by French commissions created for the purpose between 1867 and 1870, and it seemed as if the adoption of a gold standard by France in 1870 was a settled thing. Then the Franco-Prussian war broke out, and the close of the war was immediately followed by the German monetary reform. There can scarcely be any doubt that, had not Germany acted when she did, France and wide-awake Belgium would have demonetized silver, and done exactly what Germany anticipated them in doing.

Cut off from this policy, France and the Latin Union,

however, were soon forced to consider the effects of another change (the third since 1803) in their monetary system arising from unforeseen movements in the relative values of gold and silver. The convention of 1865 had been entered into because gold had become cheaper than silver. But, a very few years after the contracting powers had ratified this convention of 1865, a change in the market value of silver removed all ground for its existence. Silver began to fall[1] relatively to gold as early as 1872, and soon reached a value more nearly in accordance with the ratio of 15·5 : 1. Had the fall ended there, all further difficulty would have been avoided. But the progress of events was against this supposition. The fall of silver (which did not reach its culmination until 1876) continued, and the countries of the Latin Union were threatened with conditions the very opposite of those which existed in 1865; then they were studying how to keep gold from driving out even their subsidiary silver coins; by 1873, on the contrary, they were occupied with the question how the enormous influx of silver could be prevented: "When, then, toward the end of 1873, Prussia having announced its intention of demonetizing silver, which at that time had already undergone a sensible depreciation in the market, some of the states bound by the convention thought it necessary to protect themselves against an excessive and sudden influx of this coin, and called a new meeting of the Conference. Any restrictive measure, such as the limitation or suspension of coinage, if undertaken separately, would be ineffective so long as any of the allied states continued to issue coins which would be introduced into other states of the Union."[2]

The downward tendency of silver in 1873 led the Latin Union to fear that the demonetized silver of Germany would flood their own mints if they continued the free coinage of five-franc silver pieces at a legal ratio of 15½ : 1. Fifteen and a

---

[1] See tables in Appendix II and Chart XIII.

[2] Annex to the Monetary Convention of January 31, 1874, presented to the French Government.—"Journal des Économistes," July, 1874, p. 108.

half ounces of silver were still counted as equal to one ounce of gold at the Mint; but since in the market more than that number of ounces of silver were needed to buy one ounce of gold, naturally silver rushed to the mints of the Latin Union. In 1871-1872, before the fall in the value of silver was noticeable, there had been presented at the French Mint for coinage into five-franc pieces only 5,000,000 francs of silver bullion; in Belgium, only 33,000,000; but in 1873 alone, because it was profitable to money-brokers, there was suddenly presented at the French Mint 154,000,000, and at the Belgian Mint 111,000,000 francs. As a consequence of this movement, December 18, 1873, an act was passed by Belgium which gave the government authority to suspend the coinage of silver five-franc pieces.

This condition of things led to the meeting of delegates from the countries of the Latin Union at Paris, January 30, 1874, who there agreed to a treaty supplementary [1] to that originally formed in 1865, and determined on withdrawing from individuals the full power of free coinage by limiting to a moderate sum the amount of silver five-franc pieces [2] which should be coined by each state of the Union during the year 1874. The date of this suspension of coinage by the Latin Union is regarded by all authorities as of great import in regard to the value of silver. At the time perhaps its importance did not seem so evident.[3] The French authorities believed that the action of Germany was only a temporary inci-

---

[1] For the text of this document see "Journ. des Écon.," July, 1874, pp. 112, 113.

[2]   France................................ 60,000,000 fr.
    Belgium.............................. 12,000,000 "
    Italy................................. 40,000,000 "
    Switzerland.......................... 8,000,000 "

Italy was also allotted an extra 20,000,000 fr., and certain deposits at the Mint, for which coin warrants had been issued, were also excepted.

[3] Wolowski held that the slight fall in silver at this time was a "passing circumstance"; and that when the various countries then laboring under heavy issues of paper money began to resume payments in specie, the danger would be that there would not be enough, rather than that there would be too much, of silver.—" Journ. des Écon.," December, 1873, p. 506.

dent affecting the value of silver; they stated,[1] therefore, that "to an irregular and accidental event they [the Latin Union] opposed a temporary measure, as exceptional as the decision which called it forth." They did not then see that the action of Germany was important, not for itself, but because of its place in a series of events due to the progress of monetary ideas. We must, therefore, regard the suspension of unlimited coinage of silver by the Latin Union as a very important step, because it forms another event in the series to which the demonetization of silver by Germany belongs.

§ 4. The suspension of the free coinage of five-franc silver pieces by the Latin Union was a consequence of the falling value of silver. So long as the ratio of silver to gold remained above $1:15\frac{1}{2}$, these four countries could not continue to receive silver at their mints unless they were willing to see gold disappear from their reserves and from circulation, and to see silver alone take its place. About this decision there was no hesitation whatever; the Latin Union had no intention of giving up gold, once that it had flowed into their territories. The preference for gold over silver, when there is a free choice between the two, again received a striking illustration. And all the subsequent movements of the Latin Union have been prompted not so much by the wish to show a preference for a silver medium as by a desire to protect themselves against the loss arising from the possibility of selling the silver with which they have already burdened themselves. They would all, at this moment, gladly embrace an opportunity to place themselves on a gold basis if they could do so without serious loss in disposing of their silver.

After 1874 the Latin Union, owing to the continued decline in the value of silver, maintained their policy of restricting the coinage. In 1875, pursuant to the agreement of a year before, another monetary conference was held in Paris,

---

[1] Annex to Monetary Convention of January 31, 1874.—"Journ. des Écon.," July, 1874, p. 111.

and limited quotas[1] of silver were fixed for coinage by each state. The annual conference in 1876 lessened the total amount[2] to be coined to 120,000,000 francs for the whole Union. About this same time Holland, a country not a member of the Latin Union, took a step away from a silver medium by forbidding[3] any further coinage of silver after July 1, 1875. The various states of the Latin Union, moreover, did not coin all the silver assigned to them as their quotas. In 1875 and 1876 Switzerland cautiously did not coin any of her quota.

In studying this example of a monetary union between different states it is to be noticed that each state reserved to itself the power to suspend the coinage entirely. The agreements of the convention fixed only the maximum amounts beyond which the coinage of silver should not go. As we have already seen, Belgium had passed a law in 1873 giving the government power to suspend the coinage of silver entirely. France likewise found it expedient,[4] on August 5, 1876, to shut the doors of her Mint to silver. It will be seen, therefore, that one country after another, so long as the old ratio of $1:15\frac{1}{2}$ was adhered to, was obliged to close its mints to the coinage of silver.

In 1877 the Union suspended entirely the coinage of five-franc pieces for that year (except a sum of 10,000,000 francs

[1] For France... 75,000,000 fr.
   " Italy... 50,000,000 "
   " Belgium... 15,000,000 "
   " Switzerland .... 10,000,000 "
[2] For France... 54,000,000 fr.
   " Italy... 36,000,000 "
   " Belgium... 10,800,000 "
   " Switzerland .... 7,200,000 "
   " Greece.. 3,600,000 "

Cf. "Journ. des Écon.," March, 1876, p. 443.

[3] Cf. "Journ. des Écon.," August, 1875, p. 172. This act ran until January 1, 1877, but was at that date continued in force.

[4] "La fabrication de pièces des 5 francs en argent pourra être limitée ou suspendue par décrets," was the phrase of the act. A decree in consonance with the law was issued the next day (August 6th) after its passage. For the animus of the law, see the statement of Léon Say, "H. C. Report of 1876," Appendix, p. 92.

for Italy). This position in regard to silver, however, was only preliminary to the decisive action of the Union in a treaty of November 5, 1878. In order to prevent gold from disappearing and being replaced by silver, a policy of successive restriction was originally adopted in 1874; but in 1878 the final policy of complete suspension was accepted. It was mutually agreed by the contracting parties that the "coinage of silver five-franc pieces is provisionally suspended. It may be resumed when a unanimous agreement to that effect shall be established between all the contracting states."[1] This agreement was to hold until January 1, 1886. The Union was not, however, dissolved, because they continued their coinage of subsidiary coinage (at 835 thousandths fine) on the common terms of the original convention of 1865. The suspension of five-franc pieces was the important point of the treaty of 1878, because it was the only silver piece which bore a ratio of $15\frac{1}{2}:1$ to the gold coins.[2]

Since 1878, therefore, the chief bimetallic countries of Europe decided that, so long as they chose to retain the legal ratio of $15\frac{1}{2}:1$ between gold and silver coins, it was impossible to keep open the mints for the presentation of silver bullion. This was their "expectant attitude" toward silver; they hoped that, if the value of silver rose, the coinage of silver might be again resumed. They are evidently hoping against hope, for since then Italy has resumed specie payments, in 1883, while Switzerland and Belgium are evidently anxious to place themselves on a gold basis; and, worst of all for the continuance of a coinage convention based on a ratio of $15\frac{1}{2}:1$, silver has steadily fallen in value since 1878, and at the present writing (September, 1885) the price has fallen to $47\frac{1}{4}d.$ per ounce in London, equivalent to a ratio of more than $20:1$. In the face of such facts, the return to a bimetallic system at $15\frac{1}{2}:1$ by the Latin Union is an impossible thing. I do not think it will ever occur.

The depreciation of silver weighs heavily on France, be-

---

[1] "Report of 1878," p. 735.
[2] The coinage of gold five-franc pieces was also suspended by this treaty.

cause she has coined a vast quantity of five-franc pieces since 1865, which have entered into circulation or have accumulated in the reserves of the Bank of France; and whenever in the course of the international exchanges a payment of specie is to be made by France to a foreign country, it must be made in gold out of a fund in the bank which is not over large. France can not return to the double standard, nor can she adopt a single gold standard, because the sale of her superfluous silver, except at a very great sacrifice, is now a practical impossibility. France is forced into her present "expectant attitude" because of the quantity of silver she has to dispose of. It is her object, therefore, to continue the Latin Union as long as possible, for a dissolution of the league would necessarily oblige each state to liquidate its own issues of silver coinage. In the future each state must have its own system, and the coins of one country would not be received reciprocally by the others, and, when rejected, they would be sent home to the banks of the issuing country under such financial pressure as would make it necessary to redeem them in some form or other. Of a total sum of 6,117,000,000 francs coined by the countries composing the Union, 3,910,000,000 are still on hand,[1] of which 3,100,000,000 bear the stamp of the French Mint. In case of a dissolution of the Union, the Belgian and Italian pieces in France would be sent out for redemption in gold to the issuing

---

[1] Probably 400 millions of Belgian stamp.
         400 " Italian "
         9·5 " Swiss "
       3,100 " French "

The following statement is given by Ottomar Haupt:

STATES.	Gold stock.	Current silver.	Subsidiary silver.	Uncovered bank-notes.
	Fr.	Fr.	Fr.	Fr.
France	4,400 millions.	3,400 millions.	200 millions.	990 millions.
Belgium	360 "	300 "	33 "	244 "
Italy	730 "	170 "	170 "	709 "
Switzerland	70 "	40 "	18 "	55 "

Dr. A. Soetbeer. "Währungsfrage," p. 32.

states, and to that extent France would be temporarily better off. For this reason some persons in France are urging the dissolution of the Latin Union. The silver pieces of other states are not a legal tender in France, although the Bank of France has hitherto received such silver on sufferance. The existence of a large amount of silver in the reserves of the bank requires that its wishes should be consulted by the authorities of France in a settlement of this question. More silver is in circulation in the Latin Union than can pass current at the legal rate, and it flows to the large banking-houses and encumbers the vaults of the bank.

The treaty of 1878 expires January 1, 1886, and even now the delegates of the Union are assembled in Paris discussing the continuance of the present agreements. Belgium, which has been very energetic in dealing with economic questions, is now anxious to demonetize silver and adopt the gold standard. The same is true of Switzerland, and France stands almost alone. The negotiations looking to a renewal of the Union are not yet fully known. France demands "that each of the powers forming the Union shall bind itself to redeem at their par value all its silver five-franc pieces that may be circulating abroad if and when the Union comes to an end."[1] Belgium objects, because coins have been issued from her Mint not only for herself, but on the account of Switzerland, of Italy, and even of France. Belgium, however, will be forced in some way to redeem her coinage, and it is highly probable that the Union will be continued. At the third sitting of the Conference, which began July 20, 1885, Belgium declined to accept the demands of France, and declared that, if this was a *sine qua non* for the renewal of the treaty, she preferred to withdraw; but, whatever the result of this last Conference, it is quite clear that they have no thought whatever of adding to their burden of silver, from which it is now their problem to escape. This being true, there is not a mint in Europe now open to the free coinage of silver.

---

[1] Cf. "London Economist," August 22, 1885. It is stated that $125,000,000 of Belgian silver coins are in circulation in France.

CHART XIII.

SHOWING THE RATIO OF GOLD TO SILVER BY YEARS, FROM 1687 TO 1884.

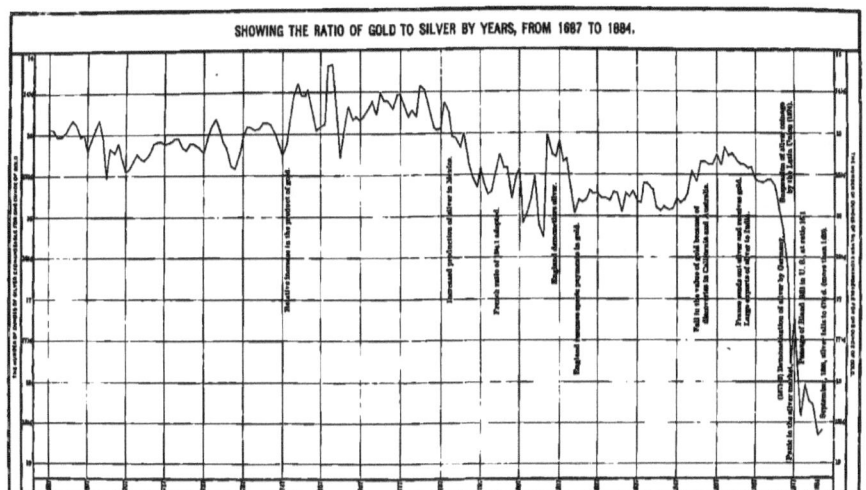

CHAPTER XII.

THE CAUSE OF THE FALL IN THE VALUE OF SILVER.

§ 1. AFTER having thus presented in the foregoing chapters of Part II the monetary events which have affected the relative values of the two precious metals since 1850, it is now intended to make a brief statement of the conclusions to be drawn from this account as to the value of silver, and to give in brief form what seems to me to have been the essential cause of the depreciation of silver. Before this can be done, however, it will be necessary to show whether a fall of silver actually did take place, and to what extent a depreciation has been proved.

At the beginning of the present century the price of silver fell until about 1825; then the course of its value remained fairly unchanged until about 1850, when the new gold was discovered; and until 1872 no great fluctuations had occurred. The movement of its value in later years may be seen by the line of Chart XIII, which shows the yearly changes since 1687. A comparison with Chart IV will show that since the discovery of America the value of silver relatively to gold has been moving steadily downward, while, as we know, gold itself has also fallen in value; but in the present century, after the effect of the Mexican production was finally realized in a generally lower level, there had been nothing of great importance to disturb its position until the later period with which we are now dealing. A glance at Chart XIII will make it clear how marked and sudden a change took place after 1872, and in the years immediately following, as compared with the general movement of silver since 1687. This sharp and distinct fall, especially after 1874, and continuing since then to 1885, has no parallel in the whole history of the precious metals. Within ten years the ratio of silver to gold has been changed from an annual average relation of about $15\frac{1}{2} : 1$ to nearly $19 : 1$.

As is well known, London is the chief silver market of the world, and prices of silver[1] are given in pence per ounce for English standard silver, $\frac{37}{40}$ fine. That is, the price of silver is estimated in the English gold currency. From 1853 to 1866 the price did not change much from about $61d.$ per ounce, which is equivalent[2] to a ratio of $15\cdot46 : 1$; from 1867 to 1872 the price was a little more than $60d.$ per ounce. By examining the table[3] of monthly prices of silver, it will be seen that the fall first began in November, 1872, when the price was about $59\frac{1}{4}d.$ Then from November, 1872, until January, 1876, there was a steady decline, as seen from the monthly prices, to about $55d.$ And in the year 1876 the price fell still more rapidly, from about $55d.$ in January to the lowest recorded price of $46\frac{3}{4}d.$ in July (equivalent to a ratio of $1 : 20\cdot17$). Since then there have been reactions toward better prices, but, on the whole, the price has steadily declined until, in September, 1885, the price is almost, if not fully, as low as it ever was in 1876.

It will appear from this statement, therefore, that silver has unquestionably fallen very seriously since 1872 in its relation to gold. But the question may very justly be asked, Has this fall been accompanied by a general increase of purchasing power in gold as regards other commodities? If so, the fall of silver relatively to gold, when other articles have

---

[1] See Appendix II, D, for London prices since 1833. Monthly quotations in each year since 1833 to 1880, by Pixley and Abell, can be found in the "French Report of the Mon. Conf. of 1881," i, p. 197. The average monthly ratio from 1845 to 1880 is given in Appendix II, F.

[2] For the computation of the ratio from the price, see Appendix II, G.

[3] Appendix II, E.

also fallen relatively to gold, will have left silver in the same relative position to other goods as before; and so it can not be said that silver has fallen, but that gold has risen, in value. This question, while eminently fair, is not capable of being answered in a brief way; and to answer it fully would lead me away from the object of this inquiry. It has been urged by Mr. Goschen and Mr. Giffen that there has been an appreciation of gold by 1879 as compared with 1873; but I shall not now consider their position, because the years to be here compared, in order to keep parallel with the movements of silver, are, on the one hand, 1871, and on the other, 1876 or 1877. And I waive for the present—what is of the utmost importance in discussing the appreciation of gold—the fact that there was a great collapse of credit in 1873 and a fall of prices due to other causes than the abundance or scarcity of specie in the world. In order to bring the fall of silver into comparison with the movement of prices between 1871 and 1877 I subjoin the following table of prices, taken[1] from the London "Economist's" figures for the first of January each year, being the prices of 22 articles, each on a scale of 100, making a total scale of 2,200, which represents the average prices of these articles in 1845–1850:

YEAR.	Index numbers.	Price of silver in pence.	Corresponding ratios.
1845–50	2200		
1857, July 1......	2996	61¾	15·27
1858, Jan. 1	2612	61 $\frac{8}{16}$	15·38
1865.............	3575	61 $\frac{1}{16}$	15·44
1866.............	3564	61¼	15·43
1867.............	3024	60 $\frac{9}{16}$	15·57
1868.............	2682 ⎫	60½	15·59
1869.............	2666	60 $\frac{7}{16}$	15·60
1870.............	2689 ⎬	60 $\frac{9}{16}$	15·57
1871.............	2590 ⎭	60 $\frac{9}{16}$	15·57
1872.............	2835	60¼	15·65
1873.............	2947	59¼	15·92
1874.............	2891	58 $\frac{5}{16}$	16·17
1875.............	2778 ⎫	56⅞	16·62
1876...	2711 ⎬	53 $\frac{1}{16}$	17·77
1877.............	2723 ⎭	54¾	17·22

[1] See the movement of the line in Chart III, which is based on these figures.

From these figures it will be seen that prices were as high in 1876 and 1877 as they were in 1875, and even higher than from 1868 to 1871 (inclusive). That is, so far as prices tell the story, it can not be said with any show of truth that gold had appreciated (that is, increased in its purchasing power, because prices had fallen). If, then, gold continued to buy about the same quantities of other goods from 1871 to 1877, and if in that time silver fell relatively to gold from about 60d. to 46$\frac{3}{4}d$. per ounce, it is quite correct to say that silver fell not merely with reference to gold, but with reference to all other commodities, including gold. As compared with 60$\frac{1}{4}d$., the average price in 1872, the fall to 46$\frac{3}{4}d$. in July, 1876, indicates a depreciation in the value of silver of more than 22 per cent; that is, silver lost general purchasing power over other commodities by July, 1876, equivalent to 22 per cent, and it is to explain this fall in the value of silver that the chapters of Part II were written. In this chapter it is intended to collect the threads which have been followed in preceding pages and to present our conclusions, based on the historical evidence which has been gathered.

§ 2. In the reasons heretofore assigned for the fall in the value of silver, nearness to the events, in my opinion, has acted to magnify immediate causes and obscure distant ones, or those acting under a general progress of events. Such an objection, it seems to me, is to be urged against the conclusions reached by the Committee of the House of Commons which reported on the "Depreciation of Silver" in 1876. Inasmuch as these conclusions have been quite generally received, it may be just to include them here before passing on to any criticism:

"Your Committee are of opinion that the evidence taken conclusively shows that the fall in the price of silver is due to the following causes:

"(1) To the discovery of new silver mines of great richness in the State of Nevada.

"(2) To the introduction of a gold currency into Germany in place of the previous silver currency. This operation commenced at the end of 1871.

"(3) To the decreased demand for silver for export to India.

" It should be added :

"(4) That the Scandinavian governments have also substituted gold for silver in their currency.

"(5) That the Latin Union, comprising France, Belgium, Switzerland, Italy, and Greece, have since 1874 limited the amount of silver to be coined yearly in the Mints of each member of the Union, suspending the privilege formerly accorded to all holders of silver bullion of claiming to have that bullion turned into coin without restriction.

"(6) That Holland has also passed a temporary act prohibiting, except on account of the Government, the coining of silver, and authorizing the coining of gold.

" It will be observed that two sets of causes have been simultaneously in operation. The increased production of the newly discovered mines, and the surplus silver thrown on the market by Germany, have affected the supply. At the same time the decreased amounts required for India, and the decreased purchases of silver by the members of the Latin Union, have affected the demand. A serious fall in the price of silver was therefore inevitable."[1]

In this very clear statement, account is taken of immediate causes, and none whatever of the more fundamental causes lying behind these operations—causes which might be supposed to show that there was some sequence in these events, and that they were controlled by a common force. Although it is not formally included in their reasons for the fall of silver, they have, however, hinted at some deeper cause. In the first place, they admit that the actual changes in the supply could not be supposed to have brought about so serious a fall in the value of silver; for, after having formally given the causes of the depreciation of silver as already recited, the Committee qualify their report by some

---

[1] " H. C. Report of 1876," p. iv.

very important statements, which to my mind come very much nearer the truth than their formal enumeration of causes: "It is, however, an important and remarkable fact . . . that, though the increased production of silver in the United States is a fact beyond question, no actual increase of imports of silver from the United States to Great Britain has taken place since the year 1873. . . . Indeed, the amount of the imports into Great Britain from the United States for the year 1875—viz., 3,092,000*l.*—is the smallest since the year 1869. In the same way, though the new currency laws of Germany affected a vast silver coinage, the sales of silver actually made up to the 26th of April in the present year [1876] do not appear to have exceeded 6,000,000*l.*, distributed over several years."[1] This Committee, moreover, show that in the early part of the century silver was produced, as compared with gold, in the proportion of 3 to 1; in 1848, of ·68 to 1; between 1852 and 1856, of ·27 to 1; and between 1857 and 1875, of ·68 to 1. Therefore, notwithstanding the new product of silver in Nevada since 1871, the relative production of silver to gold has not been very different in late years from the relation in 1848, to say nothing of the early part of the century. Consequently, the Committee decide [2] "that a review of the relations of the metals in times past shews that the fall in the price of silver is not due to any excessive production *as compared with gold.*" Although the fears of dealers may have magnified the potential supply, we may, therefore, in agreement with this conclusion, understand that the fall was not explicable on any sufficient grounds arising from an increased supply.

Indeed, the Committee only touched upon the true explanation when, leaving the question of supply and taking up the question of demand, they assert: "The fact is that, as was correctly pointed out by Mr. Giffen in his evidence, the changes have been *in the uses of the metals.* Gold has come more generally into use than before, and, indeed, the condi-

---

"H. C. Report of 1876," p. v.   [2] Ibid.

tion of trade and the situation of various countries using gold and silver respectively have entirely changed."[1]

§ 3. A change in the uses of the metals has undoubtedly taken place; and the cause of it is to be sought in the natural forces which underlie the processes of exchange and trade. The increase of commerce and the need of making large payments in wholesale transactions, while it has developed the check and clearing-house system, and all banking devices[2] by which the risk in the actual handling of large sums of metallic money has been avoided, has at the same time increased the demand for that one of the two precious metals which has the greatest value in the smallest bulk. This is the modern form of the preference, or prejudice, for gold as compared with silver, and it is most evident in the countries which have the largest commercial interests at stake.

This being the character of the monetary desires of modern nations, the opportunity of satisfying these desires, rendered possible to a very large extent by the enormous production of gold since 1850, has been, in my judgment, the cause of the fall in the value of silver. The situation, in brief, was this: In 1850 the Western world possessed a certain sum of both gold and silver (with the exception of England and the United States, chiefly silver) in use as a medium of exchange, both metals, be it observed, being in use for a common purpose—the interchange of goods. Now, there was suddenly added in 1850–1875 about $3,000,000,000 of gold. What was the effect? A very simple and natural increase in the use of gold by all the countries which could get it. But just to the extent to which the desire for gold could be satisfied by countries which had hitherto used silver wholly or in part, so far was the demand for silver as a medium of exchange

---

[1] "H. C. Report of 1876," p. v.
[2] Mulhall's "Dictionary of Statistics" states that since 1840 the banking of the world has increased eleven-fold, or three times faster than the increase of commerce, and thirty times faster than population. That in 1861–1870 the precious metals required for the interchange of the sea-borne commerce of the world was 12 per cent of the transactions, and in 1871–1880 only 8 per cent.

diminished. The new gold, therefore, because it was always preferred to silver, pushed it out of place, and, by filling the vacancy, took away from silver a part of the previous demand for the heavier metal. To the mind of the commercial world it was a substitution of a more convenient for a clumsier medium of exchange. In considering this movement in monetary progress, and comparing it with similar events in industrial progress in almost every branch of activity, no illustration seems to me more exactly to describe the change caused by the introduction of the new gold than that of steam. In former days the world carried on its exchanges by the slow, uncertain, and clumsy methods of coaches, wagons, and sails; now all is done, at less expense, more rapidly and conveniently, by railways and steamships. Both coaches and railways existed to transfer passengers and freight; so both gold and silver were used to interchange goods. Formerly coaches were our chief dependence; so was it with silver. In later years the railway has supplanted the coach because it does the same service much better, leaving the coach to do minor work in other directions; in the same way gold is supplanting silver because it serves the needs of commerce better, and silver is relegated to use as subsidiary coin for retail transactions. Consequently, when there is offered to a commercial country the choice between using gold and using silver, we should as soon expect it to prefer silver as we should expect merchants to-day to send their goods from New York to Chicago by wagons instead of by railway. This is the tendency among modern states to which we wish to call attention. Inasmuch as the production of gold from 1850 to 1875 was as great as in the 357 years preceding 1850, it can easily be seen what an opportunity was given to gratify the universal preference for gold to silver, coming as it did at the opportune moment when commerce began to expand in an unusual degree. To the extent of the surplus gold this absorption of gold could go on without interfering with its value, except to keep it from a fall. This is a striking fact in monetary history: increase the production of gold enormously, and it is eagerly absorbed, and so does not undergo much depreciation; but if the production of silver be increased to the same extent, it is not permitted to displace gold in the commercial states, as in the case of gold; and the increase of silver only creates distress to know whether the usual outlets for silver in the East are sufficient to carry off the surplus.

Thirty-five years ago England and Portugal alone[1] had a legal gold standard; all other countries, either by law or by the effect of circumstances, employed a silver currency. The United States had a double standard with but little silver in use; but Germany, France, and the countries of Continental Europe had a silver medium.[2] To-day the situation is entirely reversed. In Europe there is not a Mint open to the free coinage of silver. Gold has unquestionably become the only real medium of exchange for commercial Europe. And all this, I contend, has been brought about by two things[3]: the commercial preference for gold, and the extraordinary production of gold in California and Australia.

---

[1] "It used to be said until a few years ago that England and Portugal were the only countries where gold was the standard of value; and there were certain countries which had a double standard, but those were not very many; and all the rest used silver. Silver is the normal currency of the world, and from a natural cause, because silver is a much cheaper metal, and is suited to those small transactions which constitute the bulk of the dealings of mankind."—W. Bagehot, Q. 1,389, Report to H. C. of 1876, on "Depreciation of Silver."

[2] "In the Low Countries they struck gold ducats which circulated preferably abroad as merchandise without official value. Because of their fineness and the worth of their stamp they were highly regarded in the Orient, and especially in the Balkan peninsula; but these ducats had no circulation in the Low Countries, although their coinage was free. The only standard of the Kingdom of the Netherlands was really a silver standard. Russia, Germany, Austria, likewise struck gold ducats, friedrich d'or, and pistoles for exportation; but, like the Low Countries, they employed at home only silver money. France had, it is true, bimetallic legislation; but its circulation consisted entirely of silver. From 1789 to 1848 she had struck about four thousand millions of francs of silver money, while the amount of gold coined during the same period was only one thousand millions. Generally, in Europe, gold bore a premium; generally, the circulation, both domestic and foreign, was made up of silver."—Dr. O. J. Broch, "French Report of Mon. Conf. of 1881," 1, p. 39.

[3] Cf. also chap. viii, § 6.

In proportion as gold found a market, silver was deprived of one, since they were both in use for the same purpose.

§ 4. The operation of this cause, which has thus been only generally stated, may now be traced more in detail in each of the monetary events which have happened since 1850; and I trust that the grounds for my conclusion may be clearly seen in the history of these last thirty-five years.

The first in the series of events, after the action of the United States in 1853, caused by the new gold was the displacement of silver by gold in France as early as 1865. The willingness of France to take gold and give up silver sustained the value of the former, and to the same extent deprived the latter of a market. In other words, France, from 1853 to 1865, first began the movement in Europe against silver; and the latter would at that time have felt the effects of this change in demand by a fall in value, had not the exceptional circumstances connected with the "cotton famine" in England, and the extraordinary shipments of silver to India from 1861 to 1866, served to find a new market to counterbalance the loss of an old one.

In the whole progress of this monetary revolution caused by the new gold, whenever the substitution of gold for silver in the West threw an amount of surplus silver on the market, the part played by the Indian demand[1] was only so far important that, as the market successively failed in the West, the East was anxiously watched by dealers in silver to see how far it could take the surplus off the market and permanently absorb it. It was as if the horses, which may have been thrown out of use by the building of a railway in the United States, should have been shipped off to South America for

---

[1] "Although the metallic drain to the East is composed principally of silver, the efflux—at least in its present proportions—is not the less certainly the consequence of the increased production of gold, for the silver of which it consists has been displaced from the currencies of Europe and America by the gold of Australia and California, and the drain to the East is only not a golden one, because silver alone is in that region the recognized standard."—Cairnes, "Essays in Political Economy," p. 99.

THE CAUSE OF THE FALL IN THE VALUE OF SILVER. 171

sale in countries where railways had not yet taken away the use of wagons for transportation. But if the South American market should have become sated, the price of horses in the United States formerly used in transportation would fall, and fall in proportion to the curtailed demand at home. India and the East, therefore, play the part in this movement of silver as a drainage-ground for the West; the question always is whether the East can absorb as fast as the West produces or discards silver.

As we have said, France began the march away from silver to gold (unless we place the United States ahead in 1853). In 1867 the International Monetary Conference, in its recorded preference for the single gold standard, but expressed the universal tendencies of commercial nations at that time. When Germany anticipated France[1] in establishing a single gold standard in 1871-1873, thus following the advice of the Conference of 1867 in that respect, another mass of silver was thrown on the world's hands. Could this sum be drained off to the East? As we have seen, by 1870 India could not take as much silver as before, owing to its indebtedness to England. The value of silver accordingly began to fall; but it fell not in proportion to the sales[2] of silver by Germany (for the price did not rise when the sales stopped),

---

[1] "M. Chevalier appears to assume that, when the process now [1860] going on in France is completed, all further substitution of one metal for another will be at an end, and that the action of future supplies, concentrated on gold alone, will tell in the depreciation of this metal with proportionate effect. But we question the correctness of this assumption. We are inclined to think that the substitution of gold for silver in France is only a very striking example of a process which has been in unobserved operation over a much wider area, and which will continue after the French movement has ceased. In India, where there is an immense silver currency, the process has already begun, and signs are not wanting that it will soon assume more important dimensions."—Cairnes, "Essays in Political Economy," p. 144.

[2] The sales of silver by Germany, taken by themselves, can not be said to be the chief cause of the depreciation in silver, because other events must have had greater importance. Between 1871 and 1879 the production of silver amounted to $750,000,000; the sale of India Council Bills to $500,000,000; while the sales by Germany in all only rose to $141,000,000.

but in such a determined headlong descent, when in 1874 the Latin Union suspended free coinage of silver, as to indicate fear so very decided that it could have had its roots only in some deeper reason than the actual demonetization of silver. That is, the German sales did not much depress silver; but when, in addition to the German monetary reform, the whole Latin Union decided to give up silver rather than lose their gold, it became clear that the new gold had begun to have its perfect work. I can not think that the fall of silver is to be attributed to the action of Germany alone, or to the suspension of silver coinage by the Latin Union alone (but if to any one thing alone, then chiefly to the action of the Latin Union); but to the displacement of silver by the new gold, which had by this time accumulated momentum enough to reach a large mass of the silver currency of Europe, and so to disclose what was to be the tendency of things in modern states. To assign the incentive to Germany is to ignore the real, and to magnify the indirect or secondary, cause. During a recent hurricane in a small village a man in the street was overwhelmed by the flying timbers of a house and instantly killed. If it had been said that the man came to his death by a piece of falling timber, the statement would have been correct, but it would not have given the true cause, which was that the man came to his death by the hurricane. If he had not been killed by that one piece of timber, he would have been by any one of several others, all of which had been set in motion by the original disturbing cause, the hurricane. So in regard to the fall of silver after the demonetization by Germany. It might be said that in 1872 and 1873 the fall began; this forced the Latin Union to suspend coinage; and so it may be said that silver fell because Germany demonetized silver. And the answer is true; but true only in so far as it was true to say that the man above referred to was killed by a piece of timber. If we stop there the whole truth is not told. We need to be told that the hurricane set the timbers in motion; so we need to be told that the new gold set in motion a displacement of silver, which must con-

CHART XIV.

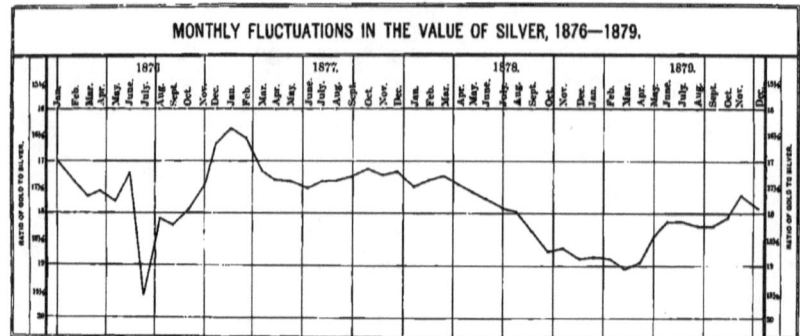

tinue as long as any surplus gold remained; and that as this new supply made it possible for Germany to put herself on an equal basis of gold with commercial states like England and the United States, and to satisfy the universal preference for gold, it left the discarded silver to find its own market; that, as a consequence of there being no unlimited absorptive power in India, this silver (or the possible rather than the actual amount) fell with a heavy weight on its own market and depressed the price.

The action of the Latin Union in 1874 and in 1878 was only a further register of events of the same kind; inasmuch as it meant that states which held large amounts of silver, and so would have done what they could for the maintenance of its value on selfish grounds, had decided to keep possession of their gold. It meant that there was no longer any market whatever for silver in Europe. The territory formerly occupied by silver was invaded by gold (first Germany, and then the Latin Union), and silver was obliged to retreat either to India and the East, or submit to a feeble decline from lack of attention. Just in proportion as the gold, augmented in quantity since 1850, covered more territory, in that proportion silver was shut off from gaining nourishment for its life from that district, and obliged to subsist on a narrower space; and now that space seems to be narrowing still more. The general influence of these causes may, therefore, be seen not merely in the sudden fall of silver in 1876, but in the subsequent downward tendency of the value of silver after 1876, as shown in Chart XIV. This chart shows the monthly fluctuations[1] of silver from the beginning of 1876 to the end of 1879. It will be noticed that the general movement of which I have been speaking, not manifesting itself in one event, but in many, has not felt the influence of a single counteracting cause like that of the attempt of the United States in 1878 to uphold the price of silver by passing the Bland-Allison Bill.

All the appeals of later days for bimetallism have united in demanding a remonetization of silver by all the above-

---

[1] For the figures see Appendix II, E and F.

mentioned countries, in order to reinvigorate the value of silver. Things, however, can not go back to the former status unless we eradicate the preference for gold, and annihilate the enormous production of gold in the last thirty-five years. The countries having gold do not complain of any disadvantage in their situation; it is the countries like France and the United States, which, having silver to dispose of and to protect, want something to be done to save them from the loss due to the late depreciation. The drift of events, in my judgment, is against them, and they must suffer for their lack of foresight in not avoiding their present predicament.

Of course, the natural result of this neglect of silver as a medium of exchange is to turn all eyes toward gold, and to consider whether there is enough gold for all countries should they all adopt the single gold standard. I shall not attempt to answer that question here. My object now is only to discover what has been the cause of the late fall in the value of silver; but a *résumé* of the series of events which I have described in Part II as acting on the value of silver may profitably be arranged in the following form [000,000 omitted]:

Date.	EVENTS.	Gold.		Silver.	
		Demand.	Supply.	Demand.	Supply.
1816....	England established single gold standard.................	[$125]			
1850–64..	France exchanges silver for gold.	1,163			$345
1867....	International Monetary Conference favored single gold standard.................				
1871–73..	Germany exchanged silver for gold.....................	414			141 [270]
1852–75..	India absorbed both gold and silver....................	440		$1,000	
1874....	Latin Union suspended coinage of silver.................				
	Denmark and Scandinavia......				9
1871–76..	Production of silver in United States in excess of previous average production, 1871–76...				100
	Total..................	$2,017		$1,000	$595
	Addition of gold, 1850–1876....		$3,000		
	Addition of silver, 1850–1876...				$1,200

This statement, therefore, leaves about $1,000,000,000 of the new gold mined from 1850 to 1875 still to be accounted [1] for, and which might have been absorbed into already existing gold currencies to satisfy any needs arising from the growth of commerce not met by the growth of banking devices. This showing does not indicate a "gold famine" at present, although, on the other hand, it discloses a large surplus of about $800,000,000 of silver left to find a place in the market.

[1] The amount of $125,000,000 claimed by Mr. Horton as constituting a new demand I do not admit as such; but I insert it in brackets in the table as a matter which has been considered as a new demand. Likewise, in the case of Germany, I insert the whole possible supply of silver in brackets. I need scarcely add that this table does not attempt to do more than approximate to the actual state of things about 1876; but yet I believe it gives the general situation with sufficient exactness to serve our purpose.

PART III.

THE UNITED STATES, 1873–1885.

PART III.
THE UNITED STATES, 1873-1885.

CHAPTER XIII.

SILVER LEGISLATION IN 1878.

§ 1. WE now take up the story of the double standard in the United States where we left it after the passage of the act of 1873, by which the coinage of the silver dollar was discontinued.

As after the legislation of 1853, so for a time after the legislation of 1873, there was complete acquiescence in the result. Our country was still laboring under the burdens of a depreciated paper, and gold was not in circulation except for the payment of customs; so that neither the silver dollar, which was worth more than a gold dollar, nor the gold pieces could have been in circulation concurrently with the depreciated United States notes. The acquiescence in the dropping of the silver dollar from our list of coins has been sometimes attributed to the fact that we had only a paper medium, and that no attention was ever paid to the relations of gold and silver coins, which were never seen in use. This, however, was not the reason. It was, simply, that the silver dollar was worth more than the gold dollar. There was no urgency whatever manifested to pay, or for the privilege of paying in the future, with the dearest of two legal coins. It was not until the fall of silver in 1875 and 1876 that the first suggestions were made for a recoinage of silver dollars. What is more, paper money still occupied the field in these years, and gold and silver were not yet in circulation. So that it was not because gold and silver were circulating in 1876 that attention was called to the position of our coins established in 1873 any more than that the acquiescence in the act of 1873 had been before due to the presence of paper money and to the absence of a metallic circulation.

§ 2. In our preceding chapters of Part II an attempt was made to point out the events which, since 1850, had affected the value of silver and gold, and to account for the diminished value of silver, which began to fall in 1872, culminated in 1876, and has continued with fluctuations to the present year, 1885. We saw that the new gold had taken away from silver a place for its employment in several states of western Europe; that silver, crowded out by its superior as a medium of exchange, was being abandoned by the chief commercial nations; and that the Latin Union, accustomed as they had been to silver, and holding as they did large amounts of silver, preferred not to give up gold, but had stopped the free coinage of silver in 1874, and wholly ceased to coin it in 1878. What the tendency of the value of silver was, and what the situation was when the United States plunged into the arena, may be seen by Chart XV. The United States took up the cause of silver in 1878, and the chart will show whether the value of silver was affected by this action. In fact, the line continued to drop after 1878 as it had been dropping before. When not a state in Europe dared open its Mint to silver, at this very time [1] the United States stupidly came forward and made the attempt to support the value of silver quite by itself. It is recorded that a very muscular and willing workman, engaged with several others in raising a huge stone to its place by means of ropes and pulleys, observed that the others had suddenly let go their hold on the ropes, and

---

[1] "There is no reason why we should move now, except that given by the man, when met with the question of an irate wife as to why he came home so late at night, who answered, 'Because all other places are shut up.'"—Senator Morrill, "Globe," vol. vii, Part I, 2d session, 45th Congress, p. 616. Hereafter, in speaking of this volume of the "Globe," I shall refer to it as vol. cxxxvi.

CHART XV.

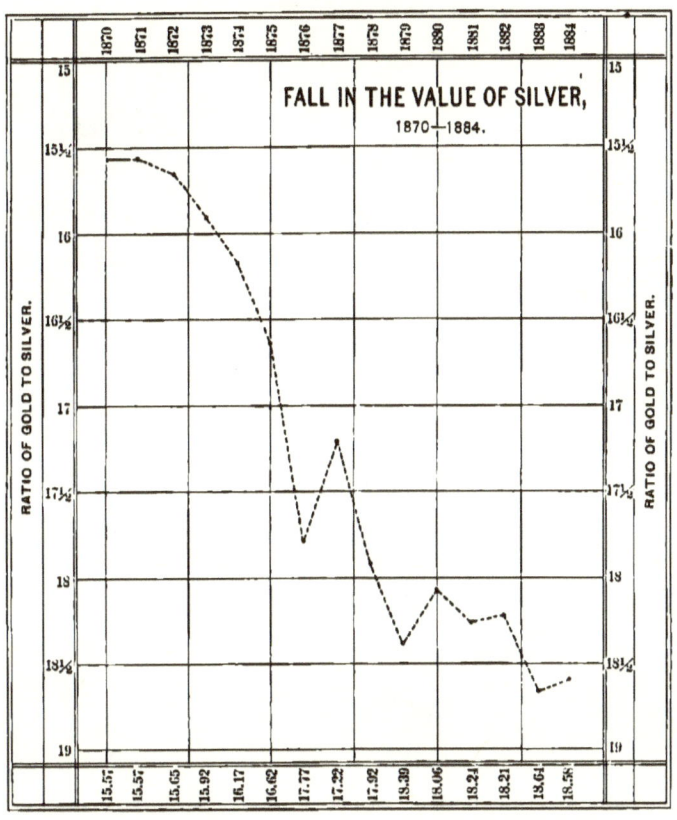

that the heavy mass was beginning to fall; confident of his strength, he by himself laid hold of the rope and tried to sustain the weight by his unaided power. The momentum of the falling stone was more than he could overcome; he was thrown upward, flung to the ground, and injured for life. The action of the United States was of a similar character. It undertook to do what all the rest of the world without us had not been able to do—namely, to keep up the value of silver in the face of the increased supply of gold. We may break the fall of silver, but we shall imperil ourselves. We shall lose by buying millions of a commodity which we must sell at a great sacrifice, the greater as we sell the more. So bold and daring an attempt, so utterly unwarranted by any financial wisdom, seems almost inexplicable to the student of economic history. So extraordinary a piece of legislation, therefore, demands as fair and cool an analysis of the reasons which caused its passage as we are able to give.

§ 3. In the summer[1] of 1876 a crop of silver bills came up in the House. July 18, 1876, Mr. W. D. Kelley introduced[2] a bill to coin the standard silver dollar and to restore its legal-tender character, which was the original of the measure finally passed. A similar bill was introduced[3] by Mr. Bland, July 25, 1876, and vigorously discussed by Mr. Hewitt on August 5th. At the next session of Congress, Mr. Bland reported[4] from the Committee on Mines and Mining, December 12, 1876, his original bill (" H. R. No. 3,635 "), of which the chief sections are as follow:

"Sec. 1. That coin-notes of the denomination of $50, and multiples thereof up to $10,000, may, in the mode hereinafter

---

[1] Mr. Bright (Tennessee) claims that he was the first to call attention to the remonetization of silver in January, 1875. See "Globe," vol. vii, Part I, 2d session, 45th Congress, p. 584.

[2] "Globe," vol. iv, Part V, 1st session, 44th Congress, p. 4704.

[3] "Globe," vol. iv, Part VI, 1st session, 44th Congress, p. 5186. "H. R. Bill No. 3,635."

[4] "Globe," vol. v, Part I, 2d session, 44th Congress, p. 149. It will be noticed that there is a great similarity in the main provision of Mr. Bland's original bill with that which at the present time (fall of 1885) is put forth as the so-called "Warner bill." Both are plans for the issue of bullion certificates.

provided, be paid by the several Mints and assay-offices . . . for the net value of gold and silver bullion deposited thereat; and of the bullion thus received not less than 75 per cent in coin or fine bars shall at all times be kept on hand for redemption of the coin-notes, gold for gold and silver for silver. The gold deposited shall be computed at its coining value, and silver at the rate of 412·8 grains standard silver to the dollar. . . .

"SEC. 4. That the coin-notes issued under the provisions of this act shall be receivable without limit for all dues to the United States; and the coin mentioned in this act shall be a legal tender for all debts of the United States, public and private, not specified to be paid in gold coin.

"SEC. 5. That the gold-coin notes issued under this act shall be redeemed on presentation in gold coin or fine bars, and silver in silver dollars or fine bars."

This bill, it will be observed, aimed rather at the unlimited issue of coin-notes, based on a fixed silver standard. But he also proposed at the same time the following substitute, which was declared to be the same as that introduced by Mr. Kelley (now numbered "H. R. No. 4,189"):

"*Be it enacted*, etc., That there shall be from time to time coined at the Mints of the United States silver dollars of the weight of 412½ grains standard silver to the dollar, as provided for in the act of January 18, 1837, and that said dollar shall be a legal tender for all debts, public and private, except where payment of gold coin is required by law."

The next day, December 13, 1876, the substitute[1] was adopted and passed by a vote of 167 to 53. The previous question being ordered, all amendments were prevented, and the debate was limited to two hours.[2] It will be seen, there-

---

[1] "I confess that I am in favor of the bill as originally introduced. I agree that the certificates authorized to be issued for bullion deposited in the Treasury would take the place of your national bank-notes."—Bland, "Globe," vol. v, Part I, 2d session, 44th Congress, p. 172.

[2] "I suppose that the officer of the United States Army who had charge of the excavations at Hell Gate, an hour before the explosion, could have given you the lay of the ground on every square foot of Hell Gate ledge; . . . but if he had pretended to tell any one, just after the explosion occurred, how the ledge lay, how deep the water was, and what the situation of the channel was in regard to navigation, he would have proved himself a charlatan and a cheat. . . . But there has been an explosion under the silver question as it stands related to gold—an explosion as much greater than the explosion under Hell Gate ledge

fore, that there was no intention whatever in the House to permit the measure to be debated. The bill, however, received no attention from the Senate during this session, and further consideration of it was, therefore, postponed to another session of Congress.

The following autumn the Kelley bill, slightly altered, was again introduced in the House (as "H. R. No. 1,093") by Mr. Bland, and, under a suspension of the rules, was passed[1] without debate, November 5, 1877, by a vote of 163 to 34. The bill which then passed the House and was sent to the Senate read as follows:

"*Be it enacted*, etc., That there shall be coined at the several Mints of the United States silver dollars of the weight of 412½ grains troy of standard silver, as provided in the act of January 18, 1837, on which shall be the devices and superscriptions provided by said act; which coins, together with all silver dollars heretofore coined by the United States of like weight and fineness, shall be a legal tender, at their nominal value, for all debts and dues, public and private, except where otherwise provided by contract; and any owner of silver bullion may deposit the same at any United States coinage-mint or assay-office to be coined into such dollars, for his benefit, upon the same terms and conditions as gold bullion is deposited for coinage under existing laws.

"Sec. 2. All acts and parts of acts inconsistent with the provisions of this act are hereby repealed."

The bill reached the Senate December 6, 1877, was made the special order for December 11th, and thereafter received prolonged and full debate. In the Senate the bill was in charge of Mr. Allison, of the Committee on Finance, who

---

as the continents of Europe, Asia, and America are greater than Hell Gate itself.... Now ... it is proposed, in the hot haste of a two hours' debate, under the tyranny of the previous question—the two hours being parceled out into fragments of five or ten minutes apiece—it is proposed in this chamber that we settle this world-wide question and determine it to-day."—Garfield, ibid., p. 167. For the names of the voters, see ibid., p. 172.

[1] Among those who voted Yea were: Bland, Buckner, Carlisle, Conger, J. D. Cox, S. S. Cox, Crittenden, Ewing, Foster, Goode, Hubbell, Hunton, Keifer, Kelley, Knott, McKinley, McMahon, Morrison, Reagan, Springer, Vance. Nay: Chittenden, Claflin, Frye, Gibson, A. S. Hewitt, Morse. See "Globe," vol. vi, 1st session, 45th Congress, p. 241.

reported the bill with important amendments, the chief of which was that one taking away from the House bill the provision granting free coinage. The last clause of the first section of the House bill (beginning "and any owner of silver bullion") was struck out, and the following words were finally inserted by a vote [1] of 49 to 22:

"And the Secretary of the Treasury is authorized and directed to purchase, from time to time, silver bullion at the market price thereof, not less than two million dollars' worth per month, nor more than four million dollars' worth per month, and cause the same to be coined monthly, as fast as so purchased, into such dollars ; and a sum sufficient to carry out the foregoing provisions of this act is hereby appropriated out of any money in the Treasury not otherwise appropriated. And any gain or seigniorage arising from this coinage shall be accounted for and paid into the Treasury, as provided under existing laws relative to the subsidiary coinage : *Provided*, That the amount of money at any one time invested in such silver bullion, exclusive of such resulting coin, shall not exceed $5,000,000 : *And provided further*, That nothing in this act shall be construed to authorize the payment in silver of certificates of deposit issued under the provisions of Section 254 of the Revised Statutes."

Another important amendment, containing the provision in regard to silver certificates, originated with Mr. Booth (California). In its after-effects this provision proved more effective in carrying out the purposes of the advocates of silver than it was expected, probably, at the time when the bill was passed :

"Sec. 3. That any holder of the coin authorized by this act may deposit the same with the Treasurer or any assistant treasurer of the United States, in sums not less than $10, and receive therefor certificates of not less than $10 each, corresponding with the denominations of the United States notes. The coin deposited for, or representing, the certificates shall be retained in the Treasury for the payment of the same on demand. Said certificates shall be receivable for customs, taxes, and all public dues, and, when so received, may be reissued."

The Senate also inserted a provision for an international

---

[1] Among the nays, as the more extreme silver advocates in the Senate, were Beck, Davis (Ill.), Garland, Jones (Nev.), Thurman, Voorhees.

monetary conference[1] of delegates from European countries to agree upon a common ratio between gold and silver. The provision for silver certificates was adopted, 49 to 15, and the whole bill, as thus amended, passed the Senate, February 15, 1878, by a vote[2] of 48 to 21.

The bill, as amended by the Senate, because of the loss of free coinage, proved very unsatisfactory to the silver party in the House, when it was returned to them for concurrence in the amendments of the Senate. There were many brief protests, but the belief was expressed by the advocates of the bill that it would be well to take what they could get from the Senate without delay, and then in the future try to gain ground by adding more extreme provisions in other bills. The measure was discussed[3] for an hour, and under the previous question was passed as it came from the Senate. The motion to concur in the amendments of the Senate was carried by a vote[4] of 203 to 72. The test vote at this time was on the motion to lay the bill on the table, which was lost by a vote[5] of 71 to 205.

The bill, having passed both Houses, was sent to President Hayes, who returned it, unsigned, February 28, 1878, accompanied by a veto message[6] expressing his objections to

[1] This was passed by a vote of 40-30. An amendment that the coinage of silver dollars should not interfere with the coinage of gold and subsidiary coins was lost, 23-46; to fix the number of standard grains in the dollar at 425, instead of 412½, which was proposed by Mr. Blaine, was lost, 23-46; to make it 440 grains, lost, 18-49; to make it 420 grains, lost, 25-44; to limit the legal-tender power of silver dollars of 412½ grains to $20, lost, 20-46; to exclude payment of duties and interest on the public debt in silver dollars, lost, 18-45. See "Globe," vol. vii, Part II, 2d session, 45th Congress, pp. 1076-1110. Hereafter, in speaking of this volume, I shall refer to it as vol. cxxxvii.

[2] Among the yeas was Mr. Windom, afterward Secretary of the Treasury in 1881.

[3] "Globe," vol. cxxxvii, pp. 1243-1285.

[4] Among the nays on this motion, or those who wanted unlimited coinage were Blackburn, Butler, Carlisle, S. S. Cox, Ewing, Knott, Mills, Reagan, Springer, Vance.

[5] Among the nays were Blackburn, Bland, Buckner, Burchard, Candler, Carlisle, Conger, J. D. Cox, S. S. Cox, Ewing, Foster, Hanna, Hiscock, Hubbell, Hunter, Keifer, Kelley, Mills, Knott, McKinley, Morrison, Reagan, Springer, Tucker, Vance.

[6] "Globe," vol. cxxxvii, pp. 1418, 1419. See, also, *infra*, § 6.

the bill. In the House, on the same day, the bill was promptly passed by a vote of 196 to 73, being more than the requisite two thirds. On the same day the Senate likewise passed the bill over the veto of the President by a vote of 46 to 19, and it became a law.

§ 4. In order to understand the existence of the party which in 1878 passed the silver bill,[1] it is necessary to keep in view the sequence of financial and political events of the preceding ten years.

The close of the Civil War brought with it the necessity of determining upon some treatment of our depreciated paper and the payment and refunding of our huge national debt. The speculative period following the war, moreover, had been scarcely equaled in our financial history; and when it was followed by the inevitable collapse of credit and prices in 1873, very large numbers of our people were caught in that uncomfortable position in which they were obliged to slowly and painfully pay back that which they had borrowed in a sanguine and speculative mood. The Western States had been largely interested in real estate speculations, and the prosperous years after the war gave them no warning of a coming downfall. The disease had acquired such a hold throughout the country as to demand a long time within which the latent fever should burn itself out and leave the body healthy, even if weak and emaciated. Weighed down by debt, and led by skillful politicians, or impelled by selfish interest, the people of the West demanded that the Government should come to the aid of debtors and, by plentiful issues of United States notes, create an inflation which should enable them to get off the shoals of debt on the high tide of rising prices. This claim of the inflationists was met by the wisdom and intelligence of the community, and a fierce and

---

[1] As it now stands, the act of 1878 ought to be called the Allison bill, because his amendments changed its whole character. As it originated in the House and was first introduced by Mr. Kelley, it might properly be known as the Kelley-Allison bill; but as it was under the charge of Mr. Bland in the House, it may be well to accept the common usage, and speak of it as the "Bland bill."

hot contest was waged, which resulted in the defeat of the former, and the veto of their bill by President Grant in 1874. This victory was followed up by the Resumption Act in 1875. Then, when, after our bonds had been mostly refunded under the act of 1870, it became also settled that the principal and interest of the Government obligations should be paid in coin, the threat of inflation from United States notes seemed to have been averted. But, although the inflationists were defeated, the conditions yet existed which produced the original inflation party. There were the demagogues, and there were the debtors. From 1876 to 1878, during which the silver discussions continued, therefore, we shall find it necessary to take into account the existence of the old inflation party if we hope to get a rational explanation of the purpose of the legislation adopted in 1878.

There was another, but related, influence also which had no little force. The older portions of the United States have naturally been the richest in accumulations of capital; the newer portions have naturally been the borrowers. Vast sums, consequently, were invested by the States of the East in railways, buildings, and all the interests of a fertile country like the West, in loans to counties and townships, while insurance companies and individuals loaned money secured by mortgages on Western farms. When the crisis of 1873 came, and debtors, having spent all the borrowed capital, were confronted with the dreary necessity of paying back all they had received, there arose a feeling (utterly irrational, but nevertheless quite human) that the creditor was cruel if he demanded his own again. On this account there was, without doubt, a very serious friction in the relations between the loaning and the borrowing States. This passed away in later years, to some extent, as the prosperity of the West allowed them to pay their indebtedness; but, at the time of which we are writing, the ancient antagonism between the debtor and creditor class was distinctly marked out, not merely between different classes, but between different sections of the country. This state of affairs was eagerly seized upon by ambitious politicians, and, in their desire to represent their constituencies, they outbid each other for favor by exaggerated appeals to this class and sectional feeling—a feeling, too, not founded on very high standards of honesty. One who has the patience to follow through the voluminous and exhausting debates of Congress during the silver discussions of 1878 must see that this factor of which I am speaking had a very important place. We may be ashamed of it, but it was true. And without an understanding of this factor it is quite impossible to comprehend the tone of the majority of arguments urged in favor of the silver bill. Among other things, for example, it was said that we should soon hear "the maddened roar of labor sounding like a trumpet-blast of prophecy."

§ 5. It is scarcely too much to say that the demand for the coinage of silver dollars began where the cry for unlimited paper money left off. The movement which resulted in the act of 1878 was but another manifestation of the same desires which led to the hot and fierce debates between the inflationists and contractionists. The evidence of this, it seems to me, is undeniable to any one who will examine the reasons urged in favor of the Bland bill in the debates of Congress. At the same time that this measure was before the country a bill was passed in the House to repeal the Resumption Act. Not, of course, that every member who voted for the silver dollar was opposed to resumption; but it was unmistakable evidence of the opinions of the majority. The debtor class were catered to, and the prejudices of class feeling invoked in favor of the Bland bill as they had been in earlier years in favor of worthless paper.

The silver advocates were largely the advocates of expansion. Said Mr. Ewing[1] in the House: "Mr. Speaker, nine tenths of the people of the United States demand the unlimited coinage of the old silver dollar with which to pay their debts and conduct their business. . . . The country is

---

[1] "Globe," vol. cxxxvii, pp. 1263, 1264.

in an agony of business distress, and looks for some relief by a gradual increase of the currency. The House bill authorized not only unlimited coinage, but coinage of silver bullion owned by citizens for immediate use in business." "If these questions are not settled," urged another member,[1] "and settled at once or before this present Congress adjourns, I say to those gentlemen that from the districts of the West and South will come a class of men who will demand, not only that silver shall be remonetized, and that the Resumption Act shall be repealed, but that the national banking law shall be repealed, and the Government of the United States shall issue all the money to be in circulation in this country." An answering echo came from the Senate:[2] "In many sections of the country it is now questionable whether, under the most favorable conditions we can hope for in the future, there can be any escape from the embarrassments that surround the debtor class except through bankruptcy. . . . In view, then, of the condition of affairs, it seems to me that any measure that tends in any degree to uphold the value of property, or to prevent its further depreciation, ought to meet the support and concurrence of all." When the bill came back from the Senate a Southern member[3] disclosed his position very clearly: "Let us force a square issue and make every one array himself either on the side of God or Mammon—the people or the gold ring. . . . The people are in no humor to be trifled with, and a veto would prove a blessing if it would have the effect I believe it would—namely, to arouse a storm which would compel a complete remonetization of silver and the repeal of the Resumption Act." Another avowal[4] was quite as frank: "I heartily sympathize with the objects of this bill in remonetizing the silver dollar and thus increasing the volume of our circulating medium." But, perhaps, the coarsest ex-

---

[1] Tipton (Illinois), ibid., p. 602.
[2] McDonald (Indiana), "Globe," vol. cxxxvi, pp. 957, 958.
[3] Turner (Georgia), "Globe," vol. cxxxvii, p. 1278.
[4] Henderson (Illinois), ibid., p. 1279.

pression of this sentiment was reserved for the lips of Mr. Bland,[1] who declared: "I give notice here and now that this war shall never cease, so long as I have a voice in this Congress, until the rights of the people are fully restored and the silver dollar shall take its place alongside the gold dollar. Meanwhile let us take what we have and supplement it immediately on appropriation bills, and, if we can not do that, I am in favor of *issuing paper money enough to stuff down the bondholders until they are sick* [Applause]."

Much more evidence could be cited, if more were necessary, to show that, in the minds of a very large number of men who urged the passage of the Bland bill, there was a hope that they might expand the currency by its provisions; and even that silver dollars would be extensively added to the circulation and create the same effects. In fact, Mr. Bland's original bill aimed rather at an issue of a new kind of legal-tender paper, limited only by the quantity of silver bullion capable of deposit, than at the legitimate union of gold and silver at a ratio which, in the beginning at least, should assure their concurrent circulation.

In fact, one is struck, on every page of the debates, with the radically different temper in which the subject of the coinage was treated in 1878 from that shown in 1853, or even in 1792. There is not a shadow of a doubt that, had silver not fallen in value in 1876, so that a dollar of silver had not become worth much less than a gold or paper dollar —and so afforded a new device for meeting existing debts, which at the same time was technically coin—we should never have heard much of the silver agitation.[2] It was born of a desire for a cheap unit in which to liquidate indebtedness.

---

[1] "Globe," vol. cxxxvii, p. 1250.

[2] The "Cincinnati Gazette," in June, 1877, said: "This notion got a start and great momentum from the apparent showing that it was cheaper than the greenback dollar. The promise of a specie dollar for payment of the bondholder and of all the 'creditor class,' cheaper than payment in legal-tender notes, was too captivating not to be received with great favor in this country, where every man is a financier and thinks that the way to pay debts is by fabricating currency."

And the demand for the free coinage of a dollar containing only ninety cents of intrinsic value received the support of all who had before marched in the ranks of the inflationists. Silver had got into politics, and was henceforth discussed politically, not scientifically.

But others, forming a smaller class, supported this measure in the belief that, even if silver had fallen in value, it was just and right to issue a coin which was of the same weight and fineness as that demonetized in 1873, and to allow debtors to pay in this money. These were persons who probably did not subscribe to the tenets of the paper-money inflationists, and honestly could not see that the arguments against cheap paper had any force in regard to an issue of coin, even if it had fallen in value. The wrong in a ninety-cent silver dollar was not apparent to men who could declare that they were in favor of "hard money." The fact that greenbacks were worth more than the silver in a dollar, and were steadier in value than it, did not affect them. If payment were offered in coin, that, they thought, was enough. This fact that, although a cheap and depreciated dollar was offered to the country, it had been very lately [1] (1873) an unlimited legal tender, and that, as the bill was finally passed, the dollars could not be issued in unlimited quantities, made it very difficult for men who did not thoroughly understand the functions performed by a proper medium of exchange to see their error, or to be convinced of it.[2] They believed that, if it had been right to

---

[1] "By it [act of 1873] one half of our money-metal is virtually abolished, silver money is abrogated, the Government, the several States, territories, cities, all corporations, and the people, are deprived of their right to pay their debts in silver coin."—Senator Merrimon, "Globe," vol. cxxxvi, p. 977.

[2] "But we are told that policy forbids restoring silver to our coinage independent of our legal right; that the quantity of metal which we propose to coin into a dollar is worth but ninety cents in gold, and a depreciation of 10 per cent in all values would follow. This is a queer argument to urge in the face of the fact that worthless paper, bearing the impress of Government authority, with no intrinsic value whatever, by being invested with the functions of money is worth nearly its face value in gold."—Senator Jones (Nevada), "Globe," vol. cxxxvi, p. 440.

pay in gold when it fell in value toward the year 1853, it was right in 1878 to pay in silver when, in turn, it fell in value. In all this class, however, it will be seen that they were influenced by the question of the ability to pay debts and existing contracts; and that they overlooked entirely the original justice of a legal-tender law—namely, that it should secure to the lender at the end of his contract only the same purchasing power[1] which he parted with when the contract was made. Of course, this section of the silver party were quite willing to see only a single standard of silver in the country. They were, therefore, not advocates of a double standard, but of a single standard[2] established in the cheapest metal, as may be seen by this utterance: "Our money system was not based on the idea that we should have both metals always and concurrently in circulation, but upon the idea that there might occur occasional variations in their value, and that it would always be to our advantage in every respect to make avail of the cheaper of the two." [3]

This wing of the silver party, however, urged the unlimited coinage of silver dollars of 412½ grains, but were

---

[1] "If I could sink low enough in my own estimation to be willing to take advantage of my creditor, and insist that it was right for me to pay him but ten cents for the dollar which I honestly owed him ; much more, if, in a legislative body, in making the law, when the question is not what the law *is* but what *it ought to be*, I should claim that it would be right or proper for me to aid in passing such a law to enable me and all other dishonest debtors to justify our dishonesty under the legal power conferred by such an act, and thus to encourage dishonesty, I should feel that all men would have the right to say of me that, but for the restraint of the law, I could be a knave and criminal."—Senator Christiancy, "Globe," vol. cxxxvi, p. 668.

[2] "But it is urged that if we remonetize silver, it, being the cheaper, will drive gold out of the country. Suppose it does; if, as is predicted by the enemies of the bill, silver will flood the country, and we pay all our debts with silver, both public and private, if this bill should become a law, where is the injury to the nation or the citizens thereof ? But it is not true that gold would be driven out. Why does it not have that effect in France ? Why did it not have that effect from the foundation of the Government down to the date of its demonetization ? "—Senator Hereford, "Globe," vol. cxxxvi, p. 205.

[3] Senator Jones, of Nevada, "Globe," vol. cxxxvii, p. 1080.

not in favor of a silver dollar containing more grains, which would bring its value more nearly to that of gold or paper. The free coinage of the silver dollar would have given to each man who brought silver bullion to the Mint the benefit of the whole difference between the intrinsic value of $412\frac{1}{2}$ grains of silver and the nominal legal-tender power given it by its face value; and this difference was to be used by any debtor to deliver himself from his obligations to just that amount without returning to his creditor any purchasing power therefor. This was repudiation of debts on a scale to the dollar marked by the descent in the intrinsic value of silver below its face value. Of course, there was no question as to the power of Congress to create a dollar of silver worth only ninety cents in gold; but, inasmuch as Congress was the lawmaking branch, it was their duty to consider not merely what they could[1] do, but what they ought to do, in view of all the demands of strict justice and honor.

Another influential section which was actively supporting the bill was made up chiefly of Senators (and their followers in the House) whose constituents were interested in silver mines. These men urged the silver bill exactly after the manner in which legislation was urged in protection of other special industries.[2] It was urged that the Government should aid

---

[1] "These rights depend on the law; the law is their definition and measure; and whatever dealings with them on our part are lawful must be right, and therefore honorable."—Senator Morgan, "Globe," vol. cxxxvi, p. 140.

[2] "It seems to me, however, that these gentlemen overlook the fact that the object in remonetizing the silver dollar is not alone to furnish money for the payment of the public debt. The main purpose is to arrest the movements inaugurated in Europe, and blindly followed in this country, to destroy a great part of the wealth of mankind. . . . The remonetization of silver aims at the restoration of commerce, manufactures, agriculture, and all our industries to their former prosperous state."—Senator Bailey, "Globe," vol. cxxxvi, p. 306. State aid was also appealed to by Senator Merrimon (North Carolina), ibid., p. 978. "This silver mania . . . seems to me to be a very peculiar disease. . . . Its intensity seems to be manifested very nearly in proportion to the proximity of the victims to the great bonanza mines. . . . It seems to have passed to the people, attacking with most severity those most deeply in debt."—Senator Christiancy, "Globe," vol. cxxxvi, p. 667. "It is needed to utilize our vast

the owners of mines in keeping up the value of silver. "I think, too, that, as silver is a product of our own country . . . it is proper that we should do whatever is well calculated to encourage its production and increase the demand for it," said Senator Hill, of Georgia. A member[1] of the House from Kentucky declared : " Our Western States and Territories are rich in silver ore. Let us remonetize silver and thereby increase the production of this metal." While a Western Congressman[2] urged : " I am also in favor of restoring silver because silver is a product of this country, and it would give it increased value to make it a legal tender. . . . Are we to allow the designing legislation of 1873 to further depreciate the value of one of our most valuable products? . . . Our mining interests have been very much embarrassed for the last few years because of this legislation."

In close alliance with this body came another class, who argued that silver had not fallen in value, but that gold had risen[3] in value, and that a dollar of 412½ grains was a just means of payment for all indebtedness. This section of the silver party displayed very much more ability than the ordinary advocate, and on questions of statistics showing a fall of prices since 1873 they were easily able to surround their position with plausible facts and arguments. Senator Matthews[4] took the following position :

---

silver mines, to employ our mining labor, and to turn the silver streams into the channels of trade. It is needed for the encouragement of our languishing industries and the employment of our starving laborers."—Bright, "Globe," vol. cxxxvi, p. 585.

[1] Durham, "Globe," vol. cxxx, December 13, 1876.
[2] Landers (Indiana), ibid., p 165.
[3] Senator Withers held that contraction had led to the panic of 1873. "Following upon this was the additional contraction caused by the act of 1873 demonetizing silver, thus reducing at once by about one half the capacity of the country to pay the bonds, depreciating largely the value of silver, and, as a natural consequence, enhancing the value of gold—all of which inured directly to the interest of the bondholder, and added from 8 to 10 per cent to the value of the bonds."—" Globe," vol. cxxxvi, pp. 849, 850. Cf. also Willard (Michigan), " Globe," vol. cxxx, p. 165.
[4] December 10, 1877, "Globe," vol. cxxxvi, p. 91.

"Then, I answer, and it can be demonstrated by an impregnable array of facts, that silver can to-day buy more of every other known product of human labor than it could in July, 1870, gold alone excepted; lands, houses, stocks of merchandise, machinery, labor, everything but gold; here, elsewhere. In Asia, in Europe, throughout the whole Continent, nowhere, measured by the average price of the general commodities of the world, has silver depreciated the breadth of a hair. . . ."

Mr. Eaton: ". . . That it can buy more land in America to-day than it could in 1870 undoubtedly is true, but less abroad."

Mr. Matthews: "What have we got to do with 'abroad'? . . . Who does not know that there is and has been throughout this country, throughout Great Britain, throughout Germany, throughout France, throughout Austria, throughout Italy, throughout the civilized world, everywhere, a most extraordinary depression in values for the last four years? And there is no cause that prevails as generally as that effect, and adequate to account for it, but the blindness of that conspiracy which has sought to exalt gold as the god and king of money."

The most zealous advocate, however, of the theory that gold had risen in value was Senator Jones, of Nevada, who quoted tables [1] of prices from 1872 to 1876 to show that general prices had fallen from 19 to 25 per cent. Then, as he found that silver had fallen only 10 per cent relatively to gold, he argued that silver had even appreciated [2] in value, instead

---

[1] "Globe," vol. cxxxvii, pp. 1017-1026. He quoted a table in the New York "Public" of May 18, 1876.

[2] "I do not hesitate to affirm that an examination of all the facts bearing upon the case . . . will demonstrate that gold again began to rise about ten years ago, and especially about five years ago, as measured by commodities, land, and labor, and that its rise is still unchecked; and that this last rise of gold, as so measured, has been so greatly in excess of its rise as compared with silver as to show that silver has not fallen in value; or, in other words, that the average fall in the gold price of commodities has been so much greater than the fall in the gold price of silver as to make the conclusion irresistible that silver, instead of having depreciated in value during the last few years, has actually appreciated, though not to the same extent as gold."—"Globe," vol. cxxxvii, p. 1019. The inconsistency of this position with that of most advocates of remonetization was distinctly pointed out by another Senator: "But, notwithstanding it is so evident and so generally admitted that the demonetization of silver, by checking a demand for it, reduced its price and increased the demand for, and the price of, gold, the argument is now started that the whole

of having fallen in value, relatively to all other commodities. This was an untenable ground, as we saw, by the comparison of prices collected from the London "Economist," in our last chapter,[1] that prices were as high in 1877 as they had been in 1867. But we do know, and every one admits, that since 1873 there had been a very marked fall in prices until 1880. The conclusion, however, that this was due to the contraction of metallic currency caused by the demonetization of silver, is a complete *non sequitur*. It overlooks one of the most important factors in regulating prices; for it ignores the collapse of credit and the fall of prices which inevitably follows in the wake of any financial crisis, and which continues until liquidation of debts arising from the speculative basis of preceding years has been somewhat completed. A fall of prices due to an enfeebled state of credit, one very important part of purchasing power, can take place without any change whatever in the quantity of the metallic medium in a country. It is, therefore, perfectly true that after the panic of 1873 prices slowly fell as liquidation went on, and that a gold dollar could buy more in 1879 than in 1872; but it was not necessarily due to any cause which affected that one factor in the exchange, gold, but to changes in the other factors. Moreover, changes which reduced the cost of production of all kinds of goods came thick and fast, and lessened the price of goods exchanged against gold without changing the absolute position of gold. That this altered the situation unfavorably to debtors is admitted; but it is an alteration of a kind which regularly happens after every unfortunate business revulsion, such as occurred in 1857 and 1866, and is no ground for talking about a cause which is supposed to be operating on gold (when it is operating on the things for which gold is exchanged).

A very large number of our legislators were, no doubt,

---

effect of the demonetization of silver was to leave silver exactly where it was, and to elevate the price and value of gold."—Senator Christiancy, "Globe," vol. cxxxvi, p. 794.

[1] Page 163.

honestly impressed with the belief that the mere gift of legal-tender power to a silver dollar worth only ninety cents, and its remonetization, would so increase its value that it would very soon become equal to the gold dollar. This was a constant and favorite argument.[1] Said Senator Allison: "Legislation gives value to the precious metals, and the commercial value simply records the condition of legislation with reference to the precious metals." It was even urged by Senator Thurman[2] that the remonetization of silver by the United States alone would stop the tendency to give up silver in other States, and would raise the value of 412½ grains of silver to the level of the gold dollar. Subsequent events did not justify this sanguine hope, as may be seen by reference to Chart XIV, showing the fluctuations and fall of silver since 1878. It was believed by many that the action of Germany alone had caused the fall of silver; and, ignorant of the fundamental forces which had shown themselves in the single case of Germany, and would have broken out elsewhere if Germany had not acted, they held that the coinage of silver by the United States would exactly fill the breach made by the withdrawal of Germany. An inspection of Chart XIII will show how fundamental a change was going on in the value of silver since 1870 as compared with the whole course of its history since 1687. It was hardly likely that a single event, such as the action of the United States, could stop so marked a fall.

Some astounding ignorance of monetary principles was, of course, exhibited. "It is said that if we authorize the coining of silver of 412½ grains to the dollar the effect will be to drive gold from the country. I deny[3] this utterly."

---

[1] Senator Wallace said: "If we coin annually one half of the world's supply of silver, its rise in value is inevitable."—"Globe," vol. cxxxvi, p. 641. Similarly Hill (Georgia), ibid., p. 850. Allison thought that the United States with the Latin Union might restore silver to its former value. "If we restore silver, shall we not practically place in circulation and in use an equivalent of the amount of silver demonetized by the action of the German Government?"— "Globe," vol. cxxxvi, p. 175.

[2] "Globe," vol. cxxxvi, pp. 786-788.

[3] Senator Johnston (Virginia), "Globe," vol. cxxxvi, p. 823.

The operation of Gresham's law was not even admitted, because, forsooth, silver was not an "inferior" currency.[1] A common fallacy, too, was that, if A owned silver bullion and had it coined at the Mint, where free coinage was allowed, a debtor B who owed a creditor C could thereby come into possession[2] of A's dollars by a miracle, and have as many dollars as he wanted. A wholesome reply to this was given[3] by Senator Bayard:

"It can not be that the laboring class are the debtor class. On the contrary, as I say, there is not a day in the year when the sun goes down when they are not the creditors of capital for the amount of their wages for that time. ... So I say, considering the great fact that each man in the community sustains the relation of creditor as well as debtor, that if he can pay his debts in this depreciated money he will be paid himself in the same money, nothing can be made of it that I can understand, excepting that a class of people who, having purchased property at exaggerated prices and finding it now

---

[1] "It is said that an inferior currency always drives away the superior, which is true in a measure; but, in my opinion, the argument will not hold good in this instance, because, first, as a currency of general use in the current transactions of trade and barter among the masses, silver is not now, and never has been, inferior to gold; second, supposing it to be the cheaper of the two, it can not drive out the superior until it becomes equal in volume to it, sufficient in quantity to fill up the channels of trade, which is not likely to occur."—Finley, "Globe," vol. cxxxvii, p. 1264.

[2] This is one example of many: "Enact this law and confidence will be restored in the public mind. ... The people of this country, and especially the people of the West, have an abiding confidence that the enactment of a law of this kind will give them not only immediate but permanent relief. ... They understand that every dollar of silver that is coined in this land adds one dollar to the material wealth of the people [!]."—Tipton (Illinois), "Globe," vol. cxxxvi, p. 601. See, also, Senator Jones, vol. cxxxvii, p. 1024. As amusing as any of the bits of rhetoric was that by which Senator Allison, without considering where the value was to come from to be exchanged for the coin, argued that very large sums of silver might be coined because the negroes of the South would take such very large quantities. "Who does not believe that if it is made a legal tender, or rather if silver dollars are coined, these colored people, like the people of China and the East Indies, will hoard this money in considerable sums, so that we shall be able to go on coining at the rate of $30,000,000 per annum for many years to come without disturbing the relative value between gold and silver?"—"Globe," vol. cxxxvi, p. 175.

[3] "Globe," vol. cxxxvi, p. 734.

shrinking in value, may have an opportunity of scaling their debts to the injury, the injustice, of their creditors."

There were, however, men who used this discussion simply as a means to an end, in catching the vulgar ear by buncombe, and went to such an extent as to merit quotation as giving specimens of the humor in the situation. Said one:[1] "Why, Senators, we had acquired Louisiana and Florida, we had carried on a war with Great Britain from 1812 to 1815, when we had hardly any gold coin, *on the credit of the silver dollar.*" Nothing, perhaps, can be better than the following[2] eulogium of a Southern Senator on silver: "It enjoys this natural supremacy among the largest number of people because the laboring people prefer it. They use it freely and confidingly. It is their familiar friend, their boon companion, while gold is a guest to be treated with severest consideration; to be hid in a place of security; not to be expended in the markets and fairs. It is a treasure, and not a tool of trade, with the laboring people. A twenty-dollar gold piece is the nucleus of a fortune, to remain hid until some freak of fortune shall add other prisoners to its cell. But twenty dollars in silver dimes is the joy of the household, 'the substance of things hoped for, the evidence of things not seen.' . . . Silver is to the great arteries of commerce what the mountain-springs are to the rivers. It is the stimulant of industry and production in the thousands of little fields of enterprise which in the aggregate make up the wealth of the nation." If anything could equal this, it was the utterance[3] of a well-known Northern Senator, Mr. Blaine:

---

[1] Beck, "Globe," vol. cxxxvi, p. 257.

[2] Morgan (Alabama), "Globe," vol. cxxxvi, p. 143.

[3] "Globe," vol. cxxxvi, p. 822. Mr. Blaine believed that the double standard was established by the Constitution! "No power was conferred on Congress to declare that either metal should not be money. Congress has, therefore, in my judgment, no power to demonetize silver any more than to demonetize gold; no power to demonetize either any more than to demonetize both. . . . If, therefore, silver has been demonetized, I am in favor of remonetizing it." But he urged a dollar of 425 grains standard silver, instead of 412½ grains, worth in 1878 only 93 cents in gold. "I think now very clearly, with the light before me, that it [the act of 1873] was a great blunder."—"Globe," vol. cxxxvii, p. 1063.

"Ever since we demonetized the old dollar we have been running our Mints at full speed, coining a new silver dollar [trade dollar] for the use of the Chinese cooly and the Indian pariah—a dollar containing 420 grains of standard silver, with its superiority over our ancient dollar ostentatiously engraved on its reverse side. . . . And shall we do less for the American laborer at home? . . . It will read strangely in history that the weightier and more valuable of these dollars is made for an ignorant class of heathen laborers in China and India, and that the lighter and less valuable is made for the intelligent and educated laboring-man who is a citizen of the United States."

The aristocratic character of the yellow metal is thus[1] well defined: "Gold is the money of monarchs; kings covet it; the exchanges of nations are effected by it. Its tendency is to accumulate in vast masses in the commercial centers, and to move from kingdom to kingdom in such volumes as to unsettle values and disturb the finances of the world." The following[2] unctuous fondness for silver was put forth by Senator Howe, afterward a delegate to the Monetary Conference of 1878: "But we are told the cheaper metal will drive out the dearer, and gold will be banished from our circulation. Silver will not drive out anything. Silver is not aggressive; it is so much like the apostle's description of wisdom that it is 'first pure, then peaceable, gentle.' . . . Put a silver and a gold dollar into the same purse and they will lie quietly together."

In fine contrast with this spirit was the manly and honest attitude taken by Senator Lamar[3] when his State Legislature in Mississippi instructed him by resolutions "to vote for the acts remonetizing silver and repealing the Resumption Act," and to use his "efforts to secure their passage." He offered to withdraw from public life rather than vote for measures which he deemed to be injurious to the country:

"Mr. President, between these resolutions and my convictions there is a great gulf. I can not pass it. . . . I have always endeavored to impress the belief that truth was better

---

[1] Senator Ingalls, "Globe," vol. cxxxvii, p. 1052.
[2] "Globe," vol. cxxxvi, p. 765.   [3] "Globe," vol. cxxxvii, p. 1061.

than falsehood, honesty better than policy, courage better than cowardice. To-day my lessons confront me. To-day I must be true or false, honest or cunning, faithful or unfaithful to my people. Even in this hour of their legislative displeasure and disapprobation I can not vote as these resolutions direct. I can not and will not shirk the responsibility which my position imposes. My duty, as I see it, I will do, and I will vote against this bill. . . . Then it will be for them to determine if adherence to my honest convictions has disqualified me from representing them."

§ 6. During the passage of the Bland-Allison bill through Congress, Senator Matthews (Ohio) introduced a concurrent resolution on which as much debate was spent as on the Bland bill itself. This resolution [1] aimed to establish the technical right of the United States to pay the principal and interest of its public debt in silver dollars of $412\frac{1}{2}$ grains:

"*Whereas*, By the act entitled 'An act to strengthen the public credit,' approved March 18, 1869, it was provided and declared that the faith of the United States was thereby solemnly pledged to the payment in coin or its equivalent of all the interest-bearing obligations of the United States, except in cases where the law authorizing the issue of such obligations had expressly provided that the same might be paid in lawful money or other currency than gold or silver; and

"*Whereas*, All the bonds of the United States authorized to be issued by the act entitled 'An act to authorize the refunding of the national debt,' approved July 14, 1870, by the terms of said act were declared to be redeemable in coin of'the then present standard value, bearing interest payable semi-annually in such coin; and

"*Whereas*, All bonds of the United States authorized to be issued under the act entitled 'An act to provide for the resumption of specie payments,' approved January 14, 1875, are required to be of the description of bonds of the United

---

[1] Introduced December 6, 1877 ("Globe," vol. cxxxvi, p. 47). Passed the Senate January 25, 1878, by a vote of 43 to 22. Passed House, without debate, January 28th, by a vote of 189 to 79. It was not a party question. It was supported by 116 Democrats and 73 Republicans, and opposed by 23 Democrats and 56 Republicans.

States described in the said act of Congress approved July 14, 1870, entitled 'An act to authorize the refunding of the national debt'; and

"*Whereas*, At the date of the passage of said act of Congress last aforesaid, to wit, the 14th day of July, 1870, the coin of the United States of standard value of that date included silver dollars of the weight of 412½ grains each, declared by the act approved January 18, 1837, entitled 'An act supplementary to the act entitled "An act establishing a Mint and regulating the coins of the United States,"' to be a legal tender of payment according to their nominal value for any sums whatever: Therefore,

"*Be it resolved by the Senate* (*the House of Representatives concurring therein*), That all the bonds of the United States issued, or authorized to be issued, under the said acts of Congress hereinbefore recited, are payable, principal and interest, at the option of the Government of the United States, in silver dollars of the coinage of the United States containing 412½ grains each of standard silver; and that to restore to its coinage such silver coins as a legal tender in payment of said bonds, principal and interest, is not in violation of the public faith, nor in derogation of the rights of the public creditor."

The question of moral and legal right was fully argued[1] by the Senate. There seems to be no doubt as to the technical right of the United States to pay interest and principal of all the public debt in silver, if the Government so chooses. But, on the other hand, it is equally beyond question that resumption of specie payments would have been rendered impossible on January 1, 1879, had it been understood from 1876 to 1878 that "coin" meant silver and not gold; because only on the explicit explanation of the Secretary of the Treasury (John Sherman) that the word "coin" would be interpreted as gold was he able to sell the bonds

---

[1] A speech by Senator Cockrell ("Globe," vol. cxxxvi, pp. 480-491) is a fair example of the arguments for the technical right to pay in silver. See, also, Matthews's speech, ibid., pp. 87-91.

needed to secure a gold reserve for resumption purposes. The passage of the Matthews resolution, in fact, was recognized as part of a plan to scale debts, public and private, by giving free coinage to silver; and, as a consequence, our bonds began to come back from Europe in large quantities. In one week there came an amount of ten millions, and in 1878 it was said by Mr. Allison that one hundred millions had been returned. This action shows distinctly enough whether there had been any tacit understanding in the minds of purchasers of bonds that they expected to be paid in gold.

When the silver bill was vetoed[1] by President Hayes, he urged as his reasons for not giving his assent to it that (1) the proposed dollar was 8 or 10 per cent less in value than it professed to be; that (2) it made the dollar a legal tender for debts contracted when the law did not recognize such coins as lawful money; that, (3) by making the dollar receivable for duties, the gold revenue of the United States would be cut off, and so necessitate the payment of principal and interest of the national debt in silver; that (4) of the bonded debt then outstanding $1,143,493,400 was issued prior to February, 1873, when no silver was in use, and $583,440,350 had been refunded since that time, when gold was the only coin for which the bonds were sold (gold being the legal unit since 1873), and so understood by the parties to the contract; that, (5) owing to the fall in the value of silver, the Administration would have been unable to sell the $250,000,000 of bonds at 4 per cent, placed on the market since 1876, had they not quieted the doubts of the purchasers by a public statement of an intention to pay the bonds in gold and not in silver; that (6) to pay the bonds in a coin less than that received would be a grave breach of public faith; and that, (7) in case the silver dollar should not rise to par with gold, the act afforded no provision for exempting pre-existing debts from this law. But these considerations did not pre-

---

[1] For the text of the message, see "Globe," vol. cxxxvii, p. 1410.

vail with a sufficient number to prevent the bill from being passed over the head of the Executive.

At the time when Congress was discussing the silver bill a commission [1] was sitting, appointed to investigate the causes of the change in the relative value of gold and silver, the effects upon trade, and to report on the policy of restoring the double standard in the United States. Three Senators, Jones (Nevada), Bogy, and Boutwell; three Representatives, Gibson, Willard, and Bland, and two "experts," Mr. Groesbeck and Professor Bowen, formed the commission. It was packed in favor of a report for the remonetization of silver, and its conclusions have never had much weight. The minority report of Prof. Bowen and Mr. Gibson is, however, excellently done. Messrs. Jones, Bogy, Williard, Bland, and Groesbeck signed the majority report, submitting the following as some of their conclusions:

(*a*) The demonetization of silver by Germany, the United States, and Scandinavia has been the chief cause of the fall in silver since 1870.

(*b*) The commercial depression since 1873 was due to the demonetization of silver, and will become chronic if gold remains as the only resource for money.

(*c*) Specie resumption by the United States is not possible until silver is remonetized.

(*d*) Remonetization of silver by the United States will deter France from wholly giving up silver.

(*e*) Remonetization of silver by the United States will introduce a period of prosperity, greater in proportion as foreigners pour into this country silver in exchange for wheat, cotton, gold, petroleum, etc. Even if the rest of the world gives up silver, the United States will have "an advantageous exchange of commodities, which we can spare, for money, which we need."

---

[1] Authorized August 15, 1876. Report ordered printed March 2, 1877, as "Senate Report No. 703," 2d session, 44th Congress.

CHAPTER XIV.

THE PRESENT SITUATION.

§ 1. THE operation of the act of 1878 has been complicated to many minds by the absence of the free coinage provision, and by the fact that only the Government of the United States can purchase bullion and have it coined into dollars of 412½ grains (at the rate of not less than $2,000,000, nor more than $4,000,000 a month). It was not apparent why this dollar, which in 1878 contained but ninety cents' worth of pure silver, could, when issued, circulate at par with a gold dollar; nor is it understood why the silver dollar is to-day at par with United States notes redeemable in gold. There are several reasons to account for this.

By the issue of a dollar piece containing an amount of silver less than its face value, such a coin is made similar in its character and qualities to an overvalued subsidiary currency, and much that is true of one is true of the other; except that, in this case, the Bland dollar is an unlimited legal tender, while subsidiary coins are a legal tender only to an amount of $10. This matter was mentioned[1] in the debates

---

[1] "I am willing to compromise . . . on this subject, and make silver more than a subsidiary coin, but I would limit its legal-tender power. Why? For the very reason of the example you have before you. The Senator from Missouri has thrown it in our faces that two of the present half-dollars are of less weight than 412½ grains, and yet they pass at par. Why? Is it because the value of the silver in them is equal to 25·8 grains of gold? No, sir; but because of the limit in legal-tender power, and because there is no other currency with which it comes in competition. For the very same reason your minor coins pass at par."—Senator Hill, "Globe," vol. cxxxvi, p. 846.

of Congress. It is well known that 100 cents of our subsidiary coin contain only 345·6 grains of pure silver, while the Bland dollar contains 371·25 grains; and yet we constantly receive for "change" two half-dollars, or four quarters, in exchange for gold, or for paper redeemable in gold, on equal terms. The reasons, therefore, which give currency to the subsidiary coins will account for the currency of the dollars of 412½ grains. In the first place, they are limited in quantity, as compared with the uses to which they can be put. Silver dollars, moreover, can enter into our common circulation only as they are sent forth from the United States Treasury in payment of its dues. At no time since the act was passed, although more than $200,000,000 have been coined, have there been more than $42,000,000 of the Bland dollars in the hands of the public and in circulation. (See Chart XVI.) And as they serve as "change" in a scarcity of one- and two-dollar United States notes (no National Bank notes being issued of denominations less than five dollars), there is an evident use for them, just as there is a use for smaller silver pieces (which are overvalued); and, if the Bland dollars had been issued on the principle that they were to supply the place of small bills, a very considerable quantity could have been permanently retained in the circulation at par.

Another fact which maintains the silver dollar at par with gold, and which is of considerable importance, arises from the provision of the act which authorizes the issue of silver certificates. Any person having not less than ten of the Bland dollars may deposit them with any assistant treasurer and receive therefor a certificate which, in size and appearance, closely resembles a United States note. The important consideration, however (and, to my mind, one of the most important provisions of the act), is that these certificates, in the words of the statute, "shall be receivable for customs, taxes, and all public dues." This is a species of daily redemption of the silver dollar; for as gold has hitherto been required (as it was during and since the war) in payment of customs, now that silver dollars are receivable equally with gold for that purpose, they must remain at par with gold until there is forced upon the circulation more than is necessary for such uses. If silver dollars alone had been made receivable for customs and taxes, their weight and inconvenience in large payments would have restricted their use; but the silver certificates remove all objections based merely on their weight. So long, therefore, as the silver dollars which get out of the United States Treasury are in quantity sufficient to satisfy only the needs caused by the absence of small notes, and the sums demanded to pay customs and taxes, there is no reason why they should depreciate in value any more than the silver subsidiary coins should depreciate.

Moreover, so long as the Government does not forcibly pay out silver, but leaves the acceptance of silver to the option of the Government creditor, no one will receive it, or give full gold value for silver, unless he thinks he can dispose of the silver also for its full face value. This, in itself, must operate to limit the quantity of silver dollars which could get into circulation. If too many pass out to satisfy the needs I have mentioned, they will begin to accumulate in the hands of merchants, then collect by deposit in the banks, and, if the United States will not withdraw or redeem them, then they must begin to depreciate, just as the smaller silver coins have depreciated in the past when issued in unnecessary quantities. No legal-tender power conferred on them by law can save them from this fate.

As may be seen by the figures and lines in Chart XVI, the number of dollar pieces out of the Treasury, but not covered by certificates, has remained about $40,000,000; the quantity of certificates outstanding, also, does not seem to be able to pass a limit of about $114,000,000; and so the steady and continued coinage of silver under the requirements of the law, after a certain point has been passed, has for its chief effect to disturb the condition of the Treasury. The decrease in the amount of outstanding certificates is followed by an increase of silver certificates owned by the Treasury;

so that the silver, either in the form of dollars or certificates, accumulates in the hands of the Government, because the limit of the capacity of the public to absorb both dollars and certificates seems to have been reached.

§ 2. It has been a mystery to many people that the silver dollar of 412½ grains should continue in circulation at par, while the trade dollar of 420 grains has fallen to its intrinsic value, and does not circulate on equal terms with the Bland dollar, which contains less silver. The co-existence of these two silver dollars has added to the complexity connected with the silver question, and it will be my plan to finish the story of the trade dollar, begun in a previous chapter,[1] in order better to understand this subject.

It will be remembered that the coinage of the trade dollar was authorized by the act of 1873. As the bill came from the Treasury officials, in 1871, it contained a provision for a dollar of 384 grains—that is, one of the weight of 100 cents of subsidiary coin. This was in the bill when it first passed the Senate, and also when, in 1872, it passed the House. January 7, 1873, however, Mr. Sherman reported the bill in the Senate so amended as to strike out the clause authorizing a dollar of the standard of the subsidiary coin, and inserted in its place the provisions[2] for the coinage of the trade dollar, which was intended purely for merchants trading with the East. This amendment was promptly accepted by the House.

At the time the act was passed a silver dollar containing 420 grains of standard silver (378 grains of pure silver) was worth 104 cents in gold; but the fall in the value of silver after 1874 seriously affected the uses originally intended for the trade dollar. The fall of silver relatively to gold in 1876 was so great that the pure silver in a trade dollar became worth less than a gold dollar; consequently money-dealers in California, where gold was the only money in use, found a profit in putting the trade dollars into circulation there. At this time, it will be recalled, this coin was a legal

---

[1] Chapter vii, § 4. [2] See the act in Appendix III, A, VI.

tender for sums of five dollars, owing to an unintentional provision of the act of 1873. Although this law limited its use to small payments, the mere fact of its circulation in the United States called attention to the inadvertence in the act of 1873, and all legal-tender power was taken away from the trade dollar by a section[1] of the act of July 22, 1876, and the Secretary of the Treasury was empowered to suspend its coinage altogether at his discretion.

As yet, however, the trade dollar had not come into use in States where gold was not in circulation, because the United States notes which occupied the place of gold were worth less than the silver coin. By 1877, however, the United States notes had so increased in value that they were worth 95 cents in gold to the dollar; but the average price of silver in 1877 was only $54\frac{3}{4}d.$, so that the 420 grains of standard weight in the trade dollar were worth only about 93 cents. As a consequence, under the quick action of money-brokers, trade dollars suddenly appeared in circulation in the United States in large quantities. It was found more profitable to put the coin into circulation at home than to export it. After 1876 the trade dollars had no legal-tender quality whatever, and, inasmuch as dishonest persons were carrying them to remote districts, where the actual nature of the coins was unknown, and were passing them at full value, the Secretary promptly used the discretion granted him by the law, and ordered a discontinuance of further coinage of these commercial dollars. In all, there were coined 35,959,360 of these pieces, and numbers of them still remain in the hands of money-dealers or individuals. They are, however, worth no more than a similar amount of bullion. The Government does not redeem them, because the Government only coined them at the expense, and for the convenience, of owners of bullion, for commercial purposes, and did not create them as legal coins. They are coins only in shape and appearance; in truth, they are only round disks of silver bullion, refined, of course, with the stamp of the United

---

[1] See Appendix III, A, X, § 2.

States on them, certifying to their weight and fineness. It has been proposed in Congress to redeem them at their face value in gold; but that will only offer to foreigners a premium on these dollars, and cause all that have gone abroad to come back again for redemption, at a loss to the Treasury equivalent to the overvaluation of the face value as compared with the value of the pure silver contained in them. Persons by whom these dollars have been received can not see why a trade dollar, which contains six and three quarters more grains of pure silver than a Bland dollar, is not equally good. But it will be found that the former is affected by none of the reasons which were assigned as giving support to the value of the latter. Having no legal-tender power whatever, the former are not receivable for customs, taxes, or any of the uses created by law for the latter.

§ 3. Inasmuch as the Treasury alone can coin the silver dollars, and since at least $24,000,000 must be coined every year, the effects of the act of 1878 are to be studied in the statements of the Treasury; so that only by following the movements of this public office can it be seen how far we have progressed in the transition from a gold to a silver basis. The relation in which the United States Treasury stands in this matter to the public may be illustrated by comparing the former to a large reservoir into which a steady stream is pouring. People about the reservoir need not be disturbed with fears of a flood until the reservoir becomes full; then, after that, unless the stream is stopped, the whole force of the stream will be directly poured upon the community without. To know what has been the effect of the act of 1878, we must inquire whether the Treasury has yet been filled with silver. So soon as that happens, then the country must prepare for the silver deluge and the disappearance of gold and of gold prices. In order to make this examination, I have prepared the accompanying tables and lines in Chart XVI from official figures given by the Treasury Department. On resuming specie payments, in January, 1879, the Secretary had a gold reserve of about $133,000,000; but, since 1878, the

CHART XVI

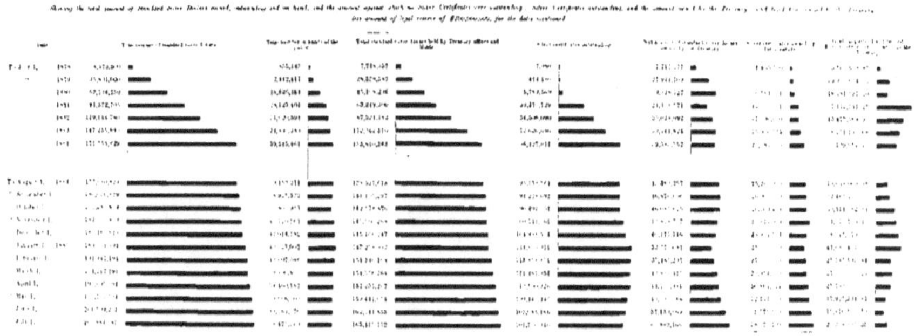

issue of silver dollars which are receivable for customs, just to the extent to which they are used by importers instead of gold, has cut off the channel by which the Government is enabled to supply itself with gold, and since 1881 the gold reserve in the Treasury has been steadily diminishing. So that now, as more and more silver has been put out by the Treasury, a large part of the sums paid in for customs duties is in silver instead of gold.[1] And, inasmuch as the United States has hitherto paid the principal and interest of all its obligations in gold, it will be found that, while the Treasury pays out gold, the supply with which it can pay is becoming gradually and constantly less. It is only a question of time, therefore, when the specie reserve of the United States shall be changed from gold to silver to an extent which will force the Secretary to pay in silver. And when this comes, then the silver current can no longer be dammed up and shut off from the country. The whole quantity of the annual coinage of silver dollars, if principal and interest of our bonds are paid in silver, will then be at once issued to the public. Then the increasing quantity, too great for the needs created by law for the dollar, will cause them to accumulate in the hands of merchants, who can then dispose of them only at their intrinsic value as bullion. So soon as any depreciation is manifest, the silver will begin to drive out the gold from circulation. We shall then have reached a silver basis, and our prices will be changed to suit the silver standard. In the existing state of trade so stupid a policy can not be too harshly condemned.

The United States Treasury receives and makes its largest payments at its principal office in New York, the Sub-Treasury in Wall Street. For its own convenience, in order to save the transfer of large sums of specie, the Sub-Treasury at New York has become a member of the New York Clearing-House Association, composed chiefly of national banks. The kind of money the Treasury pays out at its principal office, which is in New York, is, therefore, closely watched, as indi-

---

[1] In the forty-nine months, beginning January, 1881, $650,000 in silver and $102,654,000 in silver certificates were paid in for customs duties.

cating its general condition. As its dealings are with the Clearing-House, the moment it begins to pay the Clearing-House balances against it in silver the crisis will have arrived. The business community is watching with fear the faintest sign of the impending calamity. There is little doubt in my mind that an important element in the prevailing distrust of the future, and the extraordinary accumulation of unemployed capital in the surplus reserves of the banks, is the dread in the business community of silver payments. When the Treasury can no longer retain a gold basis, then the public must take care of themselves.

In a populous town there was once placed a cage of wild beasts, and in the very beginning the frailty of the bars gave timid people considerable alarm; but the mere fact that the creatures did not get out convinced passers-by, in the course of years, that there was really no danger after all, and men hurried past the animals, hearing the sounds of their baffled ferocity, but gave them no great attention. Therefore, when, on an uncomfortable day in late winter, one of the sub-keepers of the beasts carelessly sauntered in front of the cage, and casually remarked that the bars of the cage were almost gnawed through (he was sorry he could not help it), and asked the by-standers what they thought of it, it is not to be wondered at that a sudden paroxysm of alarm seized even sensible men, and that there ensued a general attempt to put a barrier between them and possible harm. The expression of seriousness under the assumed carelessness of the sub-keeper's manner seemed to imply that he was acting under directions from his superior, and that it meant something. The alarm spread at once. For many years silver dollars, like the beasts in our fable, were kept confined in the Treasury, and the Government was not forced to make payments in gold; but on the 21st of February, 1884, it was believed that the silver was to be let out. The sub-keeper of the fable was, in fact, the Sub-Treasurer in New York city, who addressed the manager of the Clearing-House Association on the probable effect of his paying Government balances at the Clearing-House[1] in silver dollars. This alarm, however, passed by, for no attempt to pay in silver was finally made at that time.

Some months after the passage of the Bland bill the Clearing-House Association (November 15, 1878) decided to refuse silver dollars for balances. But July 12, 1882, in an act extending the charters of the national banks, this decision of the New York banks was met by further legislation,[2] which forbade any national bank to join a clearing-house association that refused to accept silver certificates for balances. Inasmuch as the largest number of banks in the association were national banks, they were obliged to rescind their rule (July 14, 1882); and nominally they do not refuse to accept silver certificates, although none are offered. The banks of the country avoid the silver certificates, and, in view of the great uncertainty of the future, have accumulated a gold reserve greatly in excess of the legal requirements. In the statement for December 20, 1884, it appeared that the New York banks held $70,816,147 in gold or its representatives, and but $2,022,803 in silver and silver certificates.

In August, 1884, it was again believed that the condition of the United States Treasury required payments in silver, but the emergency was tided over. February 10, 1885, the Treasury did actually pay out silver to a certain amount to the Clearing-House, but it has not repeated the act since. In the winter session of Congress, in 1885, an attempt was made in the House late in the session to suspend the further coinage of silver dollars by adding a rider to an appropriation bill, and it came within a few votes of passing.

---

[1] On joining the Association the Treasury agreed to give thirty days' notice of its intention to change its kind of payment, which was then gold.

[2] Act of July 12, 1882, § 12. . . . "Such (gold) certificates, as also silver certificates, when held by any national banking association, shall be counted as part of its lawful reserve; and no national banking association shall be a member of any clearing-house in which *such certificates* shall not be receivable in the settlement of clearing-house balances." It is worth noticing, however, whether "such certificates" does not refer solely to gold certificates, described at length in the previous section, and already mentioned as "such certificates."

§ 4. The present Secretary of the Treasury has made it his object, evidently, to adhere to the plan of gold payments, if possible. Another session of Congress will give an opportunity to save the country from a single silver standard, with all the evils which must invariably accompany a fluctuating and unstable medium of exchange. In order to hold out against the pressure of the silver dollars, the Secretary has decided to issue no more of one- and two-dollar notes, with the expectation that the silver dollars, when issued from the Treasury, will not at once return to it, but remain in circulation in the field previously occupied by small notes.

Another plan was adopted in July, 1885, to keep the gold reserve in the Treasury intact. The associated banks of New York made a large loan of gold to the Secretary, on the deposit with them of a sum of fractional silver currency. It has been stated that on this arrangement the banks were willing to furnish $20,000,000 of gold, but that the Treasury has cared to call for only about $6,000,000. It is also said that the transaction is not a loan, but a final exchange of gold for the fractional silver.

APPENDICES.

APPENDIX I.

A.

TABLES OF THE PRODUCTION OF GOLD AND SILVER IN THE WORLD, 1493-1850.

[The mark has been computed at 25 cents (accurately ·239), and the pound sterling at $5.00 (accurately $4.8666).]

YEARS.	SOETBEER.[1]			
	Value of Average Annual Production.		Total Production.	
	Silver.	Gold.	Silver.	Gold.
1493-1520.....	$2,115,000	$4,045,500	$59,220,000	$113,274,000
1521-1544.....	4,059,000	4,994,000	97,416,000	119,856,000
1545-1560.....	14,022,000	5,985,400	224,352,000	94,968,000
1561-1580.....	13,477,500	4,770,750	269,550,000	95,415,000
1581-1600.....	18,850,500	5,147,500	377,010,000	102,950,000
1601-1620.....	19,030,500	5,942,750	380,610,000	118,855,000
1621-1640.....	17,712,000	5,789,250	354,240,000	115,785,000
1641-1660.....	16,483,500	6,117,000	329,670,000	122,340,000
1661-1680.....	15,165,000	6,458,750	303,300,000	129,175,000
1681-1700.....	15,385,500	7,508,500	307,710,000	150,170,000
1701-1720....	16,002,000	8,942,000	320,040,000	178,840,000
1721-1740.....	19,404,000	13,308,250	388,080,000	266,165,000
1741-1760.....	23,991,500	17,165,500	479,830,000	343,310,000
1761-1780.....	29,388,250	14,441,750	586,965,000	288,835,000
1781-1800.....	39,557,750	12,408,500	791,155,000	248,170,000
1801-1810.....	40,236,750	12,400,000	402,367,500	124,000,000
1811-1820.....	24,334,750	7,983,000	243,347,500	79,830,000
1820-1830.....	20,725,250	9,915,750	207,252,500	99,157,500
1831-1840.....	26,840,250	14,151,500	268,402,500	141,515,000
1841-1850....	35,118,750	38,194,250	351,187,500	381,942,500
Total........	....	....	$6,741,705,500	$3,314,553,000

[1] Petermann's "Mittheilungen," Ergänzungsheft, Nr. 57, "Edelmetall-Production," 1879, pp. 107-111. Alexander Del Mar, in the "Report of the United States Silver Commission of 1876," vol. i, pp. 61-65, gives some other figures, but they can not be depended upon, nor can his figures since 1850. For 1858 and 1859, for instance, he gives $144,000,000 as the gold product according to Sir Hector Hay, when the latter's figures are $124,000,000.

218   APPENDIX I.

B.
Annual Production of Gold and Silver in the World, 1850-1875.
[000 omitted.]

YEARS.	SOETBEER.[1]		"JOURNAL DES ÉCONOMISTES" for March, 1876.		TOOKE AND NEW-MARCH,[2] and London "Economist."		SIR HECTOR HAY.[3]		ERNEST SEYD.[4]		HORTON.[5]		YOUNG.[6]	
	Silver.	Gold.	Silver.	Gold.	Silver.	Gold.	Silver.	Gold.	Silver.	Gold.	Silver.	Gold.	Silver.	Gold.
	$	$	$	$	$	$	$	$	$	$	$	$	$	$
1849														
1850						27,100			39,000	27,100			43,900	28,400
1851						44,450			39,000	44,450			43,300	58,300
1852	30,875	137,775				67,600			40,000	67,600			42,600	86,400
1853			40,500	182,500		135,150	40,600	182,750	40,600	182,750	38,000	174,333	41,900	110,600
1854			40,500	155,000		140,400	40,600	155,450	40,600	155,450	38,000	149,500	41,600	130,770
1855			40,500	127,000		141,400	40,600	127,450	40,600	127,450	38,000	122,500	42,100	146,800
1856			40,500	135,000		151,300	40,600	135,075	40,600	135,075	38,000	130,333	43,200	146,700
1857			40,500	147,500		161,250	40,650	147,600	40,650	147,600	38,000	142,500	44,400	139,400
1858	40,725	143,725	40,500	133,000		134,225	40,650	133,275	40,650	133,275	38,000	128,500	46,000	133,100
1859			40,500	124,500		122,035	40,650	124,650	40,650	124,650	38,000	120,250	48,000	115,200
1860			40,500	124,500		107,290	46,750	124,850	40,750	124,850	38,000	120,250	50,200	103,000
1861			40,500	119,000		93,115	40,800	119,250	40,900	119,250	40,000	115,000	52,600	101,100
1862			42,500	114,000		112,270	42,700	113,800	42,700	113,900	40,000	110,000	55,300	102,600
1863	49,550	125,125	45,000	107,500		110,590	45,300	107,750	45,300	107,750	40,000	103,666	58,300	102,400
1864			49,000	107,000		100,575	49,200	106,850	49,300	106,850	46,000	103,333	63,400	101,600
1865			51,500	113,000		94,500	51,700	113,000	51,700	113,000	47,000	109,000	67,400	101,100
1866			52,500	129,000		101,270	51,950	129,300	51,950	129,300	47,250	116,750	68,900	98,200
1867			50,500	121,000		108,600	50,725	121,100	50,725	121,100	48,250	116,000	68,100	98,200
1868	60,250	133,550	54,000	116,000		103,500	54,225	111,025	54,225	114,025	50,500	112,000	68,300	98,900
1869			50,000	120,000		97,570	50,225	109,725	50,225	109,725	46,750	116,750	69,300	99,000
1870			47,500	121,000		106,415	47,500	106,225	47,500	106,225	44,500	116,000	69,300	99,600
1871			51,500	116,000		95,250	51,575	106,850	51,575	106,850	47,000	112,500	69,400	97,200
1872	88,025	119,050	61,000	116,500		108,965	61,050	107,000	61,060	107,000	56,500	103,000	72,100	91,800
1873			65,000	101,500		87,845	65,250	99,550	65,350	99,000	60,750	96,000	73,400	97,200
1874			70,500	103,500		109,730	70,250	96,300			65,500	87,333	74,700	92,000
1875			71,500	90,500		99,400	71,500	90,750			67,000	100,000	76,200	89,000
			62,000	97,500		101,765	60,500	97,500			55,750	94,000	77,700	87,400
Total	1,305,125 (25 years.)	3,317,625 (25 years.)	1,167,500 (24 years.)	2,913,000 (24 years.)		2,868,250 (27 years.)	1,390,450 (24 years.)	2,860,975 (21 years.)	1,105,300 (24 years.)	2,665,725 (24 years.)	1,108,750 (24 years.)	2,801,498 (24 years.)	1,573,900 (25 years.)	2,761,500 (27 yrs.)

[1] Petermann's "Mittheilungen," ibid., pp. 107-112. [2] Report on "Depreciation of Silver," in 1876, to House of Commons, Appendix, p. 11.
[3] Ibid., p. 11. [4] "Decline of Prosperity," p. 71. [5] "Silver and Gold," p. 23.
[6] U. S. Bureau of Statistics. See Report to House of Commons, "Depreciation of Silver," Appendix, p. 146.

C.

PRODUCTION OF GOLD AND SILVER IN THE WORLD, 1876-1886.

YEARS.	SOETBEER.		DIRECTOR OF THE U. S. MINT.	
	Silver.	Gold.	Silver.	Gold.
1876	$91,208,750	$115,756,750		
1877	96,738,750	125,165,000	$81,040,665	$113,947,173
1878	98,865,250	129,630,500	94,882,177	119,092,786
1879	95,285,250	116,699,250	96,172,628	108,778,807
1880	95,480,000	114,054,500	96,704,978	106,436,786
1881	99,168,250	110,810,250	102,168,354	103,023,078
1882	105,916,750	101,064,250	111,821,623	102,000,000
1883	108,582,000	100,822,250	115,088,000	95,392,000
1884	110,899,500	101,940,250	116,564,000	101,694,000
1885			127,257,000	102,975,000
1886			130,383,000	97,761,000

APPENDIX II.

RELATIVE VALUES OF GOLD AND SILVER.

For the time previous to the discovery of America there are many fanciful estimates of the relative values of gold and silver. Jacob[1] thus briefly sums up the situation:

"Although the amount of silver in circulation as money at all times must have been greater than that of gold, yet, as the gold has six times the durability of silver, the relative value of the two metals to each other could not be maintained unless the mines produced the two metals in proportion to the loss on them by wear respectively. It seems probable that the due proportion was kept up during the existence of the Roman power, and through the dark ages which succeeded, till the discovery of America, and till the dispersion over the world of the surplus produce of silver above that of gold. The value of gold to silver had varied but little before the mines of Potosi were discovered. Among the Romans gold to silver seldom varied more than from nine to eleven for one, that is, a pound of gold was rarely worth either more than eleven or less than nine pounds of silver; nor did the relative value of the metals fluctuate more in the long course of centuries to the time when the new sources of mineral wealth in the western world were in full activity."

A.

AVERAGE RATIOS OF SILVER TO GOLD, BY PERIODS, SINCE 1500.[2]

Years.	Ratio.	Years.	Ratio.	Years.	Ratio.
1501–1520.....	10·75 : 1	1701–1710....	15·27	1801–1810...	15·61 : 1
1521–1540.....	11·25	1711–1720....	15·15	1811–1820...	15·51
1541–1560.....	11·30	1721–1730....	15·09	1821–1830...	15·80
1561–1580.....	11·50	1731–1740....	15·07	1831–1840...	15·75
1581–1600.....	11·80	1741–1750....	14·93	1841–1850...	15·83
1601–1620.....	12·25	1751–1760....	14·56	1851–1855...	15·42
1621–1640.....	14·00	1761–1770....	14·81	1856–1860...	15·30
1641–1660.....	14·50	1771–1780....	14·64	1861–1865...	15·36
1661–1680.....	15·00	1781–1790....	14·76	1866–1870...	15·56
1681–1690.....	14·98	1791–1800....	15·42	1871–1875...	15·98
1691–1700.....	14·96				

[1] "An Historical Inquiry into the Production and Consumption of the Precious Metals," pp. 300, 301.

[2] Given by Soetbeer, in "Edelmetall-Production," Petermann's "Mittheilungen," Ergänzungsheft, Nr. 57, 1879, pp. 126, 128–131.

APPENDIX II. 221

B.

RATIOS OF GOLD TO SILVER, GIVEN YEARLY SINCE 1687.[1]

Year.	Soetbeer.	Year.	Soetbeer.	Year.	Soetbeer.	White.	Exec. Doc. 117, 1st session, 21st Congress.
1687...	14·94	1723..	15·20	1760..	14·14	14·16	14·29
1688..	14·94	1724..	15·11				
1689..	15·02	1725..	15·11	1761..	14·54	13·81	13·94
1690..	15·02	1726..	15·15	1762..	15·27	14·50	14·63
		1727..	15·24	1763..	14·99	14·58	14·71
1691..	14·98	1728..	15·11	1764..	14·70	14·78	14·91
1692..	14·92	1729..	14·92	1765..	14·83	14·56	14·69
1693..	14·83	1730..	14·81	1766..	14·80	14·28	14·41
1694..	14·87			1767..	14·85	14·32	14·45
1695..	15·02	1731..	14·94	1768..	14·80	14·45	14·58
1696..	15·00	1732..	15·09	1769..	14·72	14·32	14·45
1697..	15·20	1733..	15·18	1770..	14·62	14·22	14·35
1698..	15·07	1734..	15·39				
1699..	14·94	1735..	15·41	1771..	14·66	14·23	14·36
1700..	14·81	1736..	15·18	1772..	14·52	14·06	14·19
		1737..	15·02	1773..	14·62	14·60	14·73
1701..	15·07	1738..	14·91	1774..	14·62	14·92	15·05
1702..	15·52	1739..	14·91	1775..	14·72	14·49	14·62
1703..	15·17	1740..	14·94	1776..	14·55	14·21	14·34
1704..	15·22			1777..	14·54	13·91	14·04
1705..	15·11	1741..	14·92	1778..	14·68	14·21	14·34
1706..	15·27	1742..	14·85	1779..	14·80	14·76	14·89
1707..	15·44	1743..	14·85	1780..	14·72	14·30	14·43
1708..	15·41	1744..	14·87				
1709..	15·31	1745..	14·98	1781..	14·78	13·70	13·33
1710..	15·22	1746..	15·13	1782..	14·42	13·42	13·54
		1747..	15·26	1783..	14·48	13·66	13·78
1711..	15·29	1748..	15·11	1784..	14·70	14·77	14·90
1712..	15·31	1749..	14·80	1785..	14·92	15·07	15·21
1713..	15·24	1750..	14·55	1786..	14·96	14·76	14·89
1714..	15·13			1787..	14·92	14·70	14·83
1715..	15·11	1751..	14·39	1788..	14·65	14·58	14·71
1716..	15·09	1752..	14·54	1789..	14·75	14·76	14·89
1717..	15·13	1753..	14·54	1790..	15·04	14·88	15·01
1718..	15·11	1754..	14·48				
1719..	15·09	1755..	14·68	1791..	15·05	14·82	14·95
1720..	15·04	1756..	14·94	1792..	15·17	14·30	14·43
		1757..	14·87	1793..	15·00	14·88	15·01
1721..	15·05	1758..	14·85	1794..	15·37	15·18	15·32
1722..	15·17	1759..	14·15	1795..	15·55	14·64	14·77

[1] In parallel columns are given the various tables of different writers. Soetbeer's are taken from the official quotations of the price of silver in Hamburg by the Handels Vorstand, recorded twice a week since 1687. They are absolutely trustworthy. After 1833, Pixley and Abell's London tables are accepted by every one. The variance occurs, therefore, before 1833. Other tables than Soetbeer's do not begin until 1760.

B—Continued.

Year.	Soetbeer.	White.	Exec. Doc. 117, 1st session, 21st Congress.	Year.	Soetbeer.	White.	Exec. Doc. 117, 1st session, 21st Congress.
1796..	15·65	14·64	14·77	1815..	15·26	16·15	16·30
1797..	15·41	15·31	15·45	1816..	15·28	13·52	13·64
1798..	15·59	15·31	15·45	1817..	15·11	15·44	15·58
1799..	15·74	14·14	14·29	1818..	15 35	15·28	15·42
1800..	15·68	14·68	14·81	1819..	15·33	15·68	15·82
				1820..	15·62	15·57	15·71
1801..	15·46	14·33	14·47				
1802..	15·26	15·09	15·23	1821..	15·95	15·84	15·98
1803..	15·41	14·33	14·47	1822..	15·80	15·77	15·91
1804..	15·41	14·54	14·67	1823..	15·84	15·77	15·91
1805..	15·79	15·00	15·14	1824..	15·82	15·05	15·64
1806..	15·52	14·12	14·25	1825..	15·70	15·55	15·69
1807..	15·43	14·33	14·46	1826..	15·76	15·05	15·69
1808..	16·08	14·66	14·79	1827..	15·74	15·03	15·77
1809..	15·96	16·00	16·25	1828..	15·78	15·63	15·77
1810..	15·77	16·00	16·15	1829..	15·78	15·81	15·95
				1830..	15·82		
1811..	15·53	15·58	15·72				
1812..	16·11	14·09	15·04	1831..	15·72		
1813..	16·25	14·04	14·53	1832..	15·73		
1814..	15·04	15·71	15·85				

The table headed "White" was prepared by John White, the cashier of the United States Bank, in a Report to the Secretary of the Treasury, November 16, 1829. (See "Report of 1878," pp. 647-649; also cf. p. 624.) Accompanying White's table are the following authorities: "Mr. Mushet, Mr. Wheatly, 'Monthly Magazine,' 'Bullion Report,' Mr. Tooke, Mr. Ricardo, Chancellor of the Exchequer, Governor of the Bank." This is a varied list.

Soetbeer has pointed out that White's table is untrustworthy, because we have no knowledge what sort of quotations were used, nor how the averages were calculated. Owing to the issue of paper between 1797 and 1819, the period of the Bank Restriction Act, the Hamburg quotations would unquestionably be more reliable. Soetbeer has pointed out what seem to be palpable errors in the White table. In 1761 it is quite improbable that the ratio fell below 14 : 1 and then rose the next year 5 per cent. Moreover, in White's table the following ratios occur:

 1781...................... 13·33, corresponding to 70⅜ d.
 1782...................... 13·54,   "   69⅝ d.
 1783...................... 13·78,   "   68¼ d.
 1784...................... 14·90,   "   63¼ d.

while the Hamburg quotations give:

 1781...................... 14·78, corresponding to 63¾ d.
 1782...................... 14·42,   "   65⅝ d.
 1783...................... 14·48,   "   65¼ d.
 1784...................... 14·70,   "   64½ d.

There is absolutely no known reason to account for so sudden a change as that indicated by White's figures in 1784, while at Hamburg the ratio remained steady, or nearly so.

In addition to this, Jefferson says that the market ratio in 1782 was 1 : 14·5 in the United States, and Morris points to the fact that the ratio was nearly 1 : 15 in England ("Report of 1878," pp. 428, 441). The figures of White for the years 1812, 1813, and 1816 are undoubtedly incorrect. According to his ratios, silver changed between 1810 and 1816 from a ratio of 13·52 : 1 to 16·15 : 1, for which there appears to be no sufficient reason in the facts known to us. It seems as if the figures of 13·52 for 1816 were a mistake for 15·52.

For these reasons I can not place much, if any, reliance on White's table, and have, therefore, followed Soetbeer's figures in the course of my investigation.

The table given above, from a United States document, is evidently based on the same material as White's. Although in every ratio the figures are different from White's, yet the differences are usually very slight (except for 1812), and follow the same general direction. Even in the exceptional figures of 1781-1783, and 1816, there is the same trouble as in White's table. These figures are given in the "Report of 1878," p. 583; are made the basis of a table of ratios by Alexander Del Mar in the "Report of the United States Silver Commission of 1877," vol. i, appendix, p. 67; are stated in C. P. White's "Report, No. 278, 1833–1834," p. 96; and are quoted by H. R. Linderman, in his report as Director of the Mint, 1876, p. 46. But the table, as well as the White table, can be regarded as not sufficiently trustworthy to base any conclusions upon.

C.

PIXLEY AND ABELL'S TABLES OF THE RATIOS OF GOLD TO SILVER SINCE 1833.

Year.	Ratio.	Year.	Ratio.	Year.	Ratio.	Year.	Ratio.
1833	15·93	1847	15·80	1861	15·26	1875	16·62
1834	15·73	1848	15·85	1862	15·35	1876	17·77
1835	15·80	1849	15·78	1863	15·37	1877	17·22
1836	15·72	1850	15·70	1864	15·37	1878	17·92
1837	15·83			1865	15·44	1879	18·39
1838	15·85	1851	15·46	1866	15·43	1880	18·06
1839	15·62	1852	15·59	1867	15·57		
1840	15·62	1853	15·33	1868	15·59	1881	18·24
		1854	15·33	1869	15·60	1882	18·27
1841	15·70	1855	15·38	1870	15·57	1883	18·64
1842	15·87	1856	15·38			1884	18·58
1843	15·93	1857	15·27	1871	15·57	1885	19·39
1844	15·85	1858	15·38	1872	15·65	1886	20·78
1845	15·92	1859	15·19	1873	15·92		
1846	15·90	1860	15·29	1874	16·17		

D.

AVERAGE YEARLY PRICE OF STANDARD SILVER PER OUNCE IN LONDON, 1833–1884.

[*Taken from Pixley and Abell's Tables.*]

Year.	Price in Pence.	Year.	Price in Pence.
1833	$59\frac{3}{16}$	1859	$62\frac{1}{16}$
1834	$59\frac{8}{16}$	1860	$61\frac{11}{16}$
1835	$59\frac{11}{16}$		
1836	60	1861	$60\frac{13}{16}$
1837	$59\frac{9}{16}$	1862	$61\frac{7}{16}$
1838	$59\frac{1}{2}$	1863	$61\frac{3}{8}$
1839	$60\frac{3}{4}$	1864	$61\frac{3}{8}$
1840	$60\frac{3}{8}$	1865	$61\frac{1}{16}$
		1866	$61\frac{1}{8}$
1841	$60\frac{1}{16}$	1867	$60\frac{9}{16}$
1842	$59\frac{7}{16}$	1868	$60\frac{1}{2}$
1843	$59\frac{3}{16}$	1869	$60\frac{7}{16}$
1844	$59\frac{1}{2}$	1870	$60\frac{9}{16}$
1845	$59\frac{1}{4}$		
1846	$59\frac{5}{16}$	1871	$60\frac{1}{2}$
1847	$59\frac{11}{16}$	1872	$60\frac{5}{16}$
1848	$59\frac{1}{2}$	1873	$59\frac{1}{4}$
1849	$59\frac{3}{4}$	1874	$58\frac{5}{16}$
1850	$60\frac{1}{16}$	1875	$56\frac{7}{8}$
		1876	$52\frac{3}{4}$
1851	61	1877	$54\frac{13}{16}$
1852	$60\frac{1}{2}$	1878	$52\frac{9}{16}$
1853	$61\frac{1}{2}$	1879	$51\frac{1}{4}$
1854	$61\frac{1}{2}$	1880	$52\frac{1}{4}$
1855	$61\frac{5}{16}$		
1856	$61\frac{5}{16}$	1881	$51\frac{11}{16}$
1857	$61\frac{3}{4}$	1882	$51\frac{5}{8}$
1858	$61\frac{5}{16}$	1883	$50\frac{9}{16}$
		1884	$50\frac{5}{8}$

E.

MONTHLY QUOTATIONS OF BAR-SILVER PER OUNCE STANDARD, IN PENCE, AT LONDON, 1871–1884.

By Pixley and Abell, 27 Old Broad Street, London, E. C.

APPENDIX II. 225

F.

RATIOS OF SILVER TO GOLD, BY MONTHS,[1] FROM 1845 TO 1880.

YEARS.	JAN.	FEB.	MAR.	APR.	MAY	JUNE.	JULY.	AUG.	SEPT.	OCT.	NOV.	DEC.	Annual average.
1845	15·85	15·92	15·95	16·05	16·22	15·98	15·95	15·88	15·88	15·82	15·80	15·92	15·93
1846	15·90	15·92	15·92	15·95	15·98	15·98	15·97	15·95	15·95	15·92	15·73	15·98	15·91
1847	15·68	15·62	15·62	15·65	15·98	15·97	15·92	15·78	15·78	15·92	15·95	15·95	15·82
1848	15·95	15·90	15·93	15·95	15·97	15·85	15·85	15·77	15·78	15·77	15·83	15·85	15·87
1849	15·97	15·78	15·72	15·75	15·75	15·82	15·82	15·77	15·80	15·88	15·85	15·85	15·81
1850	15·82	15·82	15·82	15·82	15·82	15·82	15·78	15·73	15·72	15·65	15·52	15·33	15·72
1851	15·30	15·32	15·33	15·33	15·43	15·43	15·52	15·49	15·57	15·65	15·62	15·52	15·46
1852	15·52	15·59	15·62	15·68	15·75	15·73	15·64	15·62	15·62	15·40	15·32	15·35	15·58
1853	15·36	15·38	15·36	15·36	15·41	15·46	15·35	15·30	15·21	15·10	15·14	15·27	15·33
1854	15·27	15·29	15·26	15·26	15·27	15·36	15·36	15·40	15·36	15·40	15·36	15·32	15·33
1855	15·33	15·32	15·36	15·52	15·43	15·33	15·38	15·33	15·29	15·36	15·41	15·36	15·36
1856	15·40	15·38	15·47	15·46	15·43	15·43	15·40	15·35	15·24	15·21	15·15	15·18	15·34
1857	15·19	15·24	15·27	15·27	15·33	15·26	15·29	15·24	15·32	15·26	15·29	15·26	15·27
1858	15·35	15·27	15·32	15·36	15·33	15·33	15·41	15·47	15·51	15·40	15·29	15·30	15·36
1859	15·24	15·27	15·26	15·18	15·12	15·19	15·18	15·21	15·27	15·21	15·21	15·21	15·21
1860	15·18	15·19	15·18	15·29	15·30	15·40	15·44	15·36	15·36	15·30	15·29	15·32	15·35	15·30
1861	15·38	15·41	15·24	15·44	15·43	15·57	15·67	15·64	15·57	15·52	15·47	15·48	15·48
1862	15·35	15·32	15·38	15·41	15·40	15·35	15·46	15·41	15·38	15·33	15·21	15·29	15·36
1863	15·29	15·33	15·38	15·43	15·38	15·35	15·44	15·46	15·43	15·38	15·35	15·35	15·38
1864	15·23	15·35	15·33	15·51	15·46	15·40	15·41	15·38	15·33	15·46	15·47	15·39	15·39
1865	15·33	15·35	15·41	15·54	15·54	15·57	15·55	15·54	15·51	15·44	16·10	15·32	15·43
1866	15·32	15·43	15·47	15·65	15·32	15·19	15·35	15·57	15·51	15·46	15·47	15·49	15·44
1867	15·49	15·53	15·52	15·46	15·55	15·50	15·59	15·60	15·63	15·61	15·66	15·61	15·57
1868	15·62	15·59	15·54	15·55	15·59	15·62	15·61	15·64	15·66	15·64	15·59	15·54	15·61
1869	15·53	15·49	15·57	15·57	15·65	15·68	15·64	15·60	15·60	15·61	15·59	15·59	15·60
1870	15·57	15·60	15·59	15·61	15·60	15·60	15·45	15·59	15·62	15·59	15·56	15·58	15·60
1871	15·57	15·58	15·61	15·60	15·66	15·63	15·57	15·54	15·52	15·60	15·50	15·52	15·58
1872	15·50	15·45	15·51	15·54	15·68	15·70	15·68	15·68	15·61	15·70	15·85	15·79	15·64
1873	15·75	15·75	15·75	15·78	15·82	15·88	15·90	15·96	16·00	16·05	16·26	16·25	15·93
1874	16·05	16·05	16·00	16·01	16·06	16·06	16·20	16·32	16·33	16·26	16·40	16·16
1875	16·38	16·42	16·51	16·47	16·61	16·74	16·90	16·76	16·63	16·56	16·61	16·74	16·63
1876	16·98	17·38	17·07	17·55	17·80	17·24	19·59	18·07	18·21	17·96	17·50	16·65	17·80
1877	16·85	16·54	17·16	17·40	17·42	17·59	17·44	17·42	17·32	17·13	17·30	17·20	17·19
1878	17·53	17·38	17·30	17·14	17·62	17·76	17·92	17·97	18·33	18·71	18·65	18·87	17·96
1879	18·84	18·88	19·03	18·97	18·47	18·18	18·18	18·20	18·29	18·11	17·66	17·94	18·39
1880	17·96	18·05	18·14	18·13	18·09	17·97	17·90	17·90	18·02	18·11	18·22	18·19	18·06

G.

METHOD OF COMPUTING THE RATIO FROM THE LONDON PRICE OF SILVER.

Rule.—Divide the number 943 by the number of pence at which silver is quoted.

In Great Britain 1869 sovereigns are to be struck out of 40 pounds troy of gold, $\frac{11}{12}$ fine; and one ounce would be coined into $\frac{1869}{40 \times 12}$ sovereigns, or £3 17s. 10½d., or 934½d., $\frac{11}{12}$ fine. The ounce of pure gold, therefore, is worth 934½d. × $\frac{12}{11}$.

If an ounce of silver of British standard, $\frac{37}{40}$ fine, is quoted at x pence, an ounce of pure silver would be worth x × $\frac{40}{37}$ pence.

[1] Computed by Dr. O. J. Broch. See "French Report on Conference of 1881," i, p. 58.

APPENDIX II.

The ratio of the value of an ounce of pure gold to an ounce of pure silver would be, therefore,

$$\frac{934\frac{1}{2} \times 1\frac{2}{1}}{x \times \frac{40}{37}} = \frac{934\frac{1}{2} \times 1\frac{2}{1} \times \frac{37}{40}}{x} = \frac{942 \cdot 995454}{x}, \text{ or nearly } \frac{943}{x}$$

METHOD OF COMPUTING THE VALUE OF A SILVER DOLLAR FROM NEW YORK QUOTATIONS.

Rule.—Multiply the price per ounce by ·77¼.

The New York quotations, as given in the financial columns of the daily press, make allowance for changes from the London prices, due to the rate of exchange, etc.; but the quotations are for pure silver, that is, for silver 1,000 fine:

In 1,000 412½-gr. dollars are 859¾ ounces of silver 900 fine.
" "   trade   "   " 875   "   "   "   "   "
" $1,000 subsid. coin " 803¾   "   "   "   "   "

Since the New York quotations are given for silver 1,000 fine, but since our coins are made of silver 900 fine, the quotation should be multiplied by only $\frac{9}{10}$ of the actual weight of the coins. The 859⅝ ounces less $\frac{1}{10}$ is 773·4375; and to multiply this last number by the quotation would give the value of 1,000 silver dollars. But the value of one dollar can be found by multiplying the price by $\frac{11824375}{1000000}$, or, approximately, by ·77¼.

APPENDIX III.

A.

LAWS OF THE UNITED STATES RELATING TO COINAGE.

I. APRIL, 1792.—*An Act establishing a Mint, and regulating the Coins of the United States.*

SEC. 9. *And be it further enacted.* That there shall be from time to time struck and coined at the said Mint coins of gold, silver, and copper of the following denominations, values, and descriptions, viz.: EAGLES—each to be of the value of ten dollars or units, and to contain two hundred and forty-seven grains and four eighths of a grain of pure, or two hundred and seventy grains of standard gold.

[Half-eagles and quarter-eagles of corresponding weights and fineness.]

DOLLARS OR UNITS—Each to be of the value of a Spanish milled dollar as the same is now current, and to contain three hundred and seventy-one grains and four sixteenth parts of a grain of pure, or four hundred and sixteen grains of standard silver.

[Half-dollars, quarter-dollars, dimes, and half-dimes of corresponding weights and fineness.]

SEC. 11. *And be it further enacted,* That the proportional value of gold to silver in all coins which shall by law be current as money within the United States shall be as fifteen to one, according to quantity in weight, of pure gold or pure silver; that is to say, every fifteen pounds weight of pure silver shall be of equal value in all payments with one pound weight of pure gold, and so in proportion as to any greater or less quantities of the respective metals.

SEC. 14. *And be it further enacted,* That it shall be lawful for any person or persons to bring to the said Mint gold and silver bullion, in order to their being coined; and that the bullion so brought shall be there assayed and coined as speedily as may be after the receipt thereof, and that free of expense to the person or persons by whom the same shall have been brought. And as soon as the said bullion shall have been coined, the person or persons by whom the same shall have been delivered, shall, upon demand, receive in lieu thereof coins of the same species of bullion which shall have been so delivered, weight for weight, of the pure gold or pure silver therein contained: *Provided nevertheless,* That it shall be at the mutual option of the party or parties bringing such bullion, and of the director of the said Mint, to make an immediate exchange of coins for standard bullion, with a deduction of one-half per cent from the weight of pure gold, or pure silver contained in the said bullion, as an indemnification to the Mint for the time which will necessarily be required for coining the said bullion, and for the advance which shall have been so made in coins.

SEC. 16. *And be it further enacted,* That all the gold and silver coins which shall have been struck at and issued from the said Mint shall be a lawful tender in all payments whatsoever, those of full weight according to the respective values herein before declared, and those of less than full weight at values proportional to their respective weights.

[Approved, April 2, 1792. 1 Statutes at Large, 246.]

II. JUNE, 1834.—*An Act concerning the gold coins of the United States, and for other purposes.*

Be it enacted, . . . That the gold coins of the United States shall contain the following quantities of metal, that is to say: each eagle shall contain two hundred and thirty-two grains of pure gold, and two hundred and fifty-eight grains of standard gold; each half-eagle one hundred and sixteen grains of pure gold, and one hundred and twenty-nine grains of standard gold; each quarter-eagle shall contain fifty-eight grains of pure gold, and sixty-four and a half grains of standard gold; every such eagle shall be of the value of ten dollars; every such half-eagle shall be of the value of five dollars; and every such quarter-eagle shall be of the value of two dollars and fifty cents; and the said gold coins shall be receivable in all payments, when of full weight, according to their respective values; and when of less than full weight, at less values, proportioned to their respective actual weights.

SEC. 2. *And be it further enacted,* That all standard gold or silver deposited for coinage after the thirty-first of July next shall be paid for in coin, under the direction of the Secretary of the Treasury, within five days from the making of such deposit, deducting from the amount of said deposit of gold and silver one half of one per centum: *Provided,* That no deduction shall be made unless said advance be required by such depositor within forty days.

SEC. 3. *And be it further enacted,* That all gold coins of the United States, minted anterior to the thirty-first day of July next, shall be receivable in all payments at the rate of ninety-four and eight tenths of a cent per pennyweight.

[Approved, June 28, 1834. 4 Statutes at Large, 699.]

III. January, 1837.—*An Act supplementary to the act entitled "An Act establishing a Mint, and regulating the coins of the United States."*

Sec. 8. *And be it further enacted,* That the standard for both gold and silver coins of the United States shall hereafter be such that of one thousand parts by weight, nine hundred shall be of pure metal and one hundred of alloy; and the alloy of the silver coins shall be of copper; and the alloy of the gold coins shall be of copper and silver, provided that the silver do not exceed one half of the whole alloy.

Sec. 9. *And be it further enacted,* That of the silver coins, the dollar shall be of the weight of four hundred and twelve and one half grains; the half-dollar of the weight of two hundred and six and one fourth grains; the quarter-dollar of the weight of one hundred and three and one eighth grains; the dime, or tenth part of a dollar, of the weight of forty-one and a quarter grains; and the half-dime, or twentieth part of a dollar, of the weight of twenty grains and five eighths of a grain. And that dollars, half-dollars, and quarter-dollars, dimes and half-dimes, shall be legal tenders of payment, according to their nominal value, for any sums whatever.

Sec. 10. *And be it further enacted,* That of the gold coins, the weight of the eagle shall be two hundred and fifty-eight grains; that of the half-eagle one hundred and twenty-nine grains; and that of the quarter-eagle sixty-four and one half grains. And that for all sums whatever the eagle shall be a legal tender of payment for ten dollars, the half-eagle for five dollars, and the quarter-eagle for two and a half dollars.

Sec. 11. *And be it further enacted,* That the silver coins heretofore issued at the Mint of the United States, and the gold coins issued since the thirty-first day of July, one thousand eight hundred and thirty-four, shall continue to be legal tenders of payment for their nominal values, on the same terms as if they were of the coinage provided for by this act.

[Approved, January 18, 1837. 5 Statutes at Large, 136.]

IV. March, 1849.—*An Act to authorize the Coinage of Gold Dollars and Double Eagles.*

[This act authorizes the coinage of gold dollars and double eagles, "conformably in all respects to the standard for gold coins now established by law," and to be a legal tender in payment for all sums.]

[Approved, March 3, 1849. 9 Statutes at Large, 397.]

V. FEBRUARY, 1853.—*An Act amendatory of Existing Laws relative to the Half-Dollar, Quarter-Dollar, Dime, and Half-Dime.*

Be it enacted, . . . That from and after the first day of June, eighteen hundred and fifty-three, the weight of the half-dollar or piece of fifty cents shall be one hundred and ninety-two grains, and the quarter-dollar, dime, and half-dime shall be, respectively, one half, one fifth, and one tenth of the weight of said half-dollar.

SEC. 2. *And be it further enacted,* That the silver coins issued in conformity with the above section shall be legal tenders in payment of debts for all sums not exceeding five dollars.

SEC. 3. *And be it further enacted,* That, in order to procure bullion for the requisite coinage of the subdivisions of the dollar authorized by this act, the treasurer of the Mint shall, with the approval of the director, purchase such bullion with the bullion fund of the Mint. . . .

SEC. 4. *And be it further enacted,* That such coins shall be paid out at the Mint, in exchange for gold coins at par, in sums not less than one hundred dollars; and it shall be lawful, also, to transmit parcels of the same from time to time to the assistant treasurers, depositaries, and other officers of the United States, under general regulations proposed by the director of the Mint and approved by the Secretary of the Treasury: *Provided, however,* That the amount coined into quarter-dollars, dimes, and half-dimes, shall be regulated by the Secretary of the Treasury.

SEC. 5. *And be it further enacted,* That no deposits for coinage into the half-dollar, quarter-dollar, dime, and half-dime shall hereafter be received other than those made by the treasurer of the Mint, as herein authorized, and upon account of the United States.

SEC. 6. *And be it further enacted,* That, at the option of the depositor, gold or silver may be cast into bars or ingots of either pure metal or of standard fineness, as the owner may prefer, with a stamp upon the same, designating its weight and fineness; but no piece of either gold or silver shall be cast into bars or ingots of a less weight than ten ounces, except pieces of one ounce, of two ounces, of three ounces, and of five ounces, all of which pieces of less weight than ten ounces shall be of the standard fineness, with their weight and fineness stamped upon them; but in cases where the gold and silver deposited be coined or cast into bars or ingots, there shall be a charge to the depositor, in addition to the charge now made for refining or parting the metals, of one half of one per centum: . . . *Provided, however,* That nothing contained in this section shall be considered as applying to the half-dollar, the quarter-dollar, the dime, and half-dime.

SEC. 7. *And be it further enacted,* That, from time to time, there shall be struck and coined at the Mint of the United States, and the branches thereof, conformably in all respects to law, and conformably in all respects to the standard of gold coins now established by law, a coin of gold of the value of three dollars, or units. . . .

[Approved, February 21, 1853. 10 Statutes at Large, 160.]

VI. FEBRUARY, 1873.—*An Act revising and amending the Laws relative to the Mints, Assay-offices, and Coinage of the United States.*

SEC. 14. That the gold coins of the United States shall be a one-dollar piece, which, at the standard weight of twenty-five and eight tenths grains, shall be the unit of value; a quarter-eagle, or two-and-a-half-dollar piece; a three-dollar piece; a half-eagle, or five-dollar piece; an eagle, or ten-dollar piece; and a double-eagle, or twenty-dollar piece. And the standard weight of the gold dollar shall be twenty-five and eight tenths grains; of the quarter-eagle, or two-and-a-half-dollar piece, sixty-four and a half grains; of the three-dollar piece, seventy-seven and four tenths grains; of the half-eagle, or five-dollar piece, one hundred and twenty-nine grains; of the eagle, or ten-dollar piece, two hundred and fifty-eight grains; of the double-eagle, or twenty-dollar piece, five hundred and sixteen grains; which coins shall be a legal tender in all payments at their nominal value when not below the standard weight and limit of tolerance provided in this act for the single piece, and, when reduced in weight below said standard and tolerance, shall be a legal tender at valuation in proportion to their actual weight; and any gold coin of the United States, if reduced in weight by natural abrasion not more than one half of one per centum below the standard weight prescribed by law, after a circulation of twenty years, as shown by its date of coinage, and at a ratable proportion for any period less than twenty years, shall be received at their nominal value by the United States Treasury and its offices. . . .

SEC. 15. That the silver coins of the United States shall be a trade dollar, a half-dollar, or fifty-cent piece, a quarter-dollar, or twenty-five-cent piece, a dime, or ten-cent piece; and the weight of the trade dollar shall be four hundred and twenty grains troy; the weight of the half-dollar shall be twelve grams (grammes) and one half of a gram (gramme); the quarter-dollar and the dime shall be respectively one half and one fifth of the weight of said half-dollar; and said coins shall be a legal tender at their nominal value for any amount not exceeding five dollars in any one payment.

SEC. 17. That no coins, either of gold, silver, or minor coinage, shall hereafter be issued from the Mint other than those of the denominations, standards, and weights herein set forth.

SEC. 25. That the charge for converting standard gold bullion into coin shall be one fifth of one per centum; and the charges for converting standard silver into trade dollars, for melting and refining when bullion is below standard, for toughening when metals are contained in it which render it unfit for coinage, for copper used for alloy when the bullion is above standard, for separating the gold and silver when these metals exist together in the bullion, and for the preparation of bars, shall be fixed, from time to time, by the director, with the concurrence of the Secretary of the Treasury, so as to equal but not exceed, in their judgment, the actual average cost to each Mint and assay-office of the material, labor, wastage, and use of machinery employed in each of the cases aforementioned.

[Approved, February 12, 1873. 17 Statutes at Large, 424.]

NOTE.—By an act approved March 3, 1875, the coinage of a twenty-cent piece, in conformity with the provisions made as to other subsidiary silver coins, was authorized. See 18 Statutes at Large, Part III, 478.

VII. JUNE, 1874.—*Revised Statutes of the United States; Title XXXIX, Legal Tender.*

SEC. 3584. No foreign gold or silver coins shall be a legal tender in payment of debts.

SEC. 3585. The gold coins of the United States shall be a legal tender in all payments at their nominal value when not below the standard weight and limit of tolerance provided by law for the single piece, and, when reduced in weight below such standard and tolerance, shall be a legal tender at valuation in proportion to their actual weight.

SEC. 3586. The silver coins of the United States shall be a legal tender at their nominal value, for any amount not exceeding five dollars in any one payment.

SEC. 3587. The minor coins of the United States shall be a legal tender, at their nominal value, for any amount not exceeding twenty-five cents in any one payment.

[Sections 3588, 3589, 3590, contain the provisions to be found in previous acts, making United States notes, demand notes, and Treasury notes, respectively, legal tender.]

[Approved, June 22, 1874. Revised Statutes, 712.]

VIII. JANUARY, 1875.—*An Act to provide for the Resumption of Specie Payments.*

Be it enacted, . . . That the Secretary of the Treasury is hereby authorized and required, as rapidly as practicable, to cause to be coined at the mints of the United States, silver coins of the denominations of ten, twenty-five, and fifty cents, of standard value, and to issue them in

APPENDIX III. 233

redemption of an equal number and amount of fractional currency of similar denominations; or, at his discretion, he may issue such silver coins through the mints, the sub-treasuries, public depositories, and post-offices of the United States; and, upon such issue, he is hereby authorized and required to redeem an equal amount of such fractional currency until the whole amount of such fractional currency outstanding shall be redeemed.

SEC. 2. That so much of Section 3524 of the Revised Statutes of the United States as provides for a charge of one fifth of one per centum for converting standard gold bullion into coin is hereby repealed, and hereafter no charge shall be made for that service.

[Approved, January 14, 1875. 18 Statutes at Large, Part III, 296.]

IX. APRIL, 1876.—*Issue of Silver Coin.*

SEC. 2. That the Secretary of the Treasury is hereby directed to issue silver coins of the United States of the denomination of ten, twenty, twenty-five, and fifty cents of standard value, in redemption of an equal amount of fractional currency, whether the same be now in the Treasury awaiting redemption, or whenever it may be presented for redemption; and the Secretary of the Treasury may, under regulations of the Treasury Department, provide for such redemption and issue by substitution at the regular sub-treasuries and public depositories of the United States until the whole amount of fractional currency outstanding shall be redeemed. And the fractional currency redeemed under this act shall be held to be a part of the sinking-fund provided for by existing law. . . .

[Approved, April 17, 1876.]

X. JULY, 1876.—*Joint Resolution for the Issue of Silver Coin.*

Resolved, That the Secretary of the Treasury, under such limits and regulations as will best secure a just and fair distribution of the same through the country, may issue the silver coin at any time in the Treasury to an amount not exceeding ten million dollars in exchange for an equal amount of legal-tender notes; and the notes so received in exchange shall be kept as a special fund separate and apart from all other money in the Treasury, and be reissued only upon the retirement and destruction of a like sum of fractional currency received at the Treasury in payment of dues to the United States; and said fractional currency, when so substituted, shall be destroyed and held as part of the sinking-fund, as provided in the act approved April seventeen, eighteen hundred and seventy-six.

SEC. 2. That the trade dollar shall not hereafter be a legal tender, and the Secretary of the Treasury is hereby authorized to limit from time to time the coinage thereof to such an amount as he may deem sufficient to meet the export demand for the same.

SEC. 3. That, in addition to the amount of subsidiary silver coin authorized by law to be issued in redemption of the fractional currency, it shall be lawful to manufacture at the several Mints, and issue through the Treasury and its several offices, such coin to an amount that, including the amount of subsidiary silver coin and of fractional currency outstanding, shall, in the aggregate, not exceed, at any time, fifty million dollars.

[Section 4 authorizes the Secretary of the Treasury to purchase bullion for the purposes of this resolution, and requires any gain arising from the coinage thereof to be paid into the Treasury.]

[Approved, July 22, 1876. 19 Statutes at Large, 215.]

XI. FEBRUARY, 1878.—*An Act to authorize the coinage of the standard Silver Dollar, and to restore its legal-tender character.*

Be it enacted, That there shall be coined, at the several Mints of the United States, silver dollars of the weight of four hundred and twelve and a half grains troy of standard silver, as provided in the act of January eighteen, eighteen hundred and thirty-seven, on which shall be the devices and superscriptions provided by said act, which coins, together with all silver dollars heretofore coined by the United States of like weight and fineness, shall be a legal tender, at their nominal value, for all debts and dues, public and private, except where otherwise expressly stipulated in the contract. And the Secretary of the Treasury is authorized and directed to purchase, from time to time, silver bullion, at the market price thereof, not less than two million dollars worth per month, nor more than four million dollars worth per month, and cause the same to be coined monthly as fast as so purchased into such dollars; and a sum sufficient to carry out the foregoing provision is hereby appropriated out of any money in the Treasury not otherwise appropriated. And any gain or seigniorage arising from this coinage shall be accounted for and paid into the Treasury, as provided under existing laws relative to the subsidiary coinage; *Provided*, That the amount of money at any one time invested in such silver bullion, exclusive of such resulting coin, shall not exceed five million dollars. *And provided further*, That nothing in this act shall be construed to authorize the payment in silver of certificates of deposit issued under the provisions of section two hundred and fifty-four of the Revised Statutes.

SEC. 2. That, immediately after the passage of this act, the President shall invite the governments of the countries composing the Latin Union, so called, and of such other European nations as he may deem advisable, to join the United States in a conference to adopt a common ratio as between gold and silver, for the purpose of establishing, internationally, the use of bimetallic money, and securing fixity of relative value between those metals; such conference to be held at such place, in Europe or in the United States, at such time within six months, as may be mutually agreed upon by the Executives of the governments joining in the same, whenever the governments so invited, or any three of them, shall have signified their willingness to unite in the same. The President shall, by and with the advice and consent of the Senate, appoint three commissioners, who shall attend such conference on behalf of the United States, and shall report the doings thereof to the President, who shall transmit the same to Congress. Said commissioners shall each receive the sum of twenty-five hundred dollars and their reasonable expenses, to be approved by the Secretary of State; and the amount necessary to pay such compensation and expenses is hereby appropriated out of any money in the Treasury not otherwise appropriated.

SEC. 3. That any holder of the coin authorized by this act may deposit the same with the Treasurer or any Assistant Treasurer of the United States, in sums not less than ten dollars, and receive therefor certificates of not less than ten dollars each, corresponding with the denominations of the United States notes. The coin deposited for or representing the certificates shall be retained in the Treasury for the payment of the same on demand. Said certificates shall be receivable for customs, taxes, and all public dues, and, when so received, may be reissued.

SEC. 4. All acts and parts of acts inconsistent with the provisions of this act are hereby repealed.

NOTE.—The above act having been returned by the President of the United States, with his objections, to the House of Representatives, February 28, 1878, was passed by both Houses, and became a law on the same day.

XII. JUNE, 1879.—*An Act to authorize the redemption of Silver Coins.*

Be it enacted, That the holder of any of the silver coins of the United States of smaller denominations than one dollar may, on presentation of the same in sums of twenty dollars, or any multiple thereof, at the office of the Treasurer or any Assistant Treasurer of the United States, receive therefor lawful money of the United States.

SEC. 3. That the present silver coins of the United States of smaller denominations than one dollar shall hereafter be a legal tender in all sums not exceeding ten dollars in full payment of all dues, public and private.

[Approved, June 9, 1879.]

B.

French Monetary Law of 1803.

In the name of the French People,
Bonaparte, First Consul, Proclaims as law of the Republic the following decree, rendered by the Corps Legislatif the 7 germinal [28 March], year xi [1803], conformably with the proposition made by the government the 19 *ventôse*, communicated to the tribunal the next day.

DECREE.

General dispositions.

Five grammes of silver, nine tenths fine, constitute the monetary unit, which retains the name of franc.

TITLE I.

Of the fabrication of coins.

Article 1. The silver coins shall be the quarter-of-a-franc, half-franc, three-quarters-of-a-franc, one-franc, two-franc, and five-franc pieces.

Art. 2. Their fineness is fixed at nine tenths fine and one tenth alloy.

Art. 3. The weight of the quarter-of-a-franc piece shall be one gramme twenty-five centigrammes.

That of the half-franc piece, two grammes five décigrammes.

That of the three-quarters-of-a-franc piece, three grammes seventy-five centigrammes.

That of the one-franc piece, five grammes.

That of the two-franc piece, ten grammes.

That of the five-franc piece, twenty-five grammes.

Art. 4. The tolerance of fineness for silver money shall be three thousandths, outside as well as within.

Art. 5. The tolerance of weight shall be, for the quarter-of-a-franc piece, ten thousandths, outside as well as within; for the half-franc and three-quarters-of-a-franc piece, seven thousandths, outside as well as within; for the one-franc and two-franc pieces, five thousandths, outside as well as within; and for the five-franc piece, three thousandths, outside as well as within.

Art. 6. There shall be coined gold pieces of twenty francs and of forty francs.

Art. 7. Their fineness is fixed at nine tenths fine and one tenth alloy.

ART. 8. The twenty-franc pieces shall be struck at the rate of a hundred and fifty-five pieces to the kilogramme, and the forty-franc pieces at that of seventy-seven and a half.

ART. 9. The tolerance of fineness of the gold coins is fixed at two thousandths outside, the same within.

ART. 10. The tolerance of weight is fixed at two thousandths outside, the same within.

ART. 11. The expense of coinage alone can be required of those who shall bring material of gold or silver to the Mint.

These charges are fixed at nine francs per kilogramme of gold, and at three francs per kilogramme of silver.

ART. 12. When the material shall be below the monetary standard, it shall bear the charges of refining or of separation.

The amount of these charges shall be calculated on the portion of the said material which must be purified in order to raise the whole to the monetary standard.

ART. 13. There shall be coined pieces of pure copper of two hundredths, three hundredths, and five hundredths of a franc.

ART. 14. The weight of the pieces of two hundredths shall be four grammes; that of the pieces of three hundredths, six grammes; that of the pieces of five hundredths, ten grammes.

ART. 15. The tolerance of weight shall be for the copper pieces a fiftieth outside.

[ART. 16 explains the devices.]

ART. 17. The diameter of each piece shall be determined by regulations of the public administration.

[Title II deals only with the verification of the coins.]

At Paris, the 17 germinal [April 7], year xi of the Republic [1803].

[Signed.]

C.

GERMAN MONETARY LAWS OF 1871 AND 1873.

German Reichstag, 1st Legislation Period, 2d session, 1871. Law relating to the coinage of imperial gold coins, as passed by Parliament after its third reading.

We, WILHELM, by the grace of God, German Emperor, King of Prussia, etc., do ordain, in the name of the German Empire, the same having been passed by the Bundesrath and the Reichstag as follows:

SEC. 1. There shall be coined an imperial gold coin, $139\frac{1}{2}$ pieces of which shall contain one pound of pure gold.

APPENDIX III.

SEC. 2. The tenth of this gold coin shall be called "mark," and shall be divided into one hundred "pfennige."

SEC. 3. Besides the imperial gold coin of 10 marks (Sec. 1), there shall be coined imperial gold coins of 20 marks, of which $69\frac{1}{2}$ pieces shall contain one pound of pure gold.

SEC. 4. The alloy of the imperial gold coins shall consist of 900 thousandths parts gold, and 100 thousandths parts copper. Therefore, 125·55 pieces of 10 marks, 62·775 pieces of 20 marks, will each weigh one pound.

SEC. 5. The imperial gold coins are to bear on one side the imperial eagle, with the inscription "German Empire," and their value in marks; also the year of their coinage; on the other side the likeness of the sovereign, or, in the case of the free cities, their arms, with a corresponding inscription and the marks of the Mint. Diameters of coins, form, and inscription of edges of the same shall be prescribed by the Bundesrath.

SEC. 6. Until the enactment of a law for the redemption of the large silver coins, the making of the gold coins shall be conducted at the expense of the Empire, for all the states of the Confederation, at the mints of those states which have declared their readiness to do so.

The Chancellor of the Empire shall determine, with the consent of the Bundesrath, the amounts to be coined in gold, the apportionment of these amounts to the several kinds of coins and to the several mints, and the compensation to be paid in equal proportions to the several mints for the coinage of each separate kind of coin. He shall deliver to the several mints the gold requisite to the amounts of coinage assigned them.

SEC. 7. The process of coinage of the imperial gold coins will be determined by the Bundesrath, and is subject to the control of the Empire. This process shall assure the absolute accuracy of the coins in fineness and weight. So far as an absolute accuracy in each single piece can not be secured, the deviation in weight shall not be greater, either above or below, than two and one half thousandths; in fineness not more than two thousandths.

SEC. 8. All payments which are by law to be made, or which may be made, in silver coins of the thaler system, of the South German system, of the Lubeck or Hamburg current system, or in gold thalers of the Bremen system, can be made in imperial gold coins (Secs. 1 and 3) in such manner as to count the 10-mark piece equal in value to $3\frac{1}{3}$ thalers, or 5 florins 50 kreutzers, South German system, 8 marks $5\frac{1}{3}$ schillings Lubeck or Hamburg current system, $3\frac{1}{13}$ gold thalers of the Bremen system; the 20-mark piece equal in value to $6\frac{2}{3}$ thalers, or 11 florins 40 kreutzers, South German system; 16 marks $10\frac{2}{3}$ schillings, Lubeck or Hamburg current system; $6\frac{2}{13}$ gold thalers of the Bremen system.

APPENDIX III. 239

SEC. 9. Imperial gold coin whose weight shall be not more than five thousandths parts below their normal weight (Sec. 4), current weight, and whose weight shall not have been reduced by violent or unlawful injury, shall be counted as of full weight for all payments. Imperial gold coins which are of less than the above-named current weight, and which have been accepted in payment by imperial, state, provincial, or municipal treasuries, or by money and credit institutions and banks, shall not be paid out again by such treasuries or institutions.

The imperial gold coins will be taken in for remelting by and for the account of the Empire after they have lost so much of their weight by long circulation and wear as to be of less than the current weight.

All such worn gold coins shall always be accepted by all treasuries of the Empire and of the states at the value at which they were emitted.

SEC. 10. No coinage of gold coins other than those established by this law, nor of large silver coins, the coinage of metals excepted, shall take place until further action.

SEC. 11. The gold coins of the states of the German Confederation at present in circulation are to be redeemed by order and for account of the Empire in proportion to the issue of the new gold coins (Sec. 6).

The Chancellor of the Empire is authorized to provide, in like manner, for the redemption of the hitherto-made large silver coins of the states of the German Confederation, and to take from the most available funds of the imperial treasury the means necessary therefor. Concerning the execution of the above regulations, an annual account shall be given to the Reichstag at its first regular session.

SEC. 12. Pieces of standard weight may be made for adjustment and sealing which shall represent the normal weight and the current weight of the gold coins to be made according to this law; also multiples of those standard pieces. The regulations given in Sections 10 and 18 of the act dated August 17, 1868, relating to weights and measures ("Bundesgesetzblatt," p. 473), shall be binding for the adjustment and sealing of such standard pieces.

SEC. 13. In the territory of the Kingdom of Bavaria the pfennig may, if necessary, be divided into two half-pfennigs.

Berlin, November 23, 1871. The President of the German Imperial Diet, represented by

Prince von HOHENLOHE SCHILLENGSFÜRST.

(Extract from the "Journal of National Laws," 1873. Published in Berlin, July 15, 1873.)

"*Journal of National Laws*," No. 22.—No. 953, *Mint Law of July* 9, 1873.

WE, WILHELM, by the grace of God, German Emperor, King of Prussia, etc., do decree, in the name of the German Empire and the Parliament, as follows:

ARTICLE 1. In place of the various local standards now current in Germany, a national gold standard will be established. Its monetary unit is the "mark," as established in paragraph 2 of the law dated December 4, 1871, in regard to the issue of national gold coins. (See "Journal of National Laws" for 1871, p. 404.)

The date when the national standard shall be enforced within the entire territory of the Empire will be determined by an imperial decree, to be published with the consent of the Federal Council, and proclaimed at least three months in advance of that date. The state governments are authorized to introduce the national "mark" standard, even before that date, by special decree.

ART. 2. In addition to the national gold coins designated in the law of December 4, 1871, there will also be issued national gold coins of five marks, 279 pieces to be coined from each pound of fine gold. The regulations of paragraphs 4, 5, 7, 8, and 9 of that law also apply in regard to these coins, with the provision, however, that the allowance in weight (paragraph 7) above or below the standard may be four thousandths, and the difference between the standard and current weight may be eight thousandths for these coins.

ART. 3. There shall also be issued in addition to the national gold coins:

1. As silver coins, five-mark pieces, two-mark pieces, one-mark pieces, fifty-pfennig pieces, and twenty-pfennig pieces.

2. As nickel coins, ten-pfennig pieces, and five-pfennig pieces.

3. As copper coins, two-pfennig and one-pfennig pieces, in accordance with the following regulations:

¶ 1. The pound of fine silver shall produce at coinage twenty five-mark pieces, fifty two-mark pieces, one hundred one-mark pieces, two hundred fifty-pfennig pieces, five hundred twenty-pfennig pieces. The proportion of alloy is one hundred parts of copper to nine hundred parts of silver, so that ninety marks in silver coin shall weigh one pound. The process of the manufacture of these coins will be established by the Federal Council. In single coins the allowance in fineness above or below the standard shall not be more than three thousandths, and in weight, the twenty-pfennig pieces excepted, not more than ten thousandths. In quantities, however, the standard weight and fineness must be observed in silver coins.

¶ 2. The silver coins of more than one mark bear upon one side the national eagle, with the inscription "Deutsches Reich" (German Empire), and the designation of the value in marks, as well as the year of coinage; upon the other side the image of the sovereign, or, respectively, the escutcheon of the free cities, with a suitable inscription and the cipher of the Mint. The diameter of these coins, as well as the nature and milling of their edges, will be determined by the Federal Council.

¶ 3. Other silver coins, also the nickel and copper coins, bear upon one side the value, the year, and the inscription "Deutsches Reich" (German Empire), and upon the other side the national eagle and the cipher of the Mint. Particular regulations concerning composition, weight, and diameter of these coins, as well as the ornamentation of the face bearing the inscription, and the condition of the edges, will be established by the Federal Council.

¶ 4. Silver, nickel, and copper coins will be manufactured in the mints of such Federal states as desire it. The coinage and the emission of these coins, however, will be subject to the direction of the Empire. The national Chancellor will designate, with the consent of the Federal Council, the aggregate of the issues, the distribution of these amounts among the different denominations of coin and the various mints; and the compensation of these mints for the coinage of every species of coin will be ordered by the national Chancellor.

ART. 4. The aggregate issue of silver coins shall, until further orders, not exceed ten marks for each inhabitant of the Empire. At each issue of these coins a quantity of the present silver coins equal in value to the new issue must be withdrawn from circulation, and first those of "thirty-thaler" standard. Their value is to be calculated according to the regulations in paragraph 2, Article 14.

ART. 5. The aggregate issue of nickel and copper coins shall not exceed two and a half marks for each inhabitant.

ART. 6. Of the fractional coins there are to be withdrawn before the introduction of the national standard—

1. The five-pfennig, two-pfennig, and one-pfennig pieces, coined after the mark system in Mecklenburg, and the coins of the thaler standard, except the Bavarian "hellers" (farthings).

2. The fractional coins of two-pfennig and four-pfennig pieces, based upon the duodecimal division of the "groschen."

3. The fractional coins of the thaler standard, based upon any other division of the thaler less than thirty groschen, with the exception of the pieces having the value of the half-thaler. After that date no person shall be compelled to take these pieces in payment, except the depositories designated for their redemption.

ART. 7. The coinage of silver, nickel, and copper coins, as well as the withdrawal of the current silver coins and fractional coins, to be ordered by the national Chancellor, will be defrayed by the national treasury.

ART. 8. The regulation for the withdrawal of local coins, and the decrees required therefor, will be issued by the Federal Council. The publication of these measures must be made in the "Journal of the National Laws," in addition to the publication of the local ordinances. Such withdrawal can only be ordered after fixing a period of redemption of at least four weeks, and the publication of its termination at least three months in advance of the same.

ART. 9. No person shall be compelled to take in payment national silver coins to a larger amount than twenty marks, and nickel and copper coins to a larger amount than one mark. The Federal Council will designate such depositories as will disburse national gold coins in exchange for silver coins in amounts of at least 200 marks, and of nickel and copper coins in amounts of at least 50 marks, upon demand. The same authority will also establish particular rules of exchange.

ART. 10. The provisions for acceptance and exchange (Article 9) do not apply to perforated coins, or counterfeits, or such as may be reduced in weight by other causes than abrasure in usage. National silver, nickel, and copper coins, which, by long circulation or use, have lost considerably in weight or imprint, will be received in national and local depositories, but must be withdrawn at the expense of the Empire.

ART. 11. The coinage of other silver, nickel, or copper coins than those authorized by this law is strictly prohibited. The provision in paragraph 10 of the law of December 4, 1871, concerning the coinage of national gold coins ("Journal of National Laws of 1871," p. 404), reserving the authority of coining silver coins as medals, will expire December 31, 1873.

ART. 12. The coinage of the national gold coins will continue to be executed according to the rules in paragraph 6 of the law of December 4, 1871, providing for the coinage of national gold coins. (See "Journal of National Laws of 1871," p. 404.)

Private persons are privileged to have twenty-mark pieces coined at their own expense, in mints which have declared themselves ready to coin at the expense of the Empire, when they are not engaged in work for the Empire.

The rate of such coinage will be fixed by the national Chancellor, with the consent of the Federal Council, but can not exceed seven marks for each pound of fine gold. The difference between this rate and the compensation due the Mint for such coinage shall be paid into the national treasury, and must be alike in all mints. The mints are not allowed to charge higher rates for private coinage than the national treasury pays for the coinage of twenty-mark pieces.

ART. 13. The Federal Council is authorized:

1. To determine the value to which foreign gold and silver coins are limited, to be offered or received in payment, and also to prohibit the circulation of foreign coins entirely, if it is deemed advisable.

2. To determine whether or not foreign coins may be admitted in national and local depositories at a publicly known value, and, if admitted, what this value is to be. Habitual or professional transgressions of the regulations established by the Federal Council, in accord-

APPENDIX III. 243

ance with paragraph 1 of this article, will be punished by a fine of 150 marks and imprisonment for six weeks.

ART. 14. From the introduction of the national standard the following rules will be enforced:

¶ 1. All payments to be made up to that time in coins now current, or in foreign coins lawfully equalized with such domestic coins, are then to be made in national coins under reservation of Articles 9, 15, and 16.

¶ 2. The calculations of such gold coins as are not provided for by an established relation to silver coins are to be made in accordance with their proportion of lawful fineness, for which their obligation calls, to the legal fineness of national gold coins.

In the calculation of other coins the thaler is valued at 3 marks, the florin (golden) of South Germany at $1\frac{4}{7}$ marks, and the mark of Lubeck or Hamburg standard at $1\frac{1}{5}$ marks. Other coins of the same standard are to be valued in their proportion to said values. In these calculations the fractions of pfennigs of the national standard are to be counted as pfennigs if equal to, or over, half a pfennig; smaller fractions are to be ignored.

¶ 3. Obligations entered into after the introduction of the national standard, based upon former standards of money or accounts, shall be liquidated in national coins, under the regulations of paragraph 2, with reservation of the provisions in Articles 9, 15, and 16.

¶ 4. In all documents executed by courts or notaries involving considerations of money, also in all court decisions involving fines, the amounts must be expressed in the national standard, if there is any proportion thereof to the national standard as legally established; yet additional designation under the standard which the obligation originated is also permitted.

ART. 15. In the place of national coins in all payments previous to the contemplated withdrawal there will be admitted:

1. Within the entire territory of the Empire, pieces of one and two thalers of German coinage, at a value of three marks to one thaler, in lieu of all national coins.

2. Within the entire territory of the Empire, in place of national silver coin only, current silver pieces of German coinage of $\frac{1}{3}$ and $\frac{1}{6}$ thaler at a value of $\frac{1}{3}$ thaler to 1 mark and $\frac{1}{6}$ thaler to $\frac{1}{2}$ mark.

3. In all states where the thaler standard now prevails in place of the national nickel and copper coins, the following coins of the thaler standard at the designated values: $\frac{1}{12}$-thaler pieces at the value of 25 pfennigs; $\frac{1}{15}$-thaler pieces at the value of 20 pfennigs; $\frac{1}{30}$-thaler pieces at the value of 10 pfennigs; $\frac{1}{2}$-groschen pieces at the value of 5 pfennigs; $\frac{1}{5}$-groschen pieces at the value of 2 pfennigs; $\frac{1}{10}$- and $\frac{1}{12}$-groschen pieces at the value of 1 pfennig.

4. In those states where the duodecimal division of the groschen exists in place of the national nickel and copper coins, the three-pfennig pieces based upon the duodecimal division of the groschen at a value of 2½ pfennigs.

5. In Bavaria, in place of the national copper coins, the (heller) farthing pieces, at the value of ½ pfennig.

6. In Mecklenburg, in place of the national copper coins, the five-pfennig, two-pfennig, and one-pfennig pieces coined under the mark standard, at a value of 5, 2, and 1 pfennig. All coins embraced under paragraphs 3 and 4 of this article are to be admitted in payment at all public depositories within the Federal territory at the stated values until their withdrawal.

ART. 16. German gold crowns, state gold coins, and foreign gold coins, placed by law on equal footing with domestic (German) coins, as well as large silver coins of another standard than that of the thaler, are to be admitted in payment until their withdrawal in the same manner as they have been accepted hitherto under previous regulations.

ART. 17. Even before the introduction of the national standard all payments which may be made under the present laws in coins of domestic (German) standard, or in foreign coins placed by law on an equal footing with them, may be liquidated either in part or the total in national coins, reserving the provisions in Article 9 in such a manner that their value is calculated according to the provisions of paragraph 2, Article 14.

ART. 18. By January 1, 1876, all bank-notes not issued according to the national standard must be withdrawn.

From that date only bank-notes issued according to the national standard, and in amounts of not less than 100 marks, may be emitted and kept in circulation. These provisions also apply to bills hitherto issued by corporations.

All paper money issued by single states of the Confederation must be withdrawn before January 1, 1876, and is to be recalled at least six months before that date. In lieu thereof an emission of national paper money will be made according to a national law to be issued in the mean time. This national law will establish provisions concerning the emission and circulation of national paper money, as well as the facilities to be granted to the single states of the Confederation for the purpose of the withdrawal of their paper money.

In witness whereof, our signature and imperial seal,

[L. S.]   WILHELM.
COUNT V. BISMARCK.
Given at Ems, July 9, 1873.

D.

TREATY BETWEEN SWITZERLAND, BELGIUM, FRANCE, AND ITALY CONCERNING THE MONETARY UNION.

The Swiss Confederation, H. M. the King of Belgium, H. M. the French Emperor, and H. M. the King of Italy, equally animated by a desire to establish a more complete harmony between their monetary enactments, to remedy the inconveniences in regard to intercourse and transactions between the inhabitants of their respective states, which result from the difference of standard of their subsidiary silver money, and to contribute, by forming a monetary union between them, to the progress of a uniformity of weights, of measures, and of money, have resolved to conclude an agreement to this end, and have named the following as their commissioners plenipotentiary:

The Swiss Confederation: M. Kern, Envoy Extraordinary, and M. Feer-Herzog, member of the Swiss National Council.

The King of the Belgians: M. Frederic Fortamps, member of the Senate, director of the Bank of Belgium, and M. A. Kreglinger, Government Commissioner of the National Bank.

The Emperor of the French: M. de Parieu, Vice-President of the Council of State, and M. Théophile-Jules Pelouze, President of the Money Commission.

The King of Italy: M. Isaac Artom, Counselor of his Legation at Paris, and M. Valentin Protolongo, Director, Chief of Division, in the Ministry of Agriculture, Industry, and Commerce.

Who, having communicated respectively their full powers, found in good and due form, have agreed upon the following articles:

ART. 1. Switzerland, Belgium, France, and Italy are formed into a union so far as regards the weight, fineness, diameter, and circulation of their gold and silver coinage.

No change, for the present, is made in legislation relative to the copper coinage of each of the four states.

ART. 2. The high contracting parties agree not to make, nor permit to be made, with their stamp, any gold coins of other kinds than pieces of 100 fr., 50 fr., 20 fr., 10 fr., and 5 fr., determined as to weight, fineness, tolerance, and diameter, as follows:

Pieces.	Weight.	Tolerance.	Fineness.	Tolerance of Fineness.	Diameter.
100	32 gr. 258·06	1 millièm.			35 millim.
50	16 " 120·03	1 "			28 "
20	6 " 451·71	2 "	900 millièm.	2 millièm.	21 "
10	2 " 225·80	2 "			19 "
5	1 " 612·90	3 "			17 "

They will admit without distinction at their public treasuries gold coins made under the foregoing conditions, in one or any of the four states, with the reservation, however, that they exclude pieces whose weight may have been reduced by wear one half per cent below the tolerance stated above, or whose device may have disappeared.

ART. 3. The contracting governments pledge themselves not to coin, nor permit to be coined, silver five-franc pieces except of a weight, fineness, tolerance, and diameter determined herewith:

Weight.	Tolerance.	Fineness.	Tolerance of Fineness.	Diameter.
25 gram.	3 millièmes.	900 millièmes.	2 millièmes.	37 millimètres.

They will reciprocally receive the aforesaid pieces in their public treasuries, with the reservation, however, that they exclude those whose weight may have been reduced by wear one per cent below the tolerance stated above, or whose device may have disappeared.

ART. 4. The high contracting parties will not coin hereafter silver pieces of two francs, one franc, fifty centimes, and twenty centimes, except under the conditions of weight, fineness, tolerance, and diameter determined herewith:

Pieces.	Weight.	Tolerance.	Fineness.	Tolerance of Fineness.	Diameter.
2 fr.	10 gram.	5 millièm.	835 millièm.	3 millièm.	27 millim.
1 "	5 "	5 "	835 "	3 "	23 "
0·50	2·50 "	7 "	835 "	3 "	18 "
0·20	1 "	10 "	835 "	3 "	16 "

These pieces must be recoined by the governments that have issued them when they may have been reduced by wear five per cent below the tolerance above stated, or when their devices have disappeared.

ART. 5. Silver pieces of two francs, one franc, fifty centimes, and twenty centimes, coined on different terms than those stated in the preceding article, are to be retired from circulation before January 1, 1869. This term is extended to January 1, 1878, for pieces of two francs and one franc issued by Switzerland by virtue of the law of January 31, 1860.

ART. 6. Silver pieces coined under the conditions of Article 4 shall be a legal tender between individuals of the state which coined them to the amount of fifty francs at each payment.

The state issuing them shall receive them from its inhabitants without limitation of quantity.

ART. 7. The public treasuries of each of the four countries shall accept the silver money coined by any one of the other contracting states, conformably to Article 4, to the amount of one hundred francs at each payment to the aforesaid treasuries.

The governments of Belgium, France, and Italy will receive, on the

APPENDIX III.

same terms, until January 1, 1878, the Swiss coins of two francs and one franc issued according to the law of January 31, 1860, which are regarded in every respect, during the same period, as the pieces coined under the provisions of Article 4.

The whole subject to the reservations stated in Article 4 in regard to wear.

ART. 8. Each of the contracting governments binds itself to accept from individuals or public treasuries of the other states the subsidiary silver which it has issued, and to give in exchange an equal value of current coin (gold coins, or five-franc silver coins, provided the sum presented for exchange shall not be less than one hundred francs). This obligation shall extend two years from the expiration of the present treaty.

ART. 9. The high contracting parties shall issue silver pieces of two francs, one franc, fifty centimes, and twenty centimes, coined under the conditions stated in Article 4, to an amount only of six francs to each inhabitant.

This amount, based on the last census taken in each state, and the probable increase of population to the expiration of the present treaty, is fixed at:

For Belgium............................	32,000,000 francs.
" France...............................	239,000,000 "
" Italy................................	141,000,000 "
" Switzerland.........................	17,000,000 "

Of the sums which the governments also have a right to coin are included the following: The amounts, already issued by France in accordance with the law of May 25, 1864, of pieces of fifty and twenty centimes to about sixteen millions; by Italy, in accordance with the law of August 24, 1862, of pieces of two francs and one franc. and of fifty and twenty centimes, to about one hundred millions; by Switzerland, in accordance with the law of January 31, 1860, of two- and one-franc pieces, to about ten millions five hundred thousand francs.

ART. 10. The date of coinage shall hereafter be stamped on the gold and silver pieces coined in the four states.

ART. 11. The contracting governments shall state annually the amount of their issues of gold and silver coins, the progress of the withdrawal and recoinage of their old coins, all the arrangements, and all the administrative documents relative to coinage.

They shall likewise give information as to all facts affecting the reciprocal circulation of their gold and silver pieces.

ART. 12. The privilege of joining the present convention is granted to any other state which shall accept its obligations, and which shall adopt the monetary system of the Union in regard to gold and silver coins.

ART. 13. The execution of the reciprocal pledges in the present convention is relegated, so far as necessary, to the fulfillment of the formalities and rules established by the constitutional laws of those of the high contracting parties which are required to refer to them, and this they bind themselves to do as soon as possible.

ART. 14. The present convention shall remain in force until January 1, 1880. If not dissolved a year before the expiration of this term, it shall remain in full force for a new period of fifteen years, and so on, fifteen years at a time, if no objection is made.

ART. 15. The present convention shall be ratified, and the ratifications shall be exchanged at Paris within six months, or, if possible, sooner.

In testimony whereof the commissioners plenipotentiary have respectively signed the present convention under their seals.

Done in four copies, at Paris, December 23, 1865.

[Then follow the signatures.]

APPENDIX IV.

COINAGE OF GOLD AND SILVER, FROM THE ORGANIZATION OF THE UNITED STATES MINT TO 1884.

YEARS.	Silver Dollars.	Total Silver Coinage, including Dollars.	Total Gold Coinage.
1793-1795	$204,791	$370,683.80	$71,485.00
1796	72,920	79,077.50	102,727.50
1797	7,776	12,591.45	103,422.50
1798	327,536	330,291.00	205,610.00
1799	423,515	423,515.00	213,285.00
1800	220,920	224,296.00	317,760.00
1801	54,454	74,758.00	422,570.00
1802	41,650	58,343.00	423,310.00
1803	66,064	87,118.00	258,377.50
1804	19,570	100,340.50	258,642.50
1805	321	149,388.50	170,367.50
1806		471,319.00	324,505.00
1807		597,448.75	437,495.00
1808		684,300.00	284,665.00
1809		707,376.00	169,375.00
1810		638,773.50	501,435.00
1811		608,340.00	497,905.00
1812		814,029.50	290,435.00
1813		620,951.50	477,140.00
1814		561,687.50	77,270.00
1815		17,308.00	3,175.00
1816		28,575.75	
1817		607,783.50	
1818		1,070,454.50	242,940.00
1819		1,140,000.00	258,615.00
1820		501,680.70	1,319,030.00
1821		825,762.45	189,325.00
1822		805,806.50	88,980.00
1823		895,550.00	72,425.00
1824		1,752,477.00	93,200.00
1825		1,564,583.00	156,385.00
1826		2,002,090.00	92,245.00
1827		2,869,200.00	131,565.00
1828		1,575,600.00	140,145.00
1829		1,994,578.00	295,717.50
1830		2,495,400.00	643,105.00
1831		3,175,600.00	714,270.00
1832		2,579,000.00	798,435.00
1833		2,759,000.00	978,550.00
1834		3,415,002.00	3,954,270.00
1835		3,443,003.00	2,186,175.00

COINAGE OF GOLD AND SILVER, FROM THE ORGANIZATION OF THE
UNITED STATES MINT TO 1884—*Continued.*

YEARS.	Silver Dollars.	Total Silver Coinage, including Dollars.	Total Gold Coinage.
1836	$1,000	$3,606,100.00	$4,135,700.00
1837		2,096,010.00	1,148,305.00
1838		2,333,243.00	1,809,595.00
1839	300	2,176,296.00	1,355,885.00
1840	61,005	1,726,703.00	1,675,302.50
1841	173,000	1,132,750.00	1,091,597.50
1842	184,618	2,332,750.00	1,834,170.00
1843	165,100	3,834,750.00	8,108,797.50
1844	20,000	2,235,550.00	5,428,230.00
1845	24,500	1,873,200.00	3,756,447.50
1846	169,600	2,558,580.00	4,034,177.50
1847	140,750	2,379,450.00	20,221,385.00
1848	15,000	2,040,050.00	3,775,512.50
1849	62,600	2,114,950.00	9,007,761.50
1850	47,500	1,866,100.00	31,981,738.50
1851	1,300	774,397.00	62,614,492.50
1852	1,100	999,410.00	56,846,187.50
1853	46,110	9,077,571.00	39,377,909.00
1854	33,140	8,619,270.00	25,915,918.50
1855	26,000	3,501,245.00	28,977,968.00
1856	63,500	5,135,240.00	36,697,768.50
1857	94,000	1,477,000.00	15,811,563.00
1858		8,040,730.00	30,253,725.50
1859	288,500	6,187,400.00	17,296,077.00
1860	600,530	2,769,920.00	16,445,476.00
1861	559,900	2,605,700.00	60,693,237.00
1862	1,750	2,812,401.50	45,532,386.50
1863	31,400	1,174,092.80	20,695,852.00
1864	23,170	548,214.10	21,649,345.00
1865	32,900	636,308.00	25,107,217.50
1866	58,550	680,264.50	28,313,945.00
1867	57,000	986,871.00	28,217,187.50
1868	54,800	1,136,750.00	18,114,425.00
1869	231,350	840,746.50	21,828,637.50
1870	588,308	1,767,253.50	22,257,312.50
1871	657,929	1,955,905.25	21,302,475.00
1872	1,112,961	3,029,834.05	20,376,495.00
1873	977,150	2,945,795.50	35,249,337.50
1874		5,983,601.30	50,442,690.00
1875		10,070,368.00	33,553,965.00
1876		19,126,502.50	38,178,962.50
1877		28,549,935.00	44,078,199.00
1878	8,573,500	28,290,825.50 [1]	52,798,980.00
1879	27,227,500	27,227,882.50	40,986,912.00
1880	27,933,750	27,942,437.50	56,157,735.00
1881	27,637,955	27,649,966.75	78,733,864.00
1882	27,772,075	27,783,368.75	89,413,447.50
1883	28,111,119	28,835,470.15	35,936,927.50
1884	28,099,930	28,773,387.80	27,932,824.00

[1] Includes trade dollars, 412½-gr. dollars, and fractional coin.

APPENDIX V.

AVERAGE GOLD EQUIVALENT[1] OF THE SILVER DOLLAR OF 412½ GRAINS BY YEARS, ACCORDING TO OUR STANDARD OF 1 : 16.

YEAR.	Gold equivalent of a dollar of silver of 412½ grains.	YEAR.	Gold equivalent of a dollar of silver of 412½ grains.
	Cents.		Cents.
1834	101·62	1856	103·95
1835	101·20	1857	104·69
1836	101·72	1858	102·95
1837	100·98	1859	105·22
1838	100·88	1860	104·58
1839	102·36	1861	103·10
1840	102·36	1862	104·16
1841	101·83	1863	104·06
1842	100·77	1864	104·06
1843	100·34	1865	103·52
1844	100·88	1866	103·63
1845	100·46	1867	102·67
1846	100·56	1868	102·57
1847	101·20	1869	102·47
1848	100·88	1870	102·67
1849	101·30	1871	102·57
1850	101·83	1872	102·25
1851	103·42	1873	100·46
1852	102·57	1874	98·86
1853	104·26	1875	96·43
1854	104·26	1876	89·22
1855	103·95		

[1] Taken from Linderman's "Money and Legal Tender," pp. 161, 162.

APPENDIX VI.

Flow of Silver to the East.

YEARS.	Surplus of Imports [1] into British India.		Shipments of Silver to India and China from England and the Mediterranean. Sir Hector Hay.[2]	Exports of Silver from Great Britain and the Mediterranean. M. de Quetteville.[3]
	Gold.	Silver.		
1835–1836	$1,094,590	$8,059,480	....	....
1836–1837	2,098,620	6,694,410	....	....
1837–1838	2,154,350	9,834,720	....	....
1838–1839	1,294,625	13,225,650	....	....
1839–1840	1,133,215	8,252,355	....	....
1840–1841	686,560	7,008,350	....	....
1841–1842	828,115	6,416,140	....	....
1842–1843	1,055,805	14,762,225	....	....
1843–1844	2,032,615	18,477,210	....	....
1844–1845	3,550,500	9,942,805	....	....
1845–1846	2,722,380	4,662,450	....	....
1846–1847	4,234,745	6,891,245	....	....
1847–1848	5,195,580	2,470,955	....	....
1848–1849	6,744,590	1,569,520	....	....
1849–1850	5,584,965	6,368,035	....	....
1850–1851	5,766,470	10,586,125	....	$8,580,500
1851–1852	6,338,065	14,326,785	$13,150,000	13,151,190
1852–1853	5,861,505	23,025,120	23,550,000	27,795,135
1853–1854	5,307,215	11,528,720	22,900,000	22,915,085
1854–1855	3,656,450	148,000	39,900,000	39,670,645
1855–1856	12,531,225	40,971,875	70,600,000	70,544,505
1856–1857	10,456,070	55,366,235	100,750,000	100,729,605
1857–1858	13,915,365	61,094,740	28,450,000	28,464,830
1858–1859	22,132,265	38,641,710	81,750,000	81,752,455
1859–1860	21,421,170	55,737,815	54,000,000	54,011,650
1860–1861	21,162,845	26,640,045	44,300,000	44,296,760
1861–1862	25,922,125	45,432,280	73,000,000	72,998,895
1862–1863	34,240,795	62,750,775	75,650,000	75,682,665
1863–1864	44,491,530	63,983,595	84,275,000	84,283,490
1864–1865	49,199,820	50,393,990	48,700,000	48,726,490
1865–1866	28,622,380	93,843,365	35,350,000	35,397,440

[1] "Report to H. C., 1876," p. 172, and "French Report of Conference of 1881," i, p. 202.
[2] "Report to H. C., 1876," Appendix, p. 24.
[3] Ibid., p. 184.

APPENDIX VI. 253

FLOW OF SILVER TO THE EAST—*Continued.*

YEARS.	Surplus of Imports into British India.		Shipments of Silver to India and China from England and the Mediterranean. Sir Hector Hay.	Exports of Silver from Great Britain and the Mediterranean. M. de Quetteville.
	Gold.	Silver.		
1866-1867 [1]	$19,211,640	$34,815,370	$10,250,000	$10,261,120
1867-1868	23,047,335	27,969,805	17,800,000	17,792,765
1868-1869	25,796,760	43,005,110	32,800,000	32,820,740
1869-1870	27,960,585	36,601,685	11,100,000	11,079,000
1870-1871	11,410,605	4,709,685	19,500,000	19,460,615
1871-1872	17,826,720	32,564,135	32,650,000	32,663,075
1872-1873	12,716,810	3,523,220	17,350,000	17,394,960
1873-1874	6,913,190	12,256,915	38,850,000	38,853,185
1874-1875	9,367,675	23,211,010	22,700,000	22,735,590
1875-1876	7,725,655	7,776,775	....	....
1876-1877	1,036,750	35,994,360	....	....
1877-1878	2,340,645	73,381,675	....	....
1878-1879	4,480,865	19,853,470	....	....
1879-1880	8,752,470	39,348,715	....	....
1880-1881	18,275,995	19,462,870	....	....
1881-1882	24,219,920	26,895,250	....	....
1882-1883	24,654,355	37,401,135	....	....
1883-1884	27,316,580	32,030,765	....	....
	....	....	$999,325,000	$1,012,062,390

[1] Eleven months.

EXPORTS[2] OF SILVER FROM THE UNITED STATES, 1870-1885.

Year ending June 30.	To Europe.	To Asia and Oceania.	To other countries.	Total.
1870	$17,843,652	$4,924,235	$1,751,817	$24,519,704
1871	27,724,312	2,658,527	1,372,941	31,755,780
1872	26,552,179	2,856,210	920,385	30,328,774
1873	33,172,373	4,846,526	1,732,960	39,751,859
1874	24,338,142	6,911,567	1,338,276	32,587,985
1875	18,698,442	5,911,310	541,413	25,151,165
1876	17,181,411	7,591,415	556,426	25,329,252
1877	13,169,252	15,793,594	609,017	29,571,863
1878	8,104,657	16,199,797	231,216	24,535,670
1879	12,552,285	7,245,320	612,222	20,409,827
1880	5,082,074	6,822,688	1,599,132	13,503,894
1881	10,584,592	5,693,563	563,560	16,841,715
1882	11,495,148	4,427,097	907,354	16,829,599
1883	13,133,869	6,676,177	409,399	20,219,445
1884	14,413,584	10,796,459	841,383	26,051,426
1885	15,787,106	17,538,345	428,182	33,753,633

[2] From U. S. Bureau Statistics, Quarterly Report ending September 30, 1885, Table 23.

APPENDIX VII.

Coinage[1] of Gold and Silver at the French Mint, 1850–1885.

YEAR.	Gold.	Silver.
1850	$17,038,478	$17,291,697
1851	53,941,914	11,865,461
1852	5,405,654	14,383,689
1853	62,592,804	4,019,897
1854	105,305,640	424,777
1855	89,485,564	5,100,061
1856	101,656,399	10,884,442
1857	114,512,245	761,922
1858	97,737,927	1,732,713
1859	140,539,558	1,680,362
1860	85,690,485	1,606,839
1861	19,643,280	503,609
1862	42,848,398	503,879
1863	42,046,128	65,922
1864	54,768,753	1,459,321
1865	32,377,367	1,844,478
1866	73,016,585	8,964,281
1867	89,715,902	22,751,707
1868	68,015,337	25,889,053
1869	46,837,238	13,635,179
1870	11,078,960	13,810,251
1871	10,033,976	4,775,699
1872		5,367,673
1873		31,254,032
1874	4,863,940	12,121,997
1875	46,982,400	15,000,000
1876	35,298,632	10,532,263
1877	51,036,228	3,292,857
1878	37,063,620	364,284
1879	4,922,108	
1880		
1881	433,400	
1882	748,400	
1883		
1884		
1885		

[1] To 1875 from "H. C. Report, 1876," Appendix, pp. 88, 89. For 1876–1884, from Soetbeer's "Materialien zur Erläuterung und Beurtheilung der wirthschaftlichen Edelmetallverhältnisse und der Währungsfrage," p. 29.

APPENDIX VII.

Coinage[1] by Countries.

COUNTRIES.	Period.	Gold.	Silver.	RELATIVE PER CENT OF	
				Gold.	Silver.
Great Britain and Australia	1851-1884.	$1,181,869,250	$86,314,250	93·2	6·8
United States	1851-1884.	1,310,179,000	344,333,000	79·2	20·8
France	1851-1884.	1,497,081,250	228,560,000	86·8	13·2
Belgium	1851-1884.	118,259,250	89,595,500	56·9	43·1
Italy	1851-1884.	95,782,250	114,190,000	45·6	54·4
Holland	1851-1884.	32,417,750	144,059,000	18·4	81·6
Germany	1857-1884.	487,933,000	290,326,000	62·7	37·3
Austria-Hungary	1857-1884.	82,559,750	252,143,500	24·7	75·3
Russia	1851-1884.	656,497,750	145,500,000	81·9	18·1
Scandinavian states.	1873-1884.	26,532,500	10,515,500	71·6	28·4
Spain	1876-1884.	184,090,750	120,461,000	60·4	39·6
Portugal	1854-1884.	7,311,000	9,093,000	44·6	55·4
Total		$5,680,513,500	$1,835,090,750	75·6	24·4

Coinage[1] by Periods.

PERIODS.	Gold.	Silver.	RELATIVE PER CENT OF	
			Gold.	Silver.
1851-1855	$834,776,500	$114,395,000	87·9	12·1
1856-1860	896,846,750	230,572,500	79·5	20·5
1861-1865	782,691,000	176,857,500	81·6	18·4
1866-1870	644,549,500	293,045,000	68·7	31·3
1871-1875	947,836,000	346,977,000	73·2	26·8
1876-1880	972,158,500	434,624,750	69·1	30·9
1881-1884	603,655,250	238,619,000	71·7	28·3
1851-1884	$5,680,513,500	$1,835,090,750	75·6	24·4

[1] From Ad. Soetbeer's "Materialien zur Erläuterung und Beurtheilung der wirthschaftlichen Edelmetallverhältnisse und der Währungsfrage," 1885, pp. 33, 34.

APPENDIX VIII.

ANNUAL NET CONSUMPTION OF GOLD AND SILVER IN THE ARTS.[1]

COUNTRIES.	Gold.	Silver.
	Kilog.	Kilog.
United States	19,500	115,000
Great Britain	17,000	72,000
France	16,800	75,000
Germany	12,000	82,000
Switzerland	10,500	24,000
Belgium and Holland	2,900	24,000
Austria-Hungary	2,400	32,000
Italy	4,500	19,000
Russia	2,400	32,000
Other countries	2,000	40,000
Total	90,000	515,000

[1] From Soetbeer, "Materialien," etc., p. 40. At $665 for one kilogramme of gold, the value of the present annual consumption of gold is about $59,859,000; at $41·6 for one kilogramme of silver, the value of the annual consumption of silver is about $21,424,000.

INDEX.

ACT, of 1792, 21-23; of 1834, 60-64; of 1837, changes alloy, 73, 74; of 1853, 79-85; of 1873, 92; effect of act of 1873, 93; acquiescence in same, 179, 180; act of 1878, 181-186.
Alloy, in gold and silver coins, not same, 21; made the same, 73.

Bank reserves, in silver, 30, 52.
Belgium, suggests Latin Union, 148. See Latin Union.
Benton, attacks Hamilton, 18; says gold disappeared, 28; supported "Gold bill," 62, 63.
Bimetallism, arguments for, 3-5; experience of United States with, instructive, 8.
Bland bill, 173; disregards movement of silver, 180, 181; history of, 181-186; reasons for its passage, 186-201; supported by inflationists, 186-190, 193; supported on grounds of protection, 193, 194; humors of debate on, 198-200; vetoed by President, 185-203; its effects, 205-208, 210-214; why dollar of, is at par, 206, 207.

Certificates, silver, 206, 207, 213.
Clearing-House connection with Treasury, 211-213.
Coins, foreign, in use before 1792, 11; regulated by law, 54; drive out American coins, 55.
Coins, subsidiary, 1792, 21, 22; erroneous system of, in United States, 59; system of, adopted, 1853, 82; disappearance of, 1862, 87, 88; in England, 1816, 36; in Latin Union,

146-149; in United States, legal tender, 205.
Colonies, condition of coins in, 10-13.
Commission, United States Silver, report of, 204.
Conference, International Monetary, 109; of 1867, 153, 171; of 1878, 184.
Currency, condition of, before 1834, 52-57; metallic, in 1830, 54.

Debasement of standard, in 1834, 69-73; used as precedent by United States Supreme Court, 72.
Demand, effect of, on gold, 34, 35, 41.
Demonetization of silver in United States, 80-92; produced financial panic, 93; silver demonetized in 1874, 93-95; charge of fraud as to, 95-100; in Germany, 137-140, 143.
Denmark, demonetized silver, 145.
Dollar, silver, first coined, 1793, 21; not coined, 1805-1836, 31, 53; "of our fathers," 73, 74. See Act.
Dollar, Spanish, 10, 17; drives out American dollar, 53; used in China, 102.
Dunham, Mr., explains act of 1853, 78, 79, 84.

"Economist," London, index figures, 38, 39, 163, 164.

Fractional currency, paper, 87-89; foolish attempt to redeem, 89, 90; redemption of, 90, 91.
France, act of 1803, 118, 150; absorption of gold by, 119; anticipated by Germany, 135, 153; war-indem-

nity, 136; standard for silver coins, 147; loss of gold after 1803, 150; depreciation of silver serious to, 159; leads in movement away from silver, 171.
Free coinage, 22; in France, 119; in Latin Union, 148; of silver in United States, taken away, 205.

Germany, 135–145; anticipated France, 135; opportunity to get gold currency, 136; circulation in 1870, 136; acts of 1871 and 1873, 137–140; bank-notes in, 140; sales of silver, 141, 171–173; withdrawal of silver coins, 142; amount of silver to be sold, 142, 143; circulation in 1885, 144; demand for gold in, 144, 145.
Gold, preference for, by Hamilton, 13; disappearance of, 1810–1820, 28–30; rise in value of, 32–37; discoveries of, in 1848–1850, 75; effects of discoveries of, 110, 111; production of, 42; preference for, in United States, 80, 114; disappearance of, in 1862, 87; facts of production of, since 1850, 111–113, 116; effect of new gold on value of silver, 116–118, 134, 135, 145, 153, 167–170; effect on currency of France, 118, 151, 152; demand for, by Germany, 144; preference for, by Latin Union, 156; appreciation of, 163, 194–196.
Gresham's law explained, 26, 27; operation of, in 1810–1820, 28–30, 56, 57; operation of, in 1834–1853, 65–69; operation of, after 1850, 76; drives out gold and silver with paper, 87; in Europe, 147; denied, 197.
Hamilton, report on establishment of Mint, 13–18, 20, 21; why he proposed bimetallism, 14, 15; result of system of, 57, 58; on steadiness of gold, 113.
Historical method, 3, 41.
Holland, stopped coinage of silver, 157.
Horton, S. D., rise in value of gold, 33–36, 39–41; falls into error, 46–50.

India, 122–134; passion for silver ornaments in, 122–124, 129; silver money in, 124, 125, 130; absorption of silver by, 125–134; effects of cotton famine on, 126; council bills, 126, 127, 131, 132; conclusions of Government of India as to fall of silver, 128; paper money in, 130; exports of, 132; decline in imports of silver into, 133; imports of gold into, 132, 134; effect of demand of, on value of silver, 170.
Ingham, 56; advises single silver standard, 60, 70, 71.
Italy. See Latin Union.

Jefferson, proposals, 11, 12, 15, 16.
Jevons, prices, 33, 38, 39.
Johnson, Andrew, opposes act, 1853, 85.

Latin Union, cause of, 146, 149; formed, 148, 149; difficulties of, 154, 155; suspension of free coinage of silver by, 155; preference of, for gold, 156; reservations of states in, 157; cessation of silver coinage, 158, 165; "expectant attitude" of, 158; coinage by, 159; continuance of the, 160; effect of, on value of silver, 172.
Lowndes, 28, 29; on Mexican silver product, 48; report of 1819, 58; death, 61.

Matthews's resolution, 201, 202.
Mint returns, show Gresham's law, 1793–1834, 30, 31; also, in 1834–1860, 69.
Money, gold and silver, what gives value to? 113–115; effect of law on, 115.
Monometallism, argument for, 5–8.
Morris, Robert, scheme of, 11, 12, 13, 16.

Norway and Sweden, demonetized silver, 145.
Notes, legal-tender, issue of, 87; value of, in gold, 91.

Periods, division into, 8, 9; the silver, 10.
Prices, expressing value of gold, 33, 35, 36; relation of prices to value of money, 37, 38, 40; on the Continent, 1751–1830, 40.

Raguet, Condy, 35; gives reason for act of 1834, 61.
Ratio, between gold and silver, select-

ed in 1792, 15-20; ratios, 1780-1800, 19; ratios, 1801-1833, 24; ratios, 1493-1880, 42; of 1:16 in 1834, 65; difficulty of selecting, between gold and silver, 67, 68; of 15½:1 in France, 150.

Report of Grand Committee of Continental Congress, 12; of Board of Treasury, 1786, 12; of Hamilton on Mint, 13; of C. P. White on coinage, 32; of J. J. Knox on Revision of Mint Laws, 84, 97; of United States Silver Commission, 204.

Restriction Act, of England, 34.

Seigniorage, 22; imposed in 1853, and reduced in 1873, 95.

Silver, Mexican product of, 15, 44, 47, 48, 51, 70, 151; fall in value of, 1790, 20, 25, 150; production of, 42; fall in value of, after discovery of America, 44; cause of fall of value of, 1780-1820, 45-51; disappearance of, about 1840, 67; demonetization of, in United States, 80; fall in value of, in 1876, 109, 143, 154; why used by semi-civilized nations, 115; cause of fall in value of, in 1876, 116-118, 134, 135, 145, 153, 161-175, 167-170; fall of, in 1876, relatively to all goods, 163; causes assigned by H. C. Committee, 165-167.

Specie payments, suspended, 86; resumed, 89; Resumption Act, 186; reserve for, 210; resumption of, by England, 28, 33, 34.

Standard, single, of gold, accepted by United States, 80-82, 86, 99.

Supply, effect of, on value of gold and silver, 44, 45, 50.

Switzerland, reduced silver in small coins, 146, 147. See Latin Union.

Trade-dollar, authorized, 101; reasons for its coinage, 101-104; given legal-tender power, 208; this removed, 209; put into circulation in United States, 209; discontinued, 209, 210.

Treasury, how affected by Bland bill, 207, 210-213.

Unit, established in silver, 17; in gold, 101.

Value, is a ratio, 37.

Vote on passage of act of 1834, 63; of act of 1853, 85; of act of 1873, 97; of act of 1878, 183-185.

White, C. P. Report on coinage, 32, 59, 60; reports bill in 1834, 60; changed front, 62.

White, J. Prices of silver, 19, 36.

THE END.

www.ingramcontent.com/pod-product-compliance
Lightning Source LLC
Chambersburg PA
CBHW030749230426
43667CB00007B/906